Hammer Film Scores
and the Musical
Avant-Garde

ALSO BY DAVID HUCKVALE

James Bernard, Composer to Count Dracula: A Critical Biography (McFarland, 2006)

Hammer Film Scores and the Musical Avant-Garde

DAVID HUCKVALE

McFarland & Company, Inc., Publishers
Jefferson, North Carolina, and London

LIBRARY OF CONGRESS CATALOGUING-IN-PUBLICATION DATA

Huckvale, David.
    Hammer film scores and the musical avant-garde /
David Huckvale.
      p.   cm.
    Includes bibliographical references, discography, and index.

    ISBN 978-0-7864-3456-5
softcover : 50# alkaline paper ∞

    1. Motion picture music — History and criticism.
2. Avant-garde (Music)   3. Horror films — History
and criticism.   4. Hammer Film Productions.   I. Title.
ML2075.H83   2008
781.5'42 — dc22   2008016260

British Library cataloguing data are available

©2008 David Huckvale. All rights reserved

*No part of this book may be reproduced or transmitted in any form
or by any means, electronic or mechanical, including photocopying
or recording, or by any information storage and retrieval system,
without permission in writing from the publisher.*

On the cover: Oliver Reed and Yvonne Romain in *The Curse of the
Werewolf*, 1961; (background) Benjamin Frankel's manuscript score for
the film (courtesy of Xenia Frankel)

Manufactured in the United States of America

McFarland & Company, Inc., Publishers
   Box 611, Jefferson, North Carolina 28640
     www.mcfarlandpub.com

To Andrew McMillan

Acknowledgments

I'm happy to confess from the start that it was really through film in general — and Hammer Films in particular — that the emotive power of orchestral music made its first significant impact on me. Film, like society, has changed a great deal since the time of Hammer's heyday — and not necessarily for the better. Bigger budgets, digital technology and changing tastes have brought much but taken even more away. Low budgets force those who suffer under them to be even more ingenious, and nowhere is that ingenuity more apparent than in the astonishing succession of scores that Hammer and its rival, Amicus, commissioned from leading British composers of the day. I therefore owe these films a great debt of gratitude for making my life so much more interesting (especially from a musical point of view) than it would have been without them.

I also owe many thanks to the following individuals who have so generously helped me with this tribute to Hammer's adventurous music policy: Hammer's late, great musical supervisor, Philip Martell, who opened so many doors for me; the composers— David Bedford, the late James Bernard, John Cacavas, Tristram Cary, Paul Glass, John McCabe, the late Buxton Orr, the late Harry Robinson, Gerard Schurmann, and Mike Vickers; Max Charles Davies, who worked on the musical examples; and all those who have so generously helped me with illustrations and other matters of copyright: Lionel Cummings, Katie van Dyke, Eike Fess of the Arnold Schönberg Center in Vienna, Xenia Frankel, Geraldine Haese of the University of Adelaide, Marcus Hearn, Christopher Hughes, Dimitri Kennaway, Jeremy Lees, Lady Mary Lees, Anthony Lustigman, F.C.A., Lewis Mitchell of Josef Weinberger Ltd., Lesley Reid, Phillipa Saraceno, Fiona Searle, Victoria Small of Chester Music/Novello & Co., Philip Venables of the University of York Music Press, Ltd., and Samuel Wilcock of Novello and Co., Ltd. I'd also like to thank my parents, Iris and John, Gail-Nina Anderson, Anthony Sellors and Ian Spiby for their continuing support and friendship.

Table of Contents

Acknowledgments — vii
Introduction — 1

ONE. Maestros (*John Hollingsworth, Marcus Dodds and Philip Martell*) — 7
TWO. The Horror from Vienna (*Arnold Schoenberg*) — 25
THREE. Serial Killer (*Benjamin Frankel*) — 38
FOUR. Modified Modernism (*Humphrey Searle and Elisabeth Lutyens*) — 54
FIVE. The Uncanny (*Richard Rodney Bennett*) — 71
SIX. Romantics (*Harry Robinson and James Bernard*) — 88
SEVEN. Prehistoric Modernism (*Mario Nascimbene and Tristram Cary*) — 115
EIGHT. Australian Menace (*Don Banks and Malcolm Williamson*) — 133
NINE. Modern Gothic (*Mike Vickers and John Cacavas*) — 154
TEN. Catching Up with the Future (*Paul Glass*) — 178
ELEVEN. Television Terror (*John McCabe, Paul Patterson and David Bedford*) — 189

Conclusion — 204
Glossary of Musical Terms — 207
Select Discography — 211
Select Bibliography — 213
Index — 215

Introduction

Hammer films have been interpreted in a variety of ways over the years since their remarkable success in the late 1950s, throughout the 1960s and up to the early 1970s, but their relation to the musical avant-garde has attracted much less critical attention. The release of several CDs in the 1990s, and, more recently, the first complete recording of Benjamin Frankel's serial score for *The Curse of the Werewolf* (dir. Terence Fisher, 1961), have begun to reveal the full richness of the music that Hammer commissioned from composers at the cutting edge of musical modernism. My biography of James Bernard,[1] Hammer's most celebrated and prolific composer, pointed out the many innovative musical effects he incorporated into his predominantly Romantic style, and I will return to some of them in chapter six, alongside the music of Harry Robinson, but what particularly concerns me in this book is how Hammer films in particular encouraged an interaction between popular culture and composers who were also active in the world of avant-garde concert music. The horror film is one of the most popular and certainly the most persistent of all film genres, and Hammer's contribution to this genre was of international importance, not simply because of the company's innovative approach to filmmaking, but also because Hammer commissioned a group of leading British composers to write music for its films at a time when the European avant-garde was changing the language and style of music as a whole.

The tensions between high and popular art, in some circles no longer so important as they were before postmodernism shook up traditional categorizations of culture, were nonetheless very apparent at the time that Hammer and its principal competitor, Amicus, scored their horror film successes in the 1960s, and it would be fair to argue that it is on the soundtracks of these companies' hugely popular films that some of the most significant interfaces between avant-garde musical developments and popular culture are to be found. In this respect they were extremely influential — far more so than any more overtly "intellectual" platform — not only in disseminating a new musical aesthetic, but also, as we shall see, in simultaneously undermining it. Popular film, particularly the popular Romanticism that was a staple of Hammer's output, certainly absorbed aspects of the musical avant-garde, but by contextualizing it in such a way, one could either claim Hammer as a champion of musical modernism or as one of the forces that helped to derail it. Possibly both. It's certainly the case that the vast majority of people who experienced the music of such films as *The Curse of the Werewolf, Paranoiac* (dir. Freddie Francis, 1963), *The Nanny* (dir. Seth Holt, 1965) and even the TV episodes that Hammer made in the 1980s would hardly have been attracted to spending an evening listening to the concert music of Benjamin Frankel, Elisabeth Lutyens, Richard Rodney Bennett or Paul Patterson; and yet people with no particular interest in contemporary music were nonetheless experiencing it, often without being fully aware of its impact. For my own part, even though I experienced these films first on television in the mid–1970s, I too am indebted to those composers for introducing me to a wide variety of musical styles. Hammer, particularly in its later films, also blended elements of pop and jazz with both avant-garde and nineteenth-century Romantic musical idioms. The horror film soundtrack was indeed a melting pot of opposing musical cultures, and could be claimed as part of what the American composer Gunther Schuller in 1957 termed the Third Stream (the fusion of jazz and classical style), of which later Hammer composer Don Banks was also an advocate in his concert works.

Dates are always helpful. In 1954, Pierre Boulez, then leader of the European musical avant-garde, premiered his cantata for mezzo-soprano and six instruments setting for René Char's surrealist poetry collection, *Le Marteau sans Maître* ("The Hammer without a Master"). Boulez' total or integral serial style, in which not only the pitches follow a preordained order but also all the dynamic markings, aimed to remove personal emotion from music and make it a totally cerebral affair. By these means, Boulez hoped to overthrow the past and create a brave new anti-emotional, anti–Romantic world. Boulez' music is consequently of extreme complexity, being not only notoriously difficult to perform but also very challenging to listen to. Many avant-garde composers applied Boulez' techniques to their own music, priding themselves on composing without being personally involved in the process. However, as the composer and academic Reginald Smith-Brindle has pointed out, creating a new system of composition and a new set of aesthetic criteria doesn't necessarily result in the creation of great art.[2] New systems alone are not enough. They must be mastered and used for musical rather than merely cerebral means, and even then they may fail to attract a significant audience.

In December 1954, roughly two months after the premiere of Boulez' *Le Marteau sans Maître*, at the Donaueschingen Festival of Contemporary Music, the Master of Hammer Films, Sir James Carreras, gave the go-ahead for filming to begin on a feature-length adaptation of Nigel Kneale's television serial *The Quatermass Experiment* (dir. Val Guest, 1955). Instead of embracing the brave new world of the future as Boulez wanted, this film followed the path of Mary Shelley's *Frankenstein*, and concentrated, instead, on popular anxieties about science in the post-war, atomic age. Hammer went on to make two more science fiction films before turning its attention to Mary Shelley's novel in earnest, with the first of what eventually became a series of seven Frankenstein films, the last of which appeared in 1973.

Boulez, in stark contrast, was still reiterating his position in 1972, insisting that he wanted most of all to change the attitude of audiences to music and culture in general. He believed that musical life had become a museum culture, preserving the past at the expense of the present. His metaphor was that of a deadening shadow cast by the huge tree of the past. For him, as for the forward-looking Frankenstein so criticized by Mary Shelley, modern society had become more interested in preserving the old than creating the new. He drew comparisons with the decadence of the Romans in the third and fourth centuries B.C., and went on to suggest that it wasn't enough to merely add a moustache to Leonardo da Vinci's *Mona Lisa,* as the Dada artist Marcel Duchamp had once famously shocked the establishment by so doing. Boulez wanted to go one step further; he argued that the contemporary artist should destroy the *Mona Lisa* altogether. He later defended this really rather silly and immature incitement to hooliganism by explaining that what he had really meant was that audiences should stop revering the past. Such reverence, he believed, stifled what was new.[3] But it's arguable if any culture can completely sever the umbilical cord that connects it to the past and still communicate meaningfully without a shared tradition and vocabulary. Popular culture has never done that, and this is perhaps why film music, which absorbs so many different styles, reaches a much larger audience than so much contemporary concert music.

The Quatermass Experiment was the first film score by James Bernard, and with only strings and percussion at his disposal he brought some remarkably avant-garde sounds of his own to the audiences who sat, terrified, in their cinema seats. Though Bernard was not an advocate or an admirer of serialism, let alone Boulez' particular variety, his score for *Quatermass* nonetheless anticipated another trend that would become very fashionable in contemporary music circles in the 1960s. This was the tone cluster, a technique eventually made famous by Polish composer Krzystof Penderecki. As Bernard himself explained:

> I give full marks to Hammer and to Anthony Hinds [producer of *The Quatermass Experiment*], because he encouraged this. They never raised their eyebrows at the comparative weirdness of the sounds. I'd never even heard of Penderecki at that stage. In fact, I've always found atonal and twelve-note music to be unappealing. I have a thing against it, but then I found myself doing the same kind of thing — it was the sort of sound I needed for the film — all from nobody's influence.[4]

From a purely cinematic point of view, Bernard's approach anticipated Bernard Herrmann's music for *Psycho* (dir. Alfred Hitchcock, 1960). For that film,

Herrmann exploited the clash of false relations and major and minor seconds just as Bernard had done before him. In *The Quatermass Experiment* Bernard also created considerably advanced tone clusters out of superimposed sevenths on *tremolo* strings, an effect that makes a great impression when the astronaut Victor Carroon (played by Richard Wordsworth) reaches out for a vase of flowers while lying in a hospital bed during the fourth reel of the film. And for the death of the giant half-man, half-vegetable monster Carroon eventually becomes at the end of the film, Bernard instructed his string players to play on the wrong side of the bridge of their instruments. His marking, *grottesco*, sums up the effect of the sound they created — a sound that he would go on to use for the immolation of so many Hammer monsters in the future.

Bernard later tried his hand at a serial concert piece in the form of a *Passacaglia* for saxophone, which was played, with success, by Sigurd Rascher, but he never used Schoenberg's system in his film music. One composer who worked for Hammer did. This was Benjamin Frankel, who created the first British serial film score in his music for *The Curse of the Werewolf*, starring Oliver Reed in the hirsute and bloody title role; but Frankel's approach to serialism was very different from the anti–Romantic, intellectual approach of Pierre Boulez. Rather, it followed, in some ways, the serial path down which Igor Stravinsky had also wandered in his later years. Indeed, in 1959, only the year before *The Curse of the Werewolf* had been unleashed on a horror-hungry public, Stravinsky had completed his first totally serial score, *Threni*; but Stravinsky's setting of the Lamentations of Jeremiah for six soloists, choir and orchestra also permits elements of tonality to exist within it. For example, by transposing into different pitches the various forms of the series (its retrograde, inverted and retrograde-inversions — terms that will be explained in more detail in chapter three), Stravinsky was even able to bring the whole thing to a close in what could be mistaken for the key of A minor. Frankel's *Curse of the Werewolf* score resembled even more the general approach of Alban Berg's Violin Concerto, the note row of which also contains elements of tonality. Berg's Concerto consequently became one of the most popular of all serial works — much more so, it has to be said, than any of the serial works of his teacher, Schoenberg, who invented his radical system in 1924.

To this day, standard dictionaries of music, while reverentially listing the concert works of contemporary composers, still pass over their film music with a somewhat embarrassed or dismissively vague reference at best. *The New Grove Dictionary of Music and Musicians*, for example, omits none of Elisabeth Lutyens' operas and symphonic works, but merely mentions, non-specifically, that she also wrote many film, theater and radio scores. Of course, social forces are at work here that have nothing to do with music and much more to do with the snobbery of genre classification. To some, no doubt, the title of a film such as *Dr. Terror's House of Horrors* sits uncomfortably next to that of Lutyens' lyric opera, *Isis and Osiris*. Meirion and Susan Harries' biography of Lutyens, *A*

Pilgrim Soul, takes a distinctly aloof approach to Lutyens' film music. While mentioning (if only briefly) her music for horror films, they mockingly describe *The Skull* as a "deathless" work, and then blunder into a plain error of fact when they absurdly claim that Hammer's musical supervisor, Philip Martell, "did not read music."[5] Quite how they expected him to conduct so many complex scores without this essential ability they do not explain. Such an error reveals the lack of real interest, understanding and concern for film music (particularly of the horror film variety) among the biographers of concert composers who have worked in the field. Music in film is still too often dismissed as though it had no real cultural significance. Of course, not all composers regard their own film music as highly as their concert works. (Lutyens was one of these, though, naturally outrageous as she was, with her penchant for green nail polish, she nonetheless enjoyed being known as a "Horror Queen.") However, it is unwise for those who write about such composers to take their film music any less seriously than their concert works, for, as the Harries correctly point out, Lutyens was quite aware that "the audience for horror films accepted without a murmur shrill atonal music which they would have rejected with irritation in the concert hall."[6] Undoubtedly far more people have heard Lutyens' film music than anything else she wrote. More have heard Benjamin Frankel's music for *The Curse of the Werewolf* than have bought a CD of Frankel's own concert works, let alone attended a performance of Berg's Violin Concerto. More have experienced the frisson of James Bernard's tone clusters in *The Quatermass Experiment* than have experienced Penderecki's *Threnody for the Victims of Hiroshima.* Could it really be that the popular horror film has been the salvation of contemporary music? Could one make the claim that Hammer and Amicus were, in fact, among the greatest patrons of contemporary music in the twentieth century? Were werewolves, vampires, psychopaths and the other colorful monsters, so cruelly derided by films critics at the time, actually responsible for pulling contemporary music out of its avant-garde ghetto and into the mainstream of popular culture? And if so, what effect did such music have on the original intentions of the composers who had pioneered these new techniques? These are the questions this book will attempt to answer; but first we need to know a little more about Hammer's musical supervisors, who were largely responsible for bringing so much of this novel and challenging music to the screen.

Notes

1. David Huckvale, *James Bernard, Composer to Count Dracula: A Critical Biography* (Jefferson, NC: McFarland, 2006).
2. Reginald Smith-Brindle, *The New Music* (Oxford: Oxford University Press, 1982), p. 41.

3. Pierre Boulez, "Freeing Music," in *Orientations* (trans. Martin Cooper) (London: Faber and Faber, 1986), pp. 481–23.

4. James Bernard, in conversation with the author, November 1999.

5. Meirion and Susan Harries, *Elisabeth Lutyens, A Pilgrim Soul* (London: Michael Joseph, 1989), p. 152.

6. Ibid., p.228.

One

Maestros

John Hollingsworth,
Marcus Dodds and *Philip Martell*

Hammer's first musical supervisor was John Hollingsworth, but before he became involved with films he had been associate conductor of the Royal Air Force Symphony Orchestra during the Second World War. After the war, he even performed in the presence of Winston Churchill, President Roosevelt and Stalin at the Potsdam peace conference. During a tour of America with this orchestra his future path in movies was suggested when he had the opportunity to observe how films were scored in Hollywood, and before long he became the assistant of Muir Mathieson, the leading British film music conductor. At the same time, he assisted Sir Malcolm Sargent at the BBC Proms, and fulfilled his duties as one of the two chief conductors of the Royal Ballet at the Royal Opera House in London. James Bernard, whose early films for Hammer were all conducted by Hollingsworth, recalled:

> He was a bit of a loner. John was quite a strange, very dear character. All the time I knew him he lived alone in a flat in a big, modernish, sort of '30s block in Hammersmith called Latimer Court. His flat was very characterless, with box-like rooms. It wasn't very roomy or cozy. He was a tall, good-looking man with a very pleasant face — tall and imposing. I think he was a bit insecure, but when he realized he could trust Paul[1] and me, we were allowed to become chums.
>
> I used to take a taxi over from our little house in Chelsea in Bramerton Street on the morning of a recording at the crack of dawn because we were starting at nine or something hideous, and would arrive outside John's flat in Latimer Court, ring the bell and either go up or he'd come down and then we would embark in his little red MG. He liked little dashing, low sports cars. On the way home we'd always stop off at a particular pub and have some drinks with great relief that all had gone well. He was a great giggler and such fun.
>
> I never actually questioned John about his association with Hammer. I

think he was quite happy. Otherwise he'd never have stayed as long as he did. When people have died you think, "Oh, I wish I'd asked him more about that," but he wasn't a person who exactly invited heart-to-heart chats.

John had a charming sense of humor. The old Gainsborough films used to be introduced by a lady in lovely period dress with a big hat. She would turn and smile; that was the logo of Gainsborough films. John called it a "picture hat." So, when we'd come to a bit in the middle of all this dramatic Dracula stuff or Frankenstein stuff where I got a chance to have my little romantic bit, he would turn to me and say, "What? Have you got your picture hat on, dear?" before he started conducting. So we always had nice little jokes like that.

In the last few months of his life, he began to get terribly breathless—I remember that. And I also remember once taking him to Verdi's *Atilla* at Sadler's Wells opera house.[2] Paul was working or couldn't come so I took John, and I always remember thinking, "What a fool I am!" because I'd booked seats at the front of the dress circle, and I remember poor John puffing and blowing as we went up the stairs. He was very uncomplaining and just said, "Do you mind if I take it slowly?"—which we did and we enjoyed the evening, but I realized that he wasn't very well.

He had a very good friend who lived in the same block of flats called Terry Earle, and John let Terry have a key to his flat. Because John lived alone, I suppose it's always good to have a neighbor or a chum who's got a key. Terry often used to call by and say, "Hi, John," or tap on the door. Then, one morning, he tapped on his door several times and there was no reply. So finally he went into the flat and found poor John lying dead, sprawled across the bed. It seems he'd died all alone in the night while trying to reach the telephone.[3]

Outside his film work, it's still possible to hear Hollingsworth's delightful interpretations of various standard classics on the series of recordings he made with the Covent Garden Orchestra for EMI, and the Sinfonia of London for the World Record Club, of suites from Tchaikovsky's *Nutcracker, Swan Lake* and *Sleeping Beauty*. His EMI recordings with the Covent Garden Orchestra also include a representative selection of Scandinavian classics by Sibelius, Svendsen and Nielsen, along with fine interpretations of Alfvén's *Swedish Rhapsody No. 1* and Grieg's *Elegiac Melodies*. His recording, with the Royal Philharmonic Orchestra, of that prolific film composer Sir Malcolm Arnold's grotesquely comic *Tam O'Shanter* concert overture is also characteristic of his lively and dramatic style.

After Hollingsworth's death, Marcus Dodds took temporary control of Hammer's baton. Dodds, a graduate of Cambridge University and the Royal Academy of Music, was born in Edinburgh in 1918. Between 1947 and 1951 he was assistant music director to the Rank Organization, and then chorus-master with the Sadler's Wells Opera Company (1952–56). Other posts followed: principal conductor of the BBC Concert Orchestra and musical director of the

London Concert Orchestra. He also conducted many West End musicals and made a recording, with the Academy of St-Martin-in-the-Fields, of future Hammer composer Malcolm Williamson's opera *The Happy Prince*. His time at Hammer was short-lived, however,[4] and he soon handed over the baton to Philip Martell, who continued to bring some astonishingly adventurous film music to the soundtracks of Hammer's varied output from the mid–1960s right up to the end of Hammer's life as a production company in the 1980s.

Martell started his musical career at the age of five when he first took up the violin. His family lived in the east end of London and were not well-off. When he learned that a neighbor played the violin in the theater, young Philip let it be known that this was what he wanted to do as well, so his father bought him a violin and found him a teacher. (Many years later he was lucky enough to own a genuine Stradivarius, which he described, not surprisingly, as "sensational.") After studies at the Guildhall School of Music with his teacher, Benoit Hollander, he started earning money not in the theater as he had originally planned but by accompanying "silent" films. It was only later that he found work in the theater, which was how he encountered the director Val Guest; and it was through Guest that he found his eventual route into film music for the sound cinema.

I got to know Philip well in his later years. When I first met him, in 1988, he was living in a rather solemn Edwardian terraced house in London's Highgate district. Highgate seemed to me at the time a very suitable location for the home of Hammer's musical supervisor. After all, was not this the location of the famous Highgate Cemetery, that amazing Victorian Valhalla of elaborate tombs and even more celebrated corpses? Hammer itself had filmed there (only once, surprisingly) for one of the graveyard scenes in *Taste the Blood of Dracula* (dir. Peter Sasdy, 1970), while Hammer's rival company, Amicus, had taken full advantage of the picturesque solemnity of the place in the main title sequence of its portmanteau horror film *Tales from the Crypt* (Freddie Francis, 1972). Even Philip's surname was appropriate, as Martell resembled the Italian musical term *martellato*, which means "hammered."

As I emerged from Highgate Underground Station and made my way along Muswell Hill Road I wondered what I would find when I eventually arrived at No. 23 Woodland Gardens. At long last, after watching so many of the films in which his name had appeared on the credits, I stood on the doorstep of this legendary figure. I rang the bell and waited, full of expectation.

"I've always wanted to meet you!" I exclaimed, as Philip opened the door.

"So have the police," he replied, with what I soon learnt to be his characteristically wry sense of humor. He led me through to his little study at the front of the house, the first room on the left of the narrow hallway. This proved to be a rather untidy but nonetheless cozy treasure trove containing the master tapes for the music of all the Hammer films Philip had ever been involved with, stacked rather chaotically on shelves built into the right-hand alcove of the fireplace. There were also scores and papers strewn over the top of his desk in the window; and on the mantelpiece stood various photographs, one of which showed Josephine Douglas, the producer of *Dracula A.D. 1972* (dir. Alan Gibson, 1972), cutting a birthday cake on the set. "She hated working on that picture," Philip explained when I drew his attention to it. "A lovely lady. She used

City of the dead. Highgate Cemetery in 1991 (photograph by the author).

to produce the T.V. pop music show *Six-Five Special*, and she vowed she'd never make another film again after her experience on that one." Indeed, she never did. On the floor I could see several screenplays for Hammer's then recent T.V. series *The Hammer House of Mystery and Suspense*, and there were books all over the place.

It seemed that Philip lived in this room almost to the exclusion of every other room in the house. He made me a cup of tea, settled me down in a comfortable arm chair and almost immediately started telling me about the people he had worked with over his long and fascinating career — in particular the great Otto Preminger, whom he had encountered while working on Preminger's film adaptation of Bernard Shaw's play *St. Joan* in 1957. Although the music for this was being written by Viennese operetta composer Mischa Spoliansky, Preminger had wanted Philip on set every day, even if he wasn't actually needed:

> Preminger said, "You can have a dressing room, you can have a piano in there, you can have a telephone in there." I said, "But I don't want to stay here!" "...Or you can stay here and watch me shoot the picture. You can do

Hammering home a point. (Left to right) James Bernard, Philip Martell and Michael Carreras at a Hammer recording session during post-production on *She* (1964) (courtesy the J.M. Bernard Will Trust).

what you like but I want you here." I said, "I'm sorry, Otto, I can't do that. I want to work at home. I want to start thinking about the music"—and there was a lot of music—but he said, "Either you do as I want or you get off my picture. Please yourself!" So I left. Three days later I get a phone call from his assistant saying, "What the hell do you think you're up to?" I said, "Nothing." He said, "You could be down here doing something, couldn't you?" I said, "I'm not on your picture any longer." He said, "Preminger sacked you?" I said, "Yes." "Well, he's sacked the leading lady, sacked the leading man, half the technicians—they're all still here, so who do you think you are?" I said, "I'm not anybody." He said, "Well, come on down and let's stop this nonsense."

So I went back and started working again with Preminger. One day I was very honored and I was invited to take tea with him in the tea break along with three or four stooges: his yes-men. Preminger said to me, "Look, I want something on the soundtrack that represents the voices that Joan hears in her head, but I don't want it done with musical instruments." Sitting at the table was a man who said to me, "I'll give you a clue as to what might be useful: a syrinx." I said, "I don't even know what it is." He said, "Well, I've heard it and it's very beautiful and I think it might do as the voices." So Otto said, "Right! Go and get him!" But I didn't know where to get him, so I asked this man, "Where did you hear this?" "In Paris, at the exhibition." "When?" "In 1926." So Otto said, "Go to Paris and find him."

So I started hunting around and got nowhere, and then I phoned the BBC record department and I said, "Do you know anything about a syrinx?" And they said, "Yes." "Have you got one?" They said, "No, we had a record." So they found it, I heard it and knew this was going either to be the entire answer or part of the answer, but I couldn't use the record. It was old and scratchy, so I then started ringing the embassies. When we got to Rumania, they found us a syrinx player. We sent the theme that we were going to use, and then I said to Otto's assistant, "Let's bring the man over and we'll record it." So we brought the man over from Rumania. He came into the studio on Saturday morning at Shepperton, complete with interpreter and bodyguard, and proceeded to put the music on the stand and play—and it was exactly what was on the record. I said, "Well, tell him that's nice. Can he play this?" Well, you know the answer, don't you? He couldn't read music. Not a bloody note! So I kept the man there a week. We put him up in a hotel. We kept him there and I taught him note by note, every note, exactly how I wanted it held, where you should breathe— all through the interpreter, and we got it.

The only thing I'll say about Otto, which is complimentary, is that he didn't care about money. You could spend money left, right and center. I then brought in a group of musicians and put a backing to it and had the track ready. Otto came one day. He'd been to Paris. He used to dodge out of his income tax, then he came back. He said, "Have you got it?" I said, "Yes." So I played it to him. He said, "Well, that's very good!" I said, "Well, thank you, Otto." He said, "Well, play me some more." This thing was long enough to cover the titles, which was a minute and three-quarters. I said: "Otto, I didn't do any more." Then the bloody roof went up. He went berserk! "You bring him from Rumania! We keep him here for a week! We pay him a fee and all you give me is a minute and three quarters!" It was absolutely unbelievable. And that's the story of Otto. But Otto hated me because I didn't care if he fired me. The slightest reason and I'd go. Money or no money.

We came to the point where it became necessary to go into the question of the crowning at Rheims Cathedral. I don't know anything about fourteenth-century music. I went and bought books. I've got them upstairs; but then I decided, this is silly. Let's go to somebody who does know, so I went to a man who played the organ at Brompton Oratory, and told him the problem. He said, "All right, I'll work the whole thing out for you. I'll record it for you." For this I'm grateful to Otto. He didn't check money. He didn't care! This was in the days when there *was* money. We're going back a hell of a long time. So we got the music all set up, and the first battle was with Mischa Spoliansky, because there had got to be an organ voluntary for the congregation, and he wrote something that sounded a little bit like Franz Lehár. So a big fight went on, and then he started writing something that was going to be like Rachmaninoff. He and I got at loggerheads, and then I said to the organist, "You write it." So he said, "Sure!" He didn't have to write it. He knew where to find it, what to do with it. He knew how much he could decorate it. We went with him to the Festival Hall and recorded it. Preminger said to me that there had got to be a boys choir, and I'd got that too, through the same organist at Brompton Oratory. But Preminger said to me, "You know, when the service is over, what's going on? " I said, "Well, the organ is playing a voluntary and the congregation is going out. When they've all gone out two people will stay behind at the back of the cathedral. That'll be Joan of Arc and Dunois. Those two will have a conversation." Preminger said, "What I want is for the organ to disappear and the orchestra to take over." I said, "You can't do that, Otto." "What do you mean: 'I can't do that?'" I said, "They didn't have orchestras in cathedrals. The organ is playing." "I don't want the organ. I want the orchestra." I said, "Where is the orchestra coming from?" He said, "You will bring in which orchestra you want!" I said, "Where from? Coming from the sky?" He said, "Don't give me arguments, just do what I want." Well, I did a recording without the orchestra. No orchestra. What could he do? He could fire me. I did the recording and I gave it to the editor. Otto was in Paris. The editor said, "I'm not putting it into the picture. I'm sending a quarter inch tape over to Otto. So I got a phone call. I can't remember what time it was. It was somewhere early in the morning, like two o'clock, and Otto was saying, "What the hell do you think you're doing? What I ask for is what I expect to get. I won't use any of it!" And so he came back to London. I said, "This is what we've got and this is what it has to be. This is what was told to me by the organist at Brompton Oratory. There's no greater authority in this country." He said, "Incidentally, that man can't play." I said, "That man is the greatest organist in that field that there is. " He said, "I don't like it. I don't like the organ either. Throw it away. Do the whole thing again."

So I then had to go and get another organ (St. Columbus Church in Kensington somewhere, where Otto said the acoustics were much better), and get the organist who was head of the organ department at the BBC. He was brilliant! We redid the entire recording just because Otto insisted. So we finally got that done. But I didn't finish the picture. It was the only way I got my own back in the end. I had a contract which had an expiry date, and I reached the expiry date and I said to his assistant—not to Otto (I wasn't that brave), "I'm leaving tomorrow." He said, "The picture's not finished yet." I said, "Yes, but my contract is." He said, "Well, we'll give you another one." I said, "I don't want another one." As it happened, and it happened to be the truth, I'd got a theater show to do. I'd committed myself and had to go. So I got Douglas Gamley in. Dougie Gamley and Don Banks came from Australia together. Dougie lived up the road and was trying to get into the film business too; so I took Dougie down and introduced him to Otto. We ran the picture from beginning to end, and then Otto said something to Dougie, and Dougie phoned me the next day and said, "Would you mind finding someone else? I'm not putting up with that." And he was quite right not to.[5]

Preminger's awfulness was an exception. Philip never had trouble with any other director—with the possible exception of John Schlesinger:

John Schlesinger is a very difficult man. He ignores you. He doesn't enthuse you. I don't need his enthusing. I'd do it anyway. I've got a job to do. I've got to please *me*. I was with him for *Yanks* [1979] when he was shooting for three months just outside Manchester, and other than saying "Good Morning" he never spoke. He just walked straight past you. He didn't even smile or nod his head. You were just a piece of the equipment. I only had one big argument with him. What I did like about him is that he has taste in music. Part of the story of *Yanks* is that all the young people and middle-aged people were away in the war. Vanessa Redgrave was the lady of the manor, and she organized things to try and keep morale up, and decided to form an orchestra. Schlesinger asked me what size orchestra it should be. I said it shouldn't be a great big orchestra because all the males are away fighting in the war, and in any case you don't want a great big work. So I asked him, "Who would you like?" He said, "I'll have Elgar and I'll have Vaughan Williams." I said, "Sure!" So I tried to get clearance for Elgar and Vaughan Williams, and I think it worked out something like a thousand pounds a minute. He said, "All right!"—but the man who was his assistant said, "No, we're not paying that sort of money for something that isn't vital in the picture. It was just a concert in the local village hall." So we ended up with about thirty players who we brought up from London—mostly women—and we ended up with Parry and Stanford. That was all right. We didn't have any trouble with that. The only trouble we had with him was with the dance band. A dance band was wanted. He kept saying it has to be a bad dance band. I said, "No, it doesn't have to be a bad dance band because the dance bands were left untouched in the war. They were wanted to go around all the army camps and all the other places to play — and they were very good. With every dance band I suggested — it even came down to Joe Loss — he said, "No. That's much too good," which was rubbish because Joe was going around to all the military bases. But he wouldn't take that either. And there we were stuck until I got a phone call from a bloke who said he'd read in a paper that we were about to shoot this scene of the New Year's Eve dance, and that Schlesinger was looking for a dance band that would be the right one, and he said that he'd got the right one — absolutely the right one, modelled on Glenn Miller. So I said, "OK. Make me a tape and let me hear it." So they made a tape and I went and picked it up at Elstree. It wasn't very good, but, all right — that was the sort of thing that Schlesinger was after. So I told Schlesinger. He said, "Well, let's go and hear it." When we heard it he said, "That's it. That'll do fine." Well, we brought them in and we shot them, visually, and recorded them. I left the picture to go back to Hammer and they brought in Richard Bennett to do the background music for the picture. Whether it was him or whether it was the Americans, I don't know, but they took out the dance track and put in the sort of dance track I wanted from day one.[6]

One afternoon Philip took me upstairs on a rather odd tour of his home, pausing to catch his breath on the stairs and to point out the view of Alexandra Palace that could be seen from the landing window. There was an air of Miss Haversham up there, of time having stopped. What surprised me most was that every room he took me into was completely empty. Everywhere was clean and tidy, the walls seemingly freshly painted white, but there wasn't a stick of furniture anywhere, the uncarpeted floors revealing their bare boards. What had happened to all his things? It was hard to reconcile this rather desolate lifestyle with that of a man who had worked with Otto Preminger and John Schlesinger, to mention nothing of so many Hammer films.

After a brief inspection of each empty room (was Philip trying to tell me something by taking me on this odd tour? I never found out if he was) we went back downstairs.

"Have you enjoyed it all," I asked, "— your amazing life in music?" He looked at me with a sparkle in his eyes and smiled back, "It's been fantastic!" That made the desolation of his empty house, and the apparent loneliness of this now rather frail, elderly man, much less melancholy, though he was quick to add, "Of course, there's nothing happening now." And indeed, by the time I got to know him, Hammer were no longer making feature films.

In his large but similarly rather forlorn sitting room were yet more treasures: a framed production design by Scott MacGregor for Hammer's psychological shocker *Crescendo* (dir. Alan Gibson, 1970), about the widow of a famous composer and her two sons — one criminally insane, the other a paralytic drug addict. Despite the gruesome story, the set design for the film was actually a very attractive view of the exterior of a villa in the south of France, with a swimming pool and terrace. Philip explained that he'd admired the design in the studio one day, and MacGregor had had it specially framed for him. There was also a signed letter from Saint-Saëns to Philip's teacher, Hollander, rather clumsily mounted in a frame opposite the *Crescendo* design. In a mezzanine room halfway up the stairs a large refrigerator stood vibrating in the corner, and literally scattered all around it, spilling out from a floor-to-ceiling cupboard, was an avalanche of music: manuscript and photostatted scores by Elisabeth Lutyens, John McCabe, Paul Patterson, James Bernard, Harry Robinson, some splashed with milk, others covered in dust. There were more scores in the cupboard under the stairs in the kitchen, where on several occasions Philip cooked me cheese on toast and poured out mugs of tea from a big brown teapot. It was strange indeed to me that a life so full of incident and musical expertise should now be drawing to a close in this lonely old house in the middle of a quietly anonymous road of Edwardian villas. Woodland Gardens indeed exuded something of the strangely desolate atmosphere that the film director Seth Holt had captured in the street scenes of *Blood from the Mummy's Tomb* (1971): grey autumnal afternoons in suburbia, clipped hedges, staring, empty windows,

Dummy love. Stephanie Powers and James Olsen in *Crescendo* (dir. Alan Gibson, 1970).

One: Maestros (Hollingsworth, Dodds and Martell)   17

deserted rooms and implacable front doors—except the door of No. 23 was far from implacable to me. Philip opened it for me on many occasions over the coming months.

One day in the middle of winter Philip took me down to his cellar. How very gothic, I smiled to myself. What on earth would I find down there? He said I might be interested in seeing Hollander's manuscripts, which Philip's ex-wife had made him store there years ago because she thought they attracted dust and spiders. Reluctantly, he had bowed to her wishes, and there they had remained: certainly dusty, probably crawled over by spiders, and, much worse, very damp. So much of the music that had been stored down there was now so rotten that the paper literally fell to dust in my hands, like staked vampires, when I lifted them from the filthy floor. There, too, were Philip's old college diplomas and piles of other memorabilia, all covered in the mold and grime of many years' neglect. Philip was now keen to rescue his old teacher's compositions. He had plans to perform them—particularly Hollander's *Roland* Symphony. This was a gigantic, late–Romantic masterpiece, he said, and he wanted me to help him, while also entrusting me with the care of these precariously preserved manuscripts. I hadn't bargained on that. So we brought them back up into the light of day and discovered that they had all been beautifully bound in cloth boards, some deep red, others faded purple or blotchy blue, their spines embossed with exotic titles: *Gringoire* and *Sardanapalus* (a setting of Byron's play of the same name, no less), *Sappho, Caesar,* and *Les Burgraves,* to name but five. Philip sighed, imagining how his teacher must have slaved away through the night over these now neglected manuscripts in his study in Westwell Road in London's Streatham Common. (What a prosaic birthplace for such exotic children!) Few of these works had ever been published, let alone performed, but there were some published items as well, including a violin concerto, two sonatas for violin and piano, a suite for violin, a song setting of a Browning poem, "Summum Bonum," and a "dramatic vocal and symphonic poem" based on Lord Lytton's novel *The Last Days of Pompeii,* several printed copies of which had also succumbed to the corrosively damp air of their subterranean dwelling. Philip fondly reminisced about his old teacher: how kind he had been to his protegé, how disapproving he had been when Philip had started to work in the cinema rather than on the concert platform, and how "the old man," as he called him, would take Philip with him to his publishers and tell him tales of his own teacher, Saint-Saëns, and the overwhelming influence of Richard Wagner on musical life at the turn of the century. (Philip, who was Jewish, never forgave the Germans for what they had done to his family, and he always refused to record anything in Germany.)

The afternoons I spent in Philip's company followed one another rapidly as autumn turned into winter. Each time I made my way past the changing colors of the leaves in Highgate Wood to Woodland Gardens, where he was always

Title page of Benoit Hollander's setting of Robert Browning's poem "Summum Bonum" (1911) (photograph by the author).

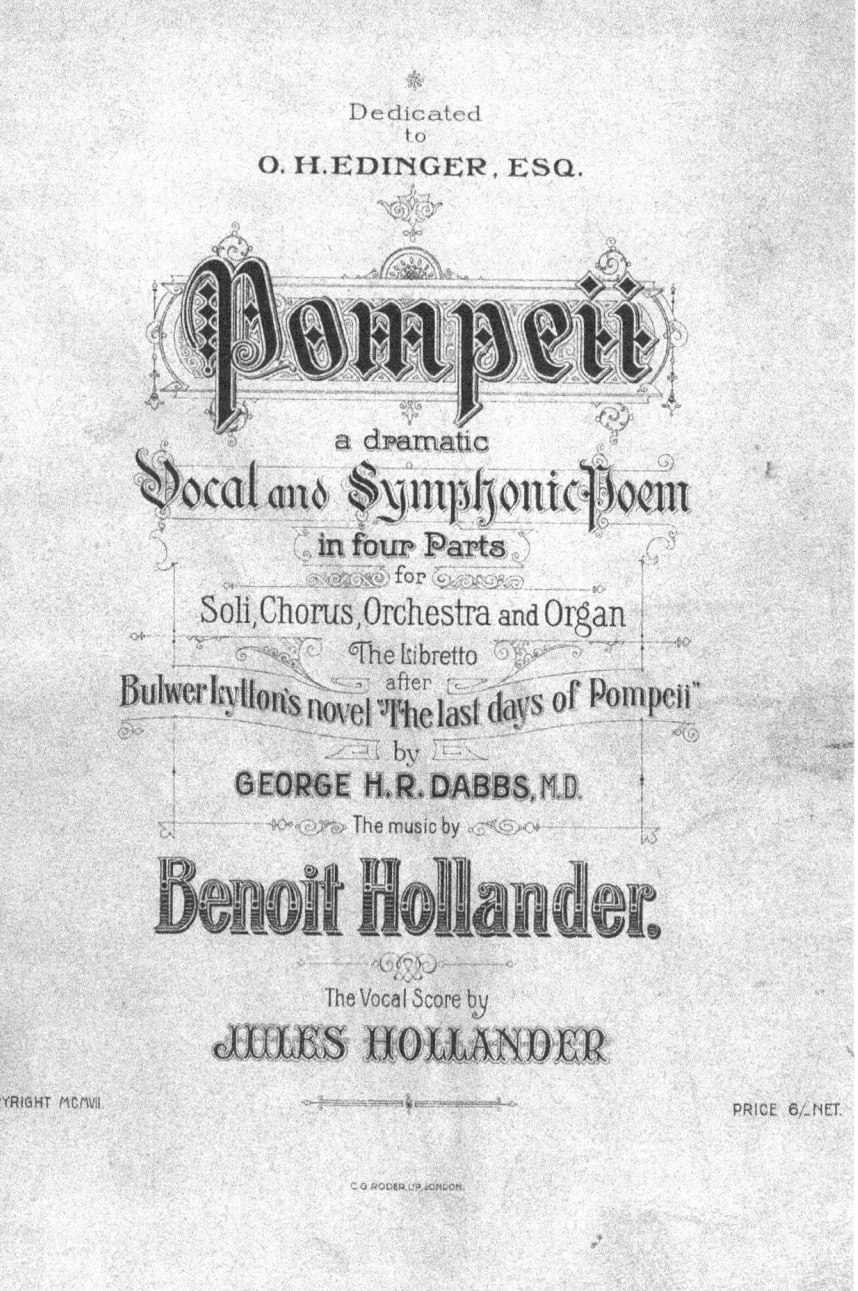

Title page of Benoit Hollander's *Pompeii* (1907) (photograph by the author).

Title page of Benoit Hollander's *Violin Concerto* (1896) (photograph by the author).

pleased to greet me. Indeed, he seemed to start relying on my visits. He wanted to collaborate with me on an autobiography, but time was running out, and with it his ability to recall clearly past events. Names eluded him, stories would start but drift into others before he finished them. Not long after I met him he suffered a stroke that left him very weak. But still he wrote me letters in a very shaky and uncertain hand, which was at odds with the inner determination he still had to get things moving:

> 25/3/89
> Dear David,
>   Glad to tell you that progress is being maintained but much much too slowly. All the plans for the recording and concerts are being held up but there is very little I can do about it — nowhere near fit enough to stand in front of the Philharmonia: would like to pick up the threads in about 2 months from now. Firstly it's necessary to sort out the music needed. Would you like to undertake this task — we'll arrange a reasonable fee for you doing it. The original plan was to perform [illegible words] at Festival Hall just to get things going on a high level. Hammer should want to go ahead with the plan — not sure I have the energy — if in due course I do undertake to conduct the concert [will?] anybody turn up! [illegible words] alternatively to perform one of Hollander's operas. So when you next visit here would it be possible for me to see the scores to chose. Could you get in touch with Malcolm [Williamson]. I have a great admiration for his talent. [A couple of illegible sentences follow]. I [illegible] Boosey for a published edition of Hollander's viola concerto which was first performed in public by YSAYE. I am not quite up to that class but will make an impression (of [illegible] sort).
>   All Good Wishes.
>   Sorry about this scribble but it's the best I can do at the moment.
>   Regards,
>   Philip

Sadly, none of Philip's plans came to anything. On the day that he was scheduled to conduct Silva Screen's recording of *Music from the Hammer Films*, he was forced to accept that his conducting days were over. He kept talking about going on a cruise to recuperate. Would I go with him? Then, when he realized that this wasn't possible in his current state of health, he even asked if I would be his nurse and look after him. But not only was I unqualified for such a role, I unfortunately had other commitments that made that impossible; and, anyway, he lived too far away from me conveniently to arrange daily visits.

One afternoon he drove me to a Chinese restaurant for lunch. The journey down Highgate Hill in his car wasn't at all advisable in his condition, but as I don't drive and he was insistent, we set off. The Chinese meal, in a deserted restaurant, was an odd affair. Philip looked really quite unwell, but

Letter from Philip Martell to the author, March 25, 1989 (photograph by the author, courtesy Philip Martell Estate).

he was still full of his plans for concerts and recordings, while the proprietor (whom Philip knew well) looked on as the dishes were served, whispering in my ear, "He's been through a hell of a lot. Make sure he gets home safely." This we eventually achieved, very late in the afternoon. The next time we met, Philip greeted me in his dressing gown, looking very poorly, encouraging me, nonetheless, to make myself at home and study the music I'd asked to look at while he took a nap. Later that afternoon I popped my head around the door of the little study that had witnessed conversations with so many composers over the years, only to find Philip fast asleep. I touched his shoulder, but he slumbered on, breathing deeply. Not having the heart to wake him, I gently pressed his hand in mine and whispered "good-bye" into his ear before letting myself out into the quiet winter evening. The windows of the houses opposite looked down accusingly at me as I made my way down the path and back to the bustle of central London. I never saw Philip again. He died on August 12, 1993.

However, Philip's contribution to musical history lives on in the scores he commissioned and frequently conducted for Hammer, scores that brought a whole new world of musical possibilities to the audiences who heard them, and which, along with those conducted and/or supervised by John Hollingsworth, and Marcus Dodds, have played an important, if underestimated role, in the history of twentieth-century British music. The more I explored what these men had commissioned from their composers, the more I realized that there was more — very much more — to Hammer than the inspiration of the nineteenth-century. Much of the music for which they had been responsible reflected what was happening in the world of twentieth century avant-garde music, and it was through Hammer's adventurous approach to film music that popular audiences had been, and continue to be, exposed to musical styles they might never otherwise have experienced.

Hammer's greatest claim to musical fame in this particular is Frankel's score for *Curse of the Werewolf*, which Frankel actually conducted himself in 1961. It's satisfying to know that it is a popular horror film that has the honor of being the first British film to have a serial score, but it wasn't the first time that horror was associated with Schoenberg's system. Indeed, as the next chapter will explain, Schoenberg himself was keen to use his music to express similar emotions and anxieties.

Notes

1. Paul Dehn, Bernard's partner, was the screenwriter for, among others, *Goldfinger* (dir. Guy Hamilton, 1964), *The Spy Who Came in from the Cold* (dir. Martin Ritt, 1965), and *Murder on the Orient Express* (dir. Sidney Lumet, 1974).
2. Hollingsworth had also been a conductor for Sadler's Wells ballet.

3. James Bernard, in conversation with the author, September 24, 1998.
4. Dodds did go on, however, to conduct Claude Bolling's score for the remake of Hammer's *Blood from the Mummy's Tomb*, called *The Awakening* (dir. Mike Newell, 1980) — see chapter 7.
5. Philip Martell, in conversation with the author, August 24, 1988.
6. Philip Martell, in conversation with the author, August 24, 1988.

Two

The Horror from Vienna
Arnold Schoenberg

Our story starts in a moonlit wood. A woman is on her way to meet her lover, but she is full of foreboding. She senses a mysterious presence that tries to hold her back and thinks she can hear someone sobbing. Night sounds of birds and animals terrify her, and she stumbles over what she thinks is a dead body, but it turns out to be only a tree trunk. In a clearing filled with curious yellow toadstools she imagines she can hear her lover calling to her and that huge yellow eyes are staring at her. Back on the road she looks for somewhere to rest and stumbles against another tree trunk, but this time it's not a tree trunk. It is indeed the corpse of her lover. She smothers it with passionate, delirious kisses, but, with the dawn, the lovers are parted forever.

This scenario is not a dream sequence from one of Hammer's psychological shockers, like *Nightmare* (dir. Freddie Francis, 1964) or *Paranoiac*, but it could so easily be. In fact, it's the plot of Arnold Schoenberg's monodrama *Erwartung* ("Expectation"), which he composed (to Marie Pappenheim's nightmare text) in 1909. He had to wait fifteen years before it was actually performed, in 1924, which was the same year that one of Germany's most celebrated film directors completed a film that should have excited Schoenberg a great deal. The film in question was Fritz Lang's cinematic version of the Germanic legends that had inspired Schoenberg's musical hero, Richard Wagner. Lang's two-part adaptation of the *Nibelungenlied* was, of course, a so-called "silent" film (sound cinema didn't appear until Al Jolson sang it into existence in 1927), but "silent" films had always been accompanied by music, and the kind of films that Germany had been making between the completion of Schoenberg's highly cinematic monodrama and its eventual performance were crying out for the kind of music that Schoenberg was writing for the stage. After the First World War, films like Robert Wiene's *Cabinet of Dr. Caligari* (1919) were all the rage, and they looked like expressionist paintings brought to life. The acting was expressionist as well (think of Conrad Veidt in his figure-hugging black leotard, his staring eyes ringed with black makeup, his every gesture a contortion). Wiene's film is often regarded as the mother of all horror films, though it was very different from Hammer's much more naturalistic approach to the macabre; and although the ghost of Schoenberg haunted the soundtracks of Hammer's films, Schoenberg himself never actually scored a movie. This is odd, as the German expressionist cinema and Schoenberg were so obviously made for each other. Schoenberg's other expressionist opera, *Die glückliche Hand* (first performed in 1924), also features horrific, nightmare imagery. In it, a fabulous monster lies on a man's back and bites the man's neck with its teeth, while a chorus of green-faced women urge the man to renounce his quest for what is unobtainable (presumably artistic perfection). Admittedly, *Die glückliche Hand* is a complex allegory about the position of the artist in society, the monster representing the anguish of existence, the man representing the isolation of the artist; but are not all these themes of anguish, isolation and the grotesque also important elements in popular horror films? One cannot help wondering why Schoenberg, who was always short of money, didn't compose the scores for films that had many themes in common with his own stage works.

The fact of the matter is that no one asked him, not in the days of the silent cinema anyway; and when sound did eventually come along, Schoenberg very quickly became disillusioned. Not that he was against the cinema in principle. It was just that commercial reality got in the way of his distinctly unrealistic ideals. Schoenberg explained his attitude to commercial cinema in an essay he wrote in 1940:

> When Berlin's UFA made its first successful experiments with talking pictures [...] I expected a renaissance of the word — of thoughts, of ideas — dealing with the highest problems of mankind! [...] How wrong I had been: a few months afterwards my dream was destroyed by the appearance of the first "full-sized" film, "full-sized" also in vulgarity, sentimentality and mere playing to the gallery.[...] The production of moving pictures abandoned entirely every attempt towards art and remained an industry, mercilessly suppressing every dangerous trait of art.[...] I had dreamed of a dramatization of [...] Strindberg's *To Damascus* [...] or even Wagner's *Parsifal*.... [T]hese works, by renouncing the law of "unity of space and time," would have found the solution to realization in sound pictures. But the industry continued to satisfy only the needs and demands of the ordinary people who filled their theatres.[1]

Schoenberg certainly never had any interest in attracting the attention of these so-called "ordinary people," but, significantly, he had tried his hand at writing film music. It was the only film score he ever wrote, but the film it "accompanied" didn't actually exist. This *Music to Accompany an Imaginary Film Scene* (or *Begleitungsmusik zu einer Lichtspielszene*, to give it its original German title) appeared in 1930. It has three sections, the titles of which suggest that he might have had the kind of horror film atmosphere of *Dr. Caligari* in mind. They are: "Threatening Danger," "Panic" and "Catastrophe." Hanns Eisler, who wrote *Composing for Films* in 1948, might, in turn, have had this piece in mind when he referred to the scene in *King Kong* (dir. Merian C. Cooper, 1933) when the giant ape hurls a New York elevated train into the streets below. "The traditional music written for such scenes," he pointed out, "has never been remotely adequate to them, whereas the shocks of modern music could meet their requirements."[2]

Schoenberg, however, had hoped that his atonal and later serial style would be equally successful in comic situations. In this Schoenberg would again have been disappointed, as his style has subsequently tended to accompany movies that occupy the same nightmare imagery as *Erwartung*. But not always. Schoenberg's own attempt at writing a *comic* serial opera, *Von Heute auf Morgen* (first performed in 1930), might not seem quite as hilarious to some members of his audience as it was for him; but, as we shall see, it was on the soundtrack of a comedy cartoon that serialism actually made its debut in film history.

The *Music to Accompany an Imaginary Film Scene* was begun two years after the premiere of Al Jolson's all-talking, all-singing *The Jazz Singer* (dir. Alan Crossland, 1927); and Schoenberg's interest in the possibilities of film at this stage in his career is documented by a letter addressed to Schoenberg from the Society of German Film Composers, in which the society agreed to answer any questions he might have about "talking pictures." When the *Imaginary Film Scene* music was eventually performed, he was rather taken aback by its success. "People do seem to like the piece," he observed. "Ought I to draw any conclusions from that as to its quality? I mean: the public apparently likes it!"[3]

Poor Schoenberg! Having suffered critical abuse for so long, any success, especially for so advanced a work, was obviously rather disorienting; but whatever the success of his music for an imaginary film scene, it was not to be repeated when he attempted to compose a real film score in Hollywood. Schoenberg's observation that Wagner's *Parsifal* would translate well to the medium of film shows how sensitive he was to the possibilities of a medium that can condense, expand or distort time and space. Indeed, the techniques of Wagner's style, which the Master of Bayreuth himself referred to as "the art of transition"[4] from one scene to another, is an important part of all film scoring. The transitional music in the first act of *Parsifal*, Wagner's last music-drama, was conceived of in almost cinematic terms. The character, Gurnemanz, who initiates Parsifal into the grail brotherhood, sings: "You see, my son, here space becomes time." He could well be singing about the potential of cinema itself. Schoenberg was steeped in Wagner, and saw himself as Wagner's legitimate musical heir. Significantly, the description Schoenberg made of several of his own stage works also uses cinematic terminology:

> In *Erwartung* the aim is to represent in *slow motion* everything that occurs during a single second of maximum spiritual excitement, stretching it out to half an hour, whereas in *Die glückliche Hand* a major drama is

compressed into about 20 minutes, as if photographed with a time-exposure. My third opera, *Von Heute auf Morgen*, is also relatively short; it lasts about an hour, but uses only the customary theatrical methods of condensing and expanding time.[5]

"Slow-motion," "time exposure"—such terms suggest that Schoenberg himself thought of the production of these operas in cinematic terms. Indeed, the elaborate lighting effects over which he took such trouble in *Die glückliche Hand* could indeed be realized most effectively in a film, rather than as a stage production. In this opera every scene has its special coloring, and the lighting within each scene is subtly changed in accordance with its varying moods. Schoenberg was an enthusiastic follower of Wagner's theory of *Gesamtkunstwerk*—or "Total Art Work"—in which all the arts combine together in a truly synthesized way. In this respect, too, the cinema is the fulfillment of Wagner's wildest dreams. Wagner's elaborate stage directions and settings are truly cinematic in scale and scope. He also anticipated the pitch black of a modern cinema by extinguishing the lights of his festival theater at Bayreuth; and the sound of his orchestra, emerging from its place under the stage, produces a similar effect to the sound of music emerging from concealed loudspeakers in the cinema. Schoenberg had a much more developed visual sense than Wagner and went so far as to design sets and costumes for some of his stage works, as well as relaxing from composition by painting his astonishing visions. Although some critics, after having seen Schoenberg's paintings, wished that they were blind as well as deaf, Schoenberg should have been a huge success in the film business.

In 1930, he might well have entertained considerable hopes for a combination of expressionist (or at least experimental) films with serial music soundtracks. If such hopes were kindled, though, they were extinguished after only two years in Hollywood. His acid comments about Hollywood, where he went to live after escaping the Nazis who had overrun his native Austria, are the result of disappointment rather than anything against cinema *per se*. It is important to consider why he should have decided to settle in Los Angeles in the first place. There were, after all, many other centers of American culture available to him, but it seems likely that one of the attractions was his own interest in film and the possibility of writing music for it. If that had been his initial expectation, everything had changed by his sixtieth birthday in 1934. By then, Schoenberg's disappointment with the realities of Hollywood was characterized by a cynical contempt of the film industry in general:

> Los Angeles (Hollywood is a sort of Floridsdorf or Mödling of Los Angeles, only with the difference that here they produce those splendid films whose highly unusual plots and wonderful sound give me so much pleasure, as you know) is a completely blank page so far as my music is concerned.[6]

Composing for an imaginary film was one thing. Composing for Hollywood was quite another, and Schoenberg soon discovered that he just wasn't suited to the commercial and practical way in which films are created and marketed. Unable to compromise his artistic integrity, he was, sadly, a miserable failure. He did, however, make one attempt to score a Hollywood film. In 1935 he was approached by Metro-Goldwyn-Meyer to write the score for a film version of Pearl S. Buck's novel *The Good Earth*. The driving force behind this enterprise was an actress who also happened to be the sister of Schoenberg's friend and former student, Eduard Steurmann. Her name was Salka Viertel, and, as she was involved in screenwriting, she had contacted Irving Thalberg of MGM with the suggestion that Schoenberg might be worth approaching. Thalberg, however, took quite a bit of impressing. It wasn't until he heard a broadcast of Schoenberg's early work, *Verklärte Nacht* ("Transfigured Night"), and discovered a lengthy article about the composer in the *Encyclopaedia Britannica* that he allowed himself to be persuaded to agree to a meeting. Viertel was dispatched to discuss the proposal with Schoenberg after she had warned the producers that Schoenberg no longer wrote in the late–Romantic style of *Verklärte Nacht*. Schoenberg was duly informed by Viertel that the current fee for film scores was around twenty-five thousand dollars, but she reminded him that there was no guarantee, despite his appearance in the *Encyclopaedia Britannica*, that the studios would not cut or alter his music. Duly warned, and no doubt tempted by the cash, Schoenberg agreed to meet Thalberg. It soon became apparent, however, that Schoenberg's ideas about film music weren't shared by the influential film producer. Viertel recorded the meeting, at which she acted as interpreter, in her memoirs:

> [Schoenberg] sat down in front of Thalberg's desk, Schoenberg refusing to part with his umbrella in case he forgot it on leaving. [...] Thalberg [...,] standing behind his desk, was explaining why he wanted a great composer for the scoring of *The Good Earth*. When he came to "Last Sunday, when I heard the lovely music you have written..." Schoenberg interrupted sharply: "I don't write lovely music." Thalberg looked baffled, then smiled and explained what he meant by "lovely music." It had to have Chinese themes, and, as the people in the film were peasants, there was not much dialogue but a lot of action. For example, there were scenes like that where the locusts eat all the grain in the fields which needed special scoring and so on. I translated what Thalberg said into German but Schoenberg [...] understood everything, and in a surprisingly literary though faulty English, he conveyed what he thought in general of music in films: that it was simply terrible.[7]

"Think of it!" Thalberg continued, "There's a terrific storm going on, the wheat field is swinging in the wind, and suddenly the earth begins to tremble. In the midst of the earthquake Oo-Lan gives birth to a baby. What an opportunity for music!"

"With so much going on," Schoenberg witheringly replied, "what do you need music for?"

And as if that wasn't bad enough, Schoenberg then made some outrageous demands. First of all he insisted that he should work personally with the actors, as the music he had in mind was to be similar to the style of his piece *Pierrot Lunnaire,* in which lines are declaimed rhythmically, with exaggerated pitch inflections, over the music. When Thalberg pointed out that the director usually handled the actors, Schoenberg generously replied that the director could do that after the actors had studied their lines with him. In the end, he left no doubt as to the terms of his contract: "I want fifty thousand dollars and an absolute guarantee that not a single note of my music will be altered. If I do commit suicide I want at least to live well on it."[8]

It's not at all surprising, then, that the deal fell through, though Schoenberg did attempt to score some of the picture. Only sketches survive, however, and the film business heard no more from him. Schoenberg may not have succeeded as a practical composer for film, but his influence on succeeding film composers has been considerable, and in many ways this influence might be seen as the most complete vindication of his musical theories.

Born in Vienna in 1874, Schoenberg was a largely self-taught composer.

Strangers in paradise. (Left to right) Charles Chaplin, Gertrud & Arnold Schoenberg and David Raksin in Los Angeles (circa 1935) (photograph by Max Munn Autrey, courtesy the Arnold Schönberg Center, Vienna).

Though always short of money, nothing would make him compromise his artistic ideals. Beginning his composing career with gigantic post–Wagnerian works such as *Gurrelieder* ("Songs of Gurre"), Schoenberg continually refined his compositional style, moving towards his major musical innovation: the system of composition known as serialism. In the wake of advanced Wagnerian chromaticism, which to Schoenberg seemed to be undermining a sense of a recognizable key, Schoenberg dispensed with keys altogether and wrote in a freely atonal style. He then decided that his music required a more formal structural system, and so began to arrange the twelve notes of the chromatic scale into what he called a note row on which an entire composition could be based. The intervals between the adjacent notes were to be as remote from traditional relationships as possible, and in order to provide developmental possibilities he suggested that there should be four versions of the note row available to the composer: the original row, the retrograde row (which presents the note row backwards), the inversion of the note row (which means that if, for example, an interval *rises* five semitones in the original row, it would *descend* five semitones in the inversion), and, finally, a retrograde inversion (which presents the inversion backwards). With these four rows at his or her disposal, the composer would now have a wealth of combinations that would be liberated from the restrictions of traditional harmonic rules. Schoenberg's principle rule was that though notes could be repeated, they should always be presented consecutively. (One could, for example, play the following sequence: 1, 2, 2, 1, 2, 3, 4, 5, 3, 4, 5, 6.) Notes could be also be played together to form chords (i.e. the first four notes of the row could form a single chord, which could then be played on its own or joined by a chord made from some or all of the remaining notes). The combinations and permutations are, of course, endless.

As I mentioned earlier, the first serial film score was, unexpectedly, for an animated cartoon called *The Cat That Hated People* (dir. Tex Avery, 1948), so Schoenberg was, after all, right about the comic potential of his new system. Scott Bradley, famous for his work on MGM's "Tom and Jerry" cartoon series, scored this surreal seven minute adventure in which a neurotic cat, disturbed by the behavior of humans, flies to the moon in a rocket. There he meets a walking diaper, a pair of lips and a dog collar, among other things, all of which reflect the imagery of the then still fashionable Surrealist movement. (Salvador Dalí had, indeed, designed the dream sequences for Alfred Hitchcock's *Spellbound* only three years before.) At one point, Bradley shares a twelve-tone row between a piccolo and an oboe, while a bassoon simultaneously plays the retrograde version of the row. It was a truly groundbreaking moment for a Hollywood film. However, it wasn't until 1955 that a full-length feature film was accompanied by a serial score. This was composed by Leonard Rosenman for *The Cobweb* (dir. Vincente Minnelli, 1955), which was set in a psychiatric sanatorium (a perhaps more obvious environment for the angst and inner turmoil so often found in Schoenberg's music). Rosenman himself explained why he took this approach:

I felt that the film really could have used this kind of treatment. I also felt that it would have set off the film as not simply a pot-boiler melodrama which happened to center around an insane asylum but rather a film in which this kind of expressionistic music could be, so to speak, mind reading or, as I say, super-real.... It was my intention not to "ape" or mimic the physical aspect of the screen *mise en scène* but it was more my intention to show what was going on inside the characters' heads..., to enter the plot and show something that wasn't immediately perceived on the screen and to try to create a kind of atmosphere that was, in my opinion, conspicuously lacking in the movie. The movie was a very refined and very slick and very well produced film. But I wanted more neurosis: much more of the inner workings of the people, which, I think, were a bit lacking in the overt action of the film.[9]

Though Rosenman was inspired by the example of Schoenberg's Piano Concerto, which he was studying at the time (and he actually uses a piano in the main title music), his desire to create a musical expression of the neurotic inner workings of the people in the film was very much the same approach as Schoenberg's.

Meanwhile, in the world of contemporary concert music, the immediate post-war period witnessed the emergence of a bewildering variety of musical styles. After the horrors unleashed on the world by Adolf Hitler, the late–Romantic, post–Wagnerian aesthetic that had informed the musical style of composers sympathetic to the Nazi regime was discredited by many of the younger generation of composers who had grown up during the second world war. A crisis took the world of contemporary music by storm, almost as destructive and partisan in its own terms as the war itself had been. Composers who had been banned by National Socialism, such as Stravinsky, Bartók and Schoenberg, were rediscovered by the European intelligentsia and formed a model for what became known as the New Music. A split soon appeared, however, between those who supported the more traditional style of Bartók and Stravinsky, and those who championed Schoenberg's radical serial style. The division between the two camps was complicated further when the traditionalist Stravinsky embraced serialism after Schoenberg's death in 1951. Serialism soon became the dominant style — aggressively so in the wake of Pierre Boulez, who regarded any contemporary music not written along serial principles as completely irrelevant to modern life. In 1952, Boulez wrote: "Anyone who has not felt — I do not say understand — but felt the necessity of the dodecaphonic language is *useless*. For everything he writes will fall short of the imperatives of his time."[10] However, Boulez and his followers felt that Schoenberg was still too contaminated with an expressionist and post–Romantic aesthetic, derived ultimately from Schoenberg's idol, Richard Wagner; and that lineage was perceived as having been corrupted by Wagner's association with Hitler (one of Wagner's most infamous admirers). Boulez acknowledged that Schoenberg had revolutionized music, but he now argued that Schoenberg's music hadn't gone far enough:

stereotyped clichés abound with Schoenberg, clichés typical of a romanticism at once ostentatious and outmoded. I mean those continual anticipations with expressive stress on the harmony note, and those false appoggiaturas; also those broken chords, tremolos, and repetitions which sound as terribly hollow and deserve only too well the name "subsidiary voices" which they have been given. Lastly there are the poor, and even ugly, rhythms, in which variations of the classical technique appear in the most disconcertingly simple way.... Let us then, without any wish to provoke indignation, but also without shame or hypocrisy, or any sense of frustration, admit the fact that SCHOENBERG IS DEAD.[11]

The article offended many, but was one of the main reasons why the avant-garde now focused its attention on the work of one of Schoenberg's pupils, Anton Webern, who soon became the figurehead of a veritable cult. Webern's style and approach to composition fitted in well with the rational anti–Romantic ideals of the younger generation, who regarded the excesses of Romanticism in general as having been largely responsible for the catastrophe into which European civilization had been plunged in 1939. Webern's approach to serialism aimed to replace extravagance and subjectivity with compression and objectivity. He also aimed to avoid all references to the past. Whereas even Schoenberg and Schoenberg's other pupil, Alban Berg, still permitted elements of tonality to survive in the arrangement of their note rows, Webern assiduously avoided triadic harmony, as well as structuring his approach to form on symmetrical mirror patterns and contrapuntal devices. His overall aim was to organize every aspect of a work intellectually, thus avoiding any element of personal, "spontaneous" emotion.

This mathematical, highly rational approach to composition eventually led to what became known as Integral Serialism, the leading proponent of which was Pierre Boulez. Integral Serialism aimed to control not only the pitches of a piece by means of a series but also every other aspect of its performance by subjecting dynamics, methods of attack, and tempo to serial procedures as well. The intention of so doing was to avoid the danger of the performer imposing his own ideas and personality onto a piece and to make the music itself as cerebral and controlled as possible. The term often used to describe such ideals was "pre-formed."

Such approaches were an attempt by the avant-garde to reject a past that they saw in an almost entirely negative light after the most catastrophic period of human history. They wished to distance themselves from the irrational impulses that had led to so much bloodshed, to wipe the board of history clean and to create a *tabula rasa* on which to compose a brave new musical world. The irony was that in its rejection of totalitarian ideology, the avant-garde ended up creating its own totalitarian aesthetic, and not everyone was happy with that. The American minimalist composer Steve Reich, for example, who was born in 1936, recalled the discomfort he felt when he was a student at a time when this avant-garde ideology was at its most influential:

When I went to music school — I was at Juilliard, and at Mills College — there was one way to write, and if you didn't write twelve-tone serial music you were just a joke. You just weren't to be taken seriously. So the only way to deal with that, for me, was to leave that world.[12]

Inevitably, the avant-garde's *tabula rasa* soon became a confusion of opposing views. Not every avant-garde composer embraced the Boulez model. While still opposing traditionalists such as Benjamin Britten and Dmitri Shostakovitch, some avant-garde composers sought less rigid and more openly expressive methods of composition. The Italian Luciano Berio (born in 1925) embraced what became known as free dodecaphony, which loosened Schoenberg's rules by using the series much more informally, as well as permitting tonal elements.

The field was made more complex by the introduction of so-called "aleatoric" music. The main exponent of this idea was the American composer John Cage (born in 1912), who felt that in order to avoid as much personal involvement as possible, the composer should set up a series of alternatives and let chance decide which one is used. (It is not surprising that Cage should eventually have "composed" that ultimate example of non-involvement, *4',33"*, in which a pianist plays nothing at all. As is the case with so many modernist ideas, however, there was nothing really new going on here. The French symbolist writer Villiers de L'Isle Adam had conceived of such "silent" music, along with the whole idea of a modernist hoax, in his story "The Secret of the Old Music," from his 1883 collection *Cruel Tales.* "The Secret of the Old Music" concerns a German composer who has written a piece for a percussion instrument called a Chinese pavilion:

> The German composer, out of Teutonic jealousy, had amused himself with Hunnish cruelty and vindictive malignity, by peppering the Chinese pavilion's part with almost insurmountable difficulties. They followed one after another, close together, ingenious, unexpected. It was a positive challenge! Let the reader judge for himself: the part consisted exclusively of *rests*. Now, even for people who are not in the profession, what could be more difficult for a Chinese pavilion to play than a *rest*? ... And it was a *crescendo* of rests that the old artist had to perform.
> He stiffened at the sight, and made an involuntary gesture of anger. But nothing in his instrument betrayed the feelings agitating him. Not one little bell moved. Not one clapper struck. Not one campanula stirred.[...] He, too, was an undoubted master.
> He played. Without flinching. With a mastery, a skill, a *brio* which filled the whole orchestra with admiration. His performance, always sober, but full of nuances, was so polished in its style, so pure in its rendering, that, strange as it may seem, the others had the impression at times that they could hear him![13]

Eventually, aleatoric methods began to influence the European avant-garde, and Boulez created his own, at first sight perhaps contradictory, concept of controlled chance.

New methods of notation rapidly proliferated to suggest new approaches to musical sound. Graphic scores permitted composers to reject traditional notation and instead indicate the pitches or the general register in which a performer should play, but not their order or indeed their rhythm. Such experiments led to the concept of tone-clusters, a stylistic idiom made famous by Krzysztof Penderecki (born in 1933), while similar effects were created by the much more traditional notation of György Ligeti (born in 1923). With the development of electronic music, new timbres were added to the traditional repertoire of orchestral sounds, leading to a diverse and sometimes bewildering complex of alternative aesthetic theories and compositional styles, which developed aloof from but nonetheless alongside the world of commercial popular music. Popular music, by contrast, never rejected tonality and traditional musical structures, and its all-pervasive influence seriously jeopardized the avant-garde's mission to re-educate the public's ears. Frustrated with the public's lack of enthusiasm to be so re-educated, along with the unstoppable triumph of tonality in pop music, avant-garde composers became increasingly remote from the public at large and closed themselves off from the "real" world, just as Frankenstein had locked himself in his laboratory to work uninterrupted on his unwanted and misunderstood experimental creation. It was largely left to film music to bring avant-garde experimentation to a popular audience.

Horror, myth and fantasy have always attracted composers because of the challenges such subjects offer to create a musical equivalent of an alternative world. Henry Purcell had thoroughly enjoyed himself composing music for witches and demons in his opera *Dido and Aeneas* (1689); and what is the finale of Mozart's opera *Don Giovanni* (1787) but a musical ghost story, in which a statue comes to life and drags the dissolute hero down to hell? In the nineteenth century, Richard Wagner had been fascinated by subjects that were not so different from the ones Hammer and Amicus were to exploit in the twentieth. Wagner was a devoted fan of Carl Maria von Weber's *singspiel*, *Der Freischütz* (1821), with its sensationally supernatural "Wolf's Glen" scene, in which deep in the heart of an enchanted forest we encounter owls, fiery wheels, wild boars, storm winds and ghostly huntsmen, while the devil in person is summoned from Hell by means of a ghastly invocation. Wagner wrote in his memoirs: "In particular, *Freischütz*, though mainly because of its spooky plot, affected my imagination with characteristic intensity. The excitement of horror and fear of ghosts constitute a singular factor in the development of my emotional life."[14] Wagner's early fascination with Heinrich Marschner's opera *Der Vampyr* (1828) led him to compose extra material for it; and his last music-drama, *Parsifal*, contains a wealth of vampiric undertones in such characters as the immortal seductress Kundry, the dangerously alluring flower maidens, the "undead" master of the grail, Titurel, and the great emphasis placed on blood throughout the entire proceedings.[15] Both Wagner and his eventual father-in-law, Franz Liszt, were also fascinated by the Faust legend. Liszt, in particular, was drawn to the character of Mephistopheles, who inspired many of his pieces. He even wrote a piano accompaniment to Gottfried Bürger's ghostly ballad "Lenore," in which the corpse of a soldier takes his still-living fiancée to the bridal couch of the tomb. The centerpiece of Giacomo Meyerbeer's seminal 1831 Grand Opera *Robert le diable* (a huge influence on Wagner's *Parsifal),* was a ballet set in a graveyard in which the hero encounters the ghosts of nuns who were not faithful to their vows during life; while Camille Saint-Saëns' most famous symphonic poem, *Danse macabre* (1877), describes a dance of death, with Death himself playing the fiddle.

As the film director John Badham wrote in his notes for the soundtrack recording of John Williams' score for *Dracula* (1979):

> The nineteenth century romantics could all say they had a descendant living late in the 20th Century. Operatic in scale, it surrounds and elevates this often told tale of the vampire King who takes a Queen for himself.
> Puccini, Verdi, Berlioz all blew it. What a great subject for an opera.[16]

Many of the writings of Edgar Allan Poe have also been set to music. Via Charles Baudelaire's French translations of Poe, which inspired the whole generation of symbolists at the end of the nineteenth century, French composer and protégée of Debussy, André Caplet, also based his *Conte fantastique (*which is really a miniature harp concerto) on "The Masque of the Red Death" (1909); while Debussy himself had toyed with the idea of an opera based on "The Fall of the House of Usher." Symbolist composer Florent Schmitt based a symphonic poem on Poe's "The Haunted Palace" (1904), and even Rachmaninoff, much enamored of things gloomy, set Poe's "The Bells" to music in 1910, just as he had been inspired to base a symphonic poem on Arnold Böcklin's even more gloomy painting *The Isle of the Dead* in 1907. (Böcklin's painting would later form the basis of one of the horror films that Boris Karloff would make for film producer Val Lewton at RKO in 1945.) The early twentieth-century British composer Joseph Holbrooke enjoyed a lifelong fascination with Poe, and not only wrote symphonic poems based on Poe's poems "The Raven," "The Bells" and "Ulalume," along with a choral symphony subtitled "Hommage to E.A. Poe," but also turned Poe's story "The Masque of the Red Death" into a ballet in 1925.

Aaron Copland also responded to the classic vampire imagery of F.W. Murnau's 1921 film *Nosferatu* with what eventually became his ballet score *Grohg* (1922–25), in which a sorcerer reanimates corpses and makes them dance for his pleasure. The British composer John Gasken based his 1990 opera *Golem* on the ancient Jewish legends that had inspired the early twentieth-century writer Gustav Meyrinck, whose novel *The Golem* went on to inspire Paul Wegener's early "horror" films on the same subject. Ghost stories by Henry James have suggested two operas to Benjamin Britten. His 1954 opera based on *The Turn of the Screw* was followed in 1970 by the television opera *Owen*

Wingrave; while in 2000, the contemporary American composer Scott Eyerly transformed Nathaniel Hawthorne's *The House of Seven Gables* into an opera, telling the macabre tale of a family that suffers under a witch's curse, set in Salem, Massachusetts.

Horror subjects in general, and the horror film in particular, have always inhabited a twilight world in the outer reaches of respectability, and film has provided the perfect platform for composers to experiment under its cover of darkness. It's no surprise that so many innovative composers should have been attracted to the horror film, and, as we shall see, the films themselves benefited beyond measure from the music they wrote for them.

Notes

1. Arnold Schoenberg, "Art and the Moving Pictures," in *Style and Idea* (ed. L. Black) (London: Faber and Faber, 1975), pp. 153–154.
2. Hanns Eisler, *Composing for Films* (Oxford: Oxford University Press, 1948), p. 36.
3. Schoenberg quoted in Carl Dalhaus, *Schoenberg and the New Music* (Cambridge: Cambridge University Press, 1987), p. 102.
4. Barry Millington (ed.), *Selected Letters of Richard Wagner* (London: Dent, 1987), p. 475 (letter from Richard Wagner to Mathilde Wesendonck, October 29, 1859).
5. Arnold Schoenberg, "New Music: My Music," 1930, in *Style and Idea* (Note 1), p. 105.
6. "Circular to my Friends on my sixtieth Birthday," 1934, in *Style and Idea* (Note 1), p. 28.
7. Salka Viertel, *The Kindness of Strangers* (New York: Holt, 1969), pp. 207–8.
8. Schoenberg quoted in Oscar Levant, *A Smattering of Ignorance* (New York: Doubleday, 1940), pp. 127–8.
9. Rosenman quoted in Roy M. Prendergast, *Film Music, a Neglected Art* (New York: Norton, 1977), p. 119.
10. Joan Peyser, *Boulez, Composer, Conductor, Enigma* (London: Cassell, 1976), p. 70.
11. Michael Hall (ed.), *Leaving Home — A Conducted Tour of Twentieth-Century Music with Simon Rattle* (London: Faber and Faber, 1996), pp. 207–8.
12. Michael Oliver (ed.), *Settling the Score — A Journey through the Music of the 20th Century* (London: Faber and Faber, 1999), p. 133.
13. Villiers de l'Isle Adam, *Cruel Tales* (trans. Robert Baldick) (Oxford: Oxford University Press, 1985), p. 117.
14. Richard Wagner, *My Life* (trans. Andrew Gray) (Cambridge: Cambridge University Press, 1983), p. 13.
15. For further information about the vampire imagery of *Parsifal* see David Huckvale, "Wagner and Vampires," in *Wagner* (ed. Stewart Spencer), vol. 18, no. 3, September 1997, pp. 127–141.
16. John Badham, sleeve notes to the LP album of John Williams' score for *Dracula*, MCA Records, 1979 (MCF 3018).

THREE

Serial Killer

Benjamin Frankel

It wasn't until 1961, thirty-eight years after Schoenberg first invented it, that serialism first appeared on the soundtrack of a British film. Perhaps surprisingly, considering the uses to which Schoenberg had put it, only one Hammer film score, *The Curse of the Werewolf*, was ever based on serial principles, though elements of atonality crop up regularly on the soundtracks of their other films. Audiences consisting of the "ordinary people" Schoenberg so despised (and who would no doubt have returned the compliment if they had been confronted with Schoenberg's own music in a concert hall) nonetheless happily absorbed his demanding musical idiom in the context of a popular horror film.

Benjamin Frankel's score for *The Curse of the Werewolf* was written towards the end of his prolific film and concert career. Born in London, in 1906, Frankel's musical education was broad and varied. As a boy he had studied music on his own in Hammersmith Public Library. At home, he learned to play the piano and violin, before studying the piano more formally in Germany. Back in London he worked as a jazz violinist in night clubs, and studied piano and composition, like Philip Martell, at the Guildhall School. After that he worked as an orchestrator and conductor for many West End musicals, writing his first film score in 1934 for *Radio Parade of 1935* (dir. Arthur B. Woods). He went on to compose over one hundred film scores alongside his eight symphonies, displaying none of the cinematic misgivings of Schoenberg by happily combining different musical styles across the board. Among the films he scored are *The Seventh Veil* (dir. Compton Bennett, 1945), *Trottie True* (Brian Desmond Hurst, 1949), *So Long at the Fair* (dir. Terence Fisher, 1950), *The Importance of Being Earnest* (dir. Anthony Asquith, 1952), *The Net* (Anthony Asquith, 1953), *The Prisoner* (dir. Peter Glenville, 1955) and *The Night of the Iguana* (dir. John Huston, 1964). Although he scored three films for Hammer, *The Curse of the Werewolf* was his most significant film project for the company. Frankel's approach to serialism has been described by his protégé and fellow film composer, Buxton Orr[1]:

Where's the Wolf? Benjamin Frankel with friend Pinkie (circa 1960) (photograph courtesy Xenia Frankel).

The special feature of Frankel's approach to serialism was his strong belief in tonality as a continuingly vital principle in musical thought, and his striking demonstration in practice that strictly serial deployment of the total chromatic is compatible with both expressive and structural use of tonality. He viewed the series as a pervasively thematic melodic line of almost infinite versatility, out of which it was possible to derive harmonies often of a startlingly bold diatonicism.[2]

However, Frankel's parallel concert and cinematic career had some unfortunate consequences. It was generally assumed that Frankel reacted to the success of his accessible film music by writing very introverted, melancholy and demandingly difficult concert music, but, as Orr pointed out, such an impression doesn't stand up to scrutiny, as one simply can't split the two sides of his career into those rigid characterizations.³ Frankel's score for *The Curse of the Werewolf* is certainly demanding, but it is also immediately effective film music. However, in 1961, when the film first appeared, there was still a prejudice against concert composers who also worked in popular film. Film music historian John Huntley was certainly of this opinion:

> Many composers went into film music and virtually destroyed their concert-hall career in doing it. William Alwyn certainly did that; Benjamin Frankel did that. It's only recently that the concert works of Alwyn and Frankel have even begun to get any kind of recognition. But, you see, in their day, "Oh, he's a film composer. Oh, we don't want him in the programme. He writes for the movies, you know, writes for the flicks"—this was very much the attitude. So some of the composers had to make a very conscious decision: make the money out of the movies; write what you like for the concert hall, but don't expect anybody to listen to it, because once you're stamped as a movie composer the concert-hall world will not want to know you.⁴

The Curse of the Werewolf is typical of Hammer's overall approach to gothic horror in its rigidly moral, Christian framework. Poor Leon, the werewolf of the title, through no fault of his own, is a congenital monster. His unavoidable destiny is to suffer for the rape of his mother by a miserable beggar who himself has been cruelly treated by a selfish aristocrat and locked up for no reason other than being poor. Leon is indeed a Christlike figure. He is born on Christmas Day (an unwanted child born on such a day is, we are told, an insult to heaven), and the first shot we see of the baby is when it is held up in front of a painting of the Madonna and Child. The sensitive Leon, who hates the sight of blood, nonetheless turns into a werewolf when the moon is full. When he eventually realizes what he is, he pleads to be killed. Like Victor Hugo's Quasimodo, this ostracized monster is eventually trapped in a belfry (the same belfry, indeed, that framed the opening shots of the film, thus emphasizing the horrible inevitability of his fate). The religious connotations are rich and significant. Leon's death atones for the sins of others, his own sin having been merely a difficulty in expressing his own sexuality. Instead of crucifixion, he is shot by his adoptive father with a silver bullet, while a crowd of colorfully dressed Spanish villagers (far more terrifying than any werewolf) bay for his blood below. The ultimate victim, Leon is truly more sinned against than sinning, and it is, of course, the consequences of his tragic destiny that the director of the film, Terence Fisher, concentrates upon. As Fisher himself once famously put it:

> If my films reflect my own personal view of the world in any way, it is in their showing of the ultimate victory of good over evil, in which I do

believe. It may take human beings a long time to achieve this, but I do believe that this is how events work out in the end.[5]

A more succinct moral view it would be hard to find, and, indeed, there is no room for moral ambiguity in any of Hammer's Gothic horror films. Even sexual ambiguity is punished (think of the probably homosexual Baron Meinster in Fisher's *Brides of Dracula*, 1960). Dr. Jekyll's disastrous sex change into his sister in Hammer's 1971 *Dr. Jekyll and Sister Hyde* was directed by Roy Ward Baker rather than Fisher, but the film's message conforms to type. Leon might also be a sexual deviant. The fact that he murders a woman of rather loose morals who has enticed him to her bed could indicate that he isn't much attracted to her. Fisher would no doubt have argued that it was simply because he was a werewolf, but sex of any kind is the great evil in all Hammer films. Vampires are evil because they awaken sexual desire. All that is primitive and instinctive must be subdued beneath the power of Christian authority figures, such as Van Helsing, who could be seen as the real monster, staking, as he does, anything that shows the slightest sexual desire. In Hammer's Gothic classics, there is good and there is evil. That, to paraphrase Keats, is all there is and all we need to know — in a Hammer film at least.

Schoenbergian serialism and atonality are fine for musical evocations of "Threatening Danger," "Panic" and "Catastrophe," but how well-suited are they to expressing their opposites? A moral universe can perhaps only be expressed in musical terms by means of oppositions and contrasts, principally of a harmonic nature. As Wagner said while composing the erotic and demonic second act of *Parsifal*: "In the first act I was very sparing of sensuous intervals, but now I am going back to my old

Oliver Reed as Leon in *The Curse of the Werewolf* (dir. Terence Fisher, 1960).

paintpot."⁶ And here, surely, lies the root of Schoenberg's basic misunderstanding of Wagner's chromaticism, a misunderstanding that could be said to be the root cause of serialism's subsequent unpopularity. Schoenberg regarded Wagner's extremes in the chromatic department as heralding the *complete* breakdown of tonality, ushering in a new musical language—first, of atonality, and second, of the serial style that Schoenberg apparently claimed, in self-confident Teutonic style, would preserve the supremacy of German music for the next one hundred years.⁷ But, of course, that didn't happen. The novelist Thomas Mann, for one, certainly felt that Schoenberg's system, while being capable of Mephistophelean irony, was incapable of discussing morality as such, because it no longer had that power of harmonic contrast, having destroyed that bedrock of musical certainty from which chromaticism may wander, in a *Parsifalian* sense, towards "evil." In his novel *Dr. Faustus*, Mann's hero, Adrian Leverkühn, is to some extent modeled on Schoenberg himself. Leverkühn's music is ironic, mocking, "hellish," "overwhelming, sardonically yelling, screeching, bawling, bleating, howling, piping, whinnying [...] icily clear, glassily transparent, of brittle dissonances indeed, but withal of an—I would like to say—inaccessibly unearthly and alien beauty of sound, filling the heart with longing without hope."⁸ Not surprisingly, Schoenberg was highly offended by Mann's opinion of his musical style and the moral implications this had on Schoenberg's character, but in many ways this argument remains academic. Living, as we do, in a world in which tonality is very much alive in popular music, and also in the constant performances of tonal classical music, the shifting sands of chromaticism can never hope to lose their traditional signification as an opposite to the solid bedrock of tonality.

Hammer's conservative approach affected many aspects of its films. Its main concern was, of course, to make money by entertaining audiences—thrilling them certainly, but not offending them. Indeed, the company had gone so far as to build the sets for a film about the Spanish Inquisition before dropping the project to avoid offending the Catholic Church. That is why *The Curse of the Werewolf* (the screenplay of which was based on Guy Endore's novel *The Werewolf of Paris*) was set, in the end, in Spain. Actor Richard Wordsworth's anecdote about his part in *The Curse of the Werewolf* is typical of the company's policy at that time. Just before shooting the rape scene in which the werewolf of the title is conceived, Terence Fisher offered Wordsworth some advice: "Oh, this is something we always do," he said. "You have a mouthful of egg white, and when you see the girl you slobber a little of it. But keep it tasteful."⁹ One could say that this desire to keep it tasteful also affected the style of the music that accompanied the film. An approach that completely abandoned traditional harmonies would perhaps have been too experimental and daring for the company at that time. Indeed, a popular film score without any elements of tonality would still be an exception today. Frankel's personal musical style, which was fully formed by 1960, fitted in well with this caution. Since the 1950s he had been strongly influenced by serialism, but, as we have seen, he firmly believed that this should be combined with more traditional elements.

The film begins with a close-up of Oliver Reed in full werewolf makeup accompanied by Frankel's astonishing main title music. Like Berg's Violin Concerto, tonal elements leven Frankel's atonal mix, based, as it is, on the following note row:

Benjamin Frankel, *The Curse of the Werewolf*— original note row.

This row contains two elements of tonality within it, which are the implied B-flat major and G-minor chords. However, the main title section is not constructed solely upon this note-row. Trombones, cellos and double-basses also have their own theme based on major and minor triads (indicated as A, B, C, and D in the lower stave, below):

Benjamin Frankel, *The Curse of the Werewolf*—1M1, bars 1–4 (Reduction).

Between them, these four chords contain the twelve pitches of the row (although they do not, of course, follow its original order), and they provide an even stronger feeling of tonality. One can hear how effectively Frankel develops the potential of the row in the latter part of 2M3 during the scene in which Yvonne Romain's jailor's daughter (who will eventually become Leon's mother) attends to the fire in the room of the old Marquis (played by Anthony Dawson). This takes place just after Clifford Evans' soundtrack narration has explained that the Marquis has become a recluse. An oboe and a flute (which are later joined by the vibraphone) exploit the opportunities that Schoenberg suggested for development of the row by transposing the pitches and repeating individual notes:

Benjamin Frankel, *The Curse of the Werewolf*— 2M3, bars 4–7.

Such a process is entirely in accordance with Schoenberg's system. However, the signification of the dissonances in Frankel's score are not liberated in the manner for which Schoenberg would have hoped. Schoenberg was keen to argue that conventional dissonances are actually "the more remote consonances of the overtone series"[10]; but the dissonant effects in Frankel's serial music function in a traditionally significatory manner. For Frankel, dissonance is a signifier of horror, pain and suffering, and this explains the reason for his abandoning serialism altogether in the next section of score. The theme that is associated with innocence throughout the film is marked *dolce cantabile*, and is quite at odds with serial procedure:

Benjamin Frankel, *The Curse of the Werewolf*—1M2, bars 13–16.

One could attempt to "justify" this melody in the same way that Berg "excused" the traditional Austrian *Ländler* that he included in his Violin Concerto—by rearranging the notes of the row to make them "fit" the tune—but such a manipulation frankly stretches things too far to justify either melody as deriving from the row itself. However, both composers' mix of tonal and serial material achieves the sense of harmonic contrast they required to suggest the tragic, nostalgic and melancholy aspects of the concerto and the film score. Frankel also indulges in some local color for the film's early scenes by exploiting the distinctively Spanish sound of the castanets.

What makes the score so remarkable is how Frankel manages to negotiate the demands of a serial structure and at the same time synchronize the music with the film's narrative. For example, he includes the dramatic effect of wind *glissandi* to accompany the murder of the old Marquis in 3M1; and when Alfredo hears a wolf howling while waiting for Leon to be born, Frankel makes sure that the "werewolf" motif, originally heard in the main title, makes its appearance on cue:

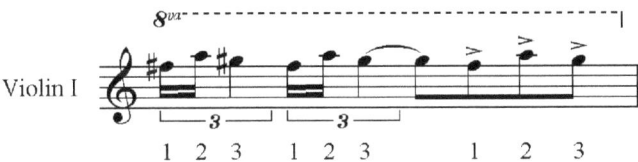

Benjamin Frankel, *The Curse of the Werewolf*—"Werewolf" Motif, 1M1, bar 7.

This "werewolf" motif is based on the opening three notes of the original series; and the series also generates the other motif associated with Leon's werewolf transformations. This second theme also appears during the thunderstorm that accompanies his baptism, and it is derived from tones nine, ten, eleven and twelve:

Benjamin Frankel, *The Curse of the Werewolf*—1M1, bar 4.

Similarly, the yearning fall of a sixth, which often accompanies the film's love scenes, is also derived from notes eleven and twelve:

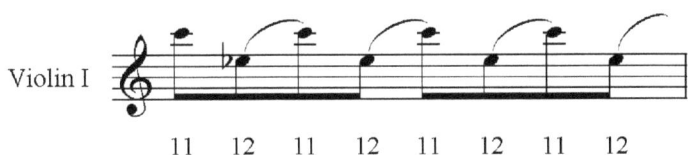

Benjamin Frankel, *The Curse of the Werewolf*—1M1, bar 9.

A notable example of the return of this motif occurs in the final love scene between Leon and Christina (played by Catherine Feller), the troubled nature of which is emphasized by a bar of oscillating tritones that precede the similarly oscillating sixths:

Benjamin Frankel, *The Curse of the Werewolf*— 8M3, bars 10-12.

Frankel calls upon the traditionally diabolic signification of these tritones, which are derived from the interval between the seventh and eighth tones of the original note row. Perhaps Frankel's most effective and memorable manipulation of the original note row accompanies the rape of the jailer's daughter by Richard Wordsworth's imprisoned beggar: an act of violence in which Leon is conceived and which thus initiates the cycle of future deaths. The same musical material accompanies all the subsequent murders. The first of these is Leon's attack on the prostitute (played by Serafina di Leo); the second is his murder of Dominique (played by George Woodbridge); and the theme returns when Leon is finally shot at the end of the film. The motif that accompanies all these acts of violence consists of a sequence of quintuplet groups, which form part of a retrograde version of the original row. Note how Frankel uses notes twelve and five to provide the supporting harmony, and that in the second bar of Example 9 the pattern is repeated, but in a different pitch:

Benjamin Frankel, *The Curse of the Werewolf*— 2M5, bars 1-2.

Frankel also skillfully transforms the emotional effect of his material through orchestration. When, for example, baby Leon is first presented to us in front of the painting of the Madonna and Child, Frankel restricts himself to a solo violin and a harp, thus creating an intimate mood that is, in fact, similar to the opening bars of Berg's Violin Concerto. Marked *teneremente* (tenderly), the violin plays a motif based on notes four, five and six of the original row, interspersed with notes one, two and three, before returning to four, five and six. Accompanying this, the harp plays a rocking figure based on notes five, six and seven of the original row.

Benjamin Frankel, *The Curse of the Werewolf*— 3M3, bars 2–5.

Similarly, in 5M2, the main title music returns, but this time scored for a string orchestra, as the Priest explains to Alfredo that only love can cure Leon's condition.

Before Leon is born, while his mute mother is lying in bed, Frankel again manages to create a completely different mood but still base his material on the row. Marked *mistico,* the somber, chant-like theme that is intoned in unison by the strings is derived from notes one, two and three of the original row as shown on the following page (3M3, bars 1–2).

As the werewolf is chased through the streets by the angry mob, Frankel's breathtaking finale resembles the furious intensity of Bernard Herrmann's almost contemporaneous music for *North by Northwest* (dir. Alfred Hitchcock, 1959). Herrmann's relentless fandango for that film is, correctly, in three beats in the bar. It would have been appropriate if the Spanish-set *Curse of the Werewolf* also ended with a fandango, but Frankel uses common time instead. He does, however, set up a very percussive, syncopated rhythm characteristic of Spanish music in general, and bases his opening idea on the minor triad that is implied in the middle of the original row (notes four, five and six) as shown on the following page (10M2, bars 1–2).

However, he now moves away from the constraints of the row considerably. Indeed, in several passages the strings play what strongly resemble conventional minor scales. Consequently, the music is much more tonal in effect,

Benjamin Frankel, *The Curse of the Werewolf*— 3M3, bars 1–2.

Benjamin Frankel, *The Curse of the Werewolf*—10M2, bars 1–2.

with an overwhelming sweep and intensity worthy of Shostakovitch in his terrifying satire on Stalin in the *Scherzo* of his Tenth Symphony, which was composed eight years before *The Curse of the Werewolf*, in 1953.

After a reprise of the "Rape" motif, as the werewolf climbs into the belfry, Alfredo aims his rifle and dispatches him with the transformative silver bullet. Leon dies and the curse is lifted. Frankel supports this action with a tragic postlude for wind and brass, marked *maestoso* at first, and then, when the strings join in, *con intensita*. The serialism with which the film began now seems a thing of the past, and the score actually ends in D major.

The Curse of the Werewolf was released on May 1, 1961. It made a star of Oliver Reed and remains a classic example of Terence Fisher's Gothic style. Hammer was now riding high on a tidal wave of horror, and *The Curse of the Werewolf* completed Hammer's appropriation of the quartet of classic monsters that included Dracula, Frankenstein's Creature and the Mummy. The significance of Frankel's music, however, took a while longer to be fully appreciated.

There had never been a British film score like it, but for years it was critically ignored, no doubt because it accompanied a film in a genre that was considered the lowest of the low by many critics at the time. It is significant that even by the mid–1970s a serious study of film music by John Huntley and Roger Manvell failed to list *The Curse of the Werewolf* in an appendix that claimed to be "a record of the principle events and film music compositions from 1895–1972."[11]

Even Hammer itself failed to appreciate the novelty of Frankel's approach. According to Frankel's stepson, Dimitri Kennaway, it was Philip Martell who rejected Frankel's subsequent score for the company's extremely expensive adaptation of Dennis Wheatley's novel *Uncharted Seas* (which reached the cinema under the title *The Lost Continent,* produced and directed by Michael Carreras in 1968). Arriving at Frankel's home during the recording sessions, Martell apparently insisted on so many changes that an argument ensued, the result of which was that Carreras decided to commission an entirely new score from someone else.[12] He eventually chose Gerard Schurmann, the British composer of Dutch origin who had been born in Indonesia in 1928. Schurmann's very chromatic, contrapuntal style was unusually complex for films at the time but well-suited to horror and fantasy. Having scored Hammer's earlier war drama, *The Camp on Blood Island* (dir. Val Guest, 1958), Schurmann went on to score the non–Hammer horror film, *Horrors of the Black Museum* (dir. Arthur Crabtree) in 1959, which, like his music for *The Lost Continent,* later formed part of his magnum opus for the concert hall, *Six Studies of Francis Bacon,* and thus providing a striking continuity between his music for both the soundtrack and the concert hall. In *Horrors of the Black Museum,* Michael Gough plays a crime writer who injects a serum into his assistant's bloodstream. The serum gives the assistant homicidal tendencies—and, consequently, increasingly violent ideas for Gough's crime novels. The film's most famous moment concerns a so-called "binocular murder," in which fiendish spikes pierce the eyes of whoever pulls the binoculars' focus; and for this Schürmann created a searing "terror" motif that would later serve the nightmare visions of Francis Bacon (a close friend of the composer) very well. The binocular murder scene had been passed by the censors before the music was added, but Schurmann's music was so effective that when the censors saw the film with its completed soundtrack they insisted that certain frames be deleted to tone down the horrific effect of the sequence. Schurmann's music for *Horrors of the Black Museum* thereby joined the elite company of Edmund Meisel's original music score for Sergei Eisenstein's revolutionary film *Battleship Potemkin* (1925), which some German towns at the time of its first release regarded as a danger to public safety. The nervous authorities allowed the film to be shown but actually banned the music![13]

Like Frankel, Schürmann never "wrote down" for the cinema. Indeed, his music for *The Lost Continent* rather overwhelmed Philip Martell, who was particularly nervous about conducting it. Martell apparently complained that

The opening bars of Benjamin Frankel's manuscript score for the main title music for *The Curse of the Werewolf* (1961) (photograph by the author, courtesy Xenia Frankel).

Schurmann had written "too many notes" (rather in the manner of Emperor Joseph II's opinion of Mozart's Singspiel, *Die Entführung aus dem Serail*). Contrary to the cavalier impression Martell often liked to give with regard to his dealings with directors and producers, he was, in fact, very concerned to give them what they wanted. "Will Michael like it?" was his continual concern during the recording sessions.[14] As it turned out, Carreras loved it—though he also commissioned "groovier" music from Roy Phillips, including a *bossa-nova* theme tune performed by the pop group The Peddlers for the main title, which led to a curiously eclectic concoction. Schurmann, on friendly terms with Frankel at the time, has always been keen to point out that had he known who he was replacing he would never have accepted the job. Frankel's unused score for *The Lost Continent* remains a tantalizing enigma.

Despite the fact that Frankel was Chairman of the British Section of the International Society of Contemporary Music (I.S.C.M.), his score for *The Curse of the Werewolf* is in so many ways contrary to the approach to music advocated by Pierre Boulez and his acolytes at the time of the film's release. In a speech he gave at Darmstadt in the summer of 1961, where a festival of contemporary music had been thriving since its foundation in 1921, Boulez had this to say:

> ... all argument is fruitless when faced with the fetishists who proclaim tradition, nature, the human heart, moderation, "keeping in touch," perspective, order, moderation, "keep left, but not too far," moderation in originality, [...] laws, of imprescriptible rights, moderation, moderation, moderation ... I really must stop. Let these whirling dervishes enjoy their palinodes, as they go on turning, like a demented top, in the narrow circle of their petty obsessions.[15]

Simultaneous with Boulez' aggressively modernist musical agenda, British architects of the time were also responding to continental ideas. Emerging from the ruins of what the Luftwaffe had reduced to rubble, Sir Basil Spence's new Coventry Cathedral was completed in 1962, its interior a celebration of unadorned concrete, and strongly reminiscent of the multi-storey car parks that were rising at the same time over the horizons of many provincial British towns. The decorative elements of many a Victorian town hall were being whitewashed, if not demolished entirely, while Peter and Alison Smithson's designs for Hunstanton secondary modern school (a model of the modernist spirit of the times), with its factory aesthetic inspired by Mies van der Rohe, had already been accommodating students for eight years. Architectural historian David Watkin's description of Hunstanton as "A ruthless intellectual excerise [...] that makes no concessions to charm or comfort"[16] could have been applied to many other modernist buildings (and, indeed, much of the avant-garde music of the time too).

Hammer films, by contrast, were offering the public a series of period-dress Gothic fantasies set amidst lovingly detailed recreations of nineteenth-century decor. However, Peter Cushing's vampire hunter, Professor Van Helsing, contrasted starkly with Edward van Sloane's portrayal of the same character in Universal's *Dracula* (dir. Tod Browning, 1931). Cushing's steely approach reflected the youthful, energetic, professional spirit of the late 1950s. His Van Helsing is intolerant of amateurs, and always approaches the subject of vampires in a ruthlessly scientific manner. As his descendent, Lorrimer Van Helsing (also played by Cushing), says in *Dracula A.D. 1972*, "Oh no, there was nothing ludicrous about it. He was a scientist." Hammer's approach to the character of Count Dracula was also in this no-nonsense, matter-of-fact manner. Lee's Dracula never changed into a wolf or a bat or dissolved into an eerie mist. He was an entirely corporeal, immensely physical and very modern monster. (In *The Satanic Rites of Dracula* he even becomes a corporate property developer.) No archaic middle-European menace for him when he first greets Jonathan Harker from the top of the stairs in his immaculately clean and efficiently run castle. Similarly, there are no swirling mists, mysterious gypsies or Romantic forests in *The Curse of the Werewolf*. Leon's condition, despite the Christian frame of reference, is treated far more psychologically — far more naturalistically. Indeed, if Émile Zola or August Strindberg had ever written a horror film screenplay, this would surely have been it, for the film painstakingly explores Leon's heredity and environment to such an extent that a great deal of time has passed before we are introduced to the adult Leon, and still more until we actually see the werewolf itself. Without putting too fine a point on it, this is indeed the *Nana* or *Miss Julie* of horror films.

Such a mix of nineteenth-century decor and the much more modern concerns that are played out against it suggests that Hammer's films were both responding to and simultaneously distancing themselves from the spirit of the times. As Peter Hutchings has pointed out:

> Certainly there are distinctively conservative elements present in Hammer horror, particularly the stress laid throughout on the need for authoritative leadership.[...] It does seem from this that Hammer's privileging of the professional at this moment in social history enabled it, in an almost prescient fashion, to tap into a widespread feeling that British society was in transition.[...] But a paradox still remains. While Hammer horror films need to be seen very much as addressing the social context within which they were fashioned, account also has to be taken of the fact that, despite their "modernity," they were set in the past. Clearly the films' engagement with present-day matters was, at the very least, veiled or coded.[... The] period settings permitted a conservative nostalgia for a fixed social order, one in which those who were powerless were legitimate prey.[17]

Hammer's modern cult of professionalism and its contradictory nostalgia, so reassuring at a time of disorientating social change, was also reflected, perhaps even more profoundly, in Frankel's music for the psychologically disturbing yet simultaneously reassuring historical horrors of *The Curse of the Werewolf*. His tonal serialism was an apt musical metaphor for this dichotomy, a dichotomy that would be explored in various ways, in rather different Hammer films, by a variety of subsequent composers.

Notes

1. Buxton Orr was a cousin of actress Phyllida Law. Law explained in *The Magic Roundabout Story* (BBC [Timeshift series], 2003, produced by Merryn Threadgould) that Buxton Orr's first name intriguingly inspired that of the evil Blue Cat in the English version of the animated film *Dougal and the Blue Cat* (dir. Serge Danot, 1972). The writer and narrator of that film, Eric Thompson, was Law's husband. Orr was himself the composer of several horror films scores, including *Corridors of Blood* (dir. Robert Day, 1958) and *Dr. Blood's Coffin* (dir. Sidney J. Furie, 1960).

2. Buxton Orr's entry for Benjamin Frankel in Stanley Sadie (ed.), *Grove Dictionary of Music and Musicians* (London: MacMillan, 1980), p. 800.

3. Ibid., p. 799.

4. Michael Oliver (ed.), *Settling the Score* (London: Faber and Faber, 1999), p. 163; John Huntley transcribed from the author's interview with him for BBC Radio 3's "Music and Movies," part of the *Settling the Score* series in 1998.

5. Allen Ayles, Robert Adkinson, and Nicholas Fry, *The House of Horror* (London: Lorrimer, 1984), p. 15.

6. Entry for Friday, April 8, 1878, in Cosima Wagner, *Diaries*, vol. 2 (trans. Geoffrey Skelton) (London: Collins, 1978).

7. This comment is attributed to Arnold Schoenberg by his pupil Josef Rufer, who claimed he heard the composer say this to him during a walk in July 1921. This attribution is, however, unreliable, and Schoenberg may indeed never have said it at all. The source of the quotation is to be found in Rufer's *Das Werk Arnold Schönbergs*, Kassel, 1959.

8. Thomas Mann, *Dr. Faustus* (trans. H.T. Lowe-Porter) (London: Secker and Warburg, 1976), p. 378.

9. John Bronson, *The Horror People* (London: Macdonald and Jane's, 1976), pp. 115–16.

10. Arnold Schoenberg, *Theory of Harmony* (trans. Roy E. Carter) (London: Faber and Faber, 1983), p. 329.

11. Roger Manvell and John Huntley, *The Technique of Film Music* (London: Focal Press, 1975) p. 265–286.

12. Dimitri Kennaway, in correspondence with the author, March 9, 2007.

13. See Roy M. Prendergast, *Film Music: A Neglected Art* (New York: Norton, 1992), pp. 15–16.

14. Gerard Schurmann, in conversation with the author, March 22, 2007.

15. Pierre Boulez, *Orientations* (trans. Martin Cooper) (London: Faber and Faber, 1985), p. 43.

16. David Watkin, *English Architecture* (London: Thames and Hudson, 1992), p. 196.

17. Peter Hutchings, *Hammer and Beyond: The British Horror Film* (Manchester: Manchester University Press, 1993), pp. 64–65.

Four

Modified Modernism
Humphrey Searle and Elisabeth Lutyens

Frankel's serial score for *The Curse of the Werewolf* was not the only "first" for a British film composer. Elisabeth Lutyens was actually the first *female* composer to score a British feature film. It was called *Penny and the Pownall Case*, directed by Slim Hand in 1948, and it was the same movie in which Christopher Lee also made his motion picture debut. Lutyens was at the cutting edge of musical modernism in 1950s Britain, and, along with Frankel and Humphrey Searle, she helped bring new musical ideas to reluctant post-war English audiences. Her relations with Frankel, however, were soured when Lutyens' husband, Edward Clark, brought a slander action against him. Clark had been a BBC producer much in sympathy with the new music, and eventually became Chairman of the London Section of the I.S.C.M. After the break-up of Lutyens' first marriage with singer Ian Glennie, she eventually married Clark in 1942. But the world of new music was split by many factions. In 1955, Frankel, who had succeeded Clark as Chairman of the London Section of the I.S.C.M., had accused his predecessor, according to Lutyens' account of the affair, of fraudulently claiming expenses from the Society. Clark immediately sued him for slander. The background to all this was, needless to say, a boiling complex of musical politics, envy, resentment and, alas, anti–Semitism (Frankel was Jewish, while Lutyens, though not quite as paranoid as the notoriously anti–Semitic Richard Wagner, was nonetheless no particular friend of Israel herself). Frankel responded to Clark's accusation of slander by claiming he had not made the accusation of fraud, but that if he had, it would nonetheless have been true. The hearing took two days in the High Court in London. Clark failed to prove the slander but nonetheless emerged with his integrity intact. As a result, Lutyens ever afterwards referred to Frankel as a "composer and ex-colleague."[1] Her relations with Humphrey Searle, however, remained cordial.

Searle was born in Oxford in 1915 and studied composition in Vienna with Anton Webern, who made a considerable impact on his own style. In 1938 he joined the BBC as a radio producer, but with the coming of the second world war he experienced a very different set of circumstances when he became involved with the training of paratroopers. Immediately after the war he assisted the historian Hugh Trevor-Roper with his book about *The Last Days of Hitler*, and was subsequently involved in a variety of musical organizations, including Sadler's Wells Ballet, the Society for the Promotion of New Music and the Composers' Guild. He also became General Secretary of the I.S.C.M. Nearly all of Searle's compositions since 1946, with the exception of his music for film, had been based on serial techniques, but it's important to realize that Searle was also a dedicated champion of Franz Liszt. Searle's own piano sonata, written to commemorate the 140th anniversary of Liszt's birth, employs both Liszt's device of thematic metamorphosis and the much more up-to-date technique of serialism. Searle was, in fact, a natural Romantic, despite these modernist tendencies, and nowhere is this more the case than in his only Hammer film score, *The Abominable Snowman* (dir. Val Guest, 1957). Searle's score for that adventure film is indeed comparable to Ralph Vaughan Williams' music for *Scott of the Antarctic* (dir. Charles Frend, 1948), and both films tell similar tales of exploration in the snowy wastes (though, so far as we know, Scott never encountered any Yetis). Searle's music has a Romantic sonority and traditional melodic sweep here that hardly suggests it was composed by a champion of musical modernism.

Searle's route to film composition lay via a ballet he had composed for the choreographer Kenneth MacMillan called *Noctambules*, which was about a magician who can make everyone's dreams come true. It had been Malcolm Arnold who had suggested Searle's name to Muir Mathieson, after having seen a performance of *Noctambules*. Mathieson was the musical director of Alexander Korda's London Film Productions, and had brought famous names such as Vaughan Williams, Sir Arthur Bliss, and Sir William Walton to the British film soundtrack. Searle soon joined Mathieson's roster of composers of documentary scores, which John Hollingsworth also helped to conduct. Nonetheless, Searle never found writing film music easy, as he explained in his memoirs, *Quadrille with a Raven*:

Humphrey Searle in the 1960s (photograph courtesy Fiona Searle).

I found it difficult to learn the technique of writing film music, which has to fit the action on the screen down to a third of a second, but I eventually saw that, if the tempo is 1–60 or a multiple thereof, one can work out the lengths mathematically and still produce an interesting score. The chief trouble is that the music is the last element to be added to the film, and the composer cannot even start work on it until the film has been finally cut; even after giving the measurements to the composer the film editors sometimes change their minds about the length of individual shots, so that adjustments have to be made at the recording session itself, where time is money, especially when a copyist is in attendance to write out new orchestral parts on the spot. In addition, producers sometimes have only a rudimentary idea about music, or cannot convey their exact wishes to the composer. In one feature film for which I wrote the score, the producer and director were at loggerheads, each telling me to write the music in different ways, and scores often have to be written very much against time. Writing film music can nevertheless be interesting and rewarding, and I have never despised it as an art; but I feel that film music should stay in the cinema and not be made into orchestral suites, with certain exceptions such as the film scores of Bliss and Walton.[...] My most interesting feature film was "*The Haunting*," in which I worked with Robert Wise, the producer and director of "*West Side Story*" and "*The Sound of Music*," a kind, quietly spoken man and the opposite of the usual image of the Hollywood tycoon.[2]

The Haunting is Searle's only true horror film score. Released in 1959, two years before *The Curse of the Werewolf*, the atonal note clusters and more experimental orchestral effects that Searle employs (such as flutter-tongue flutes and an array of decorative percussion) operate in opposition to the much more tonal and traditionally Romantic material, thus providing the required musical contrasts with which he symbolizes the forces of good and evil. Indeed, one should really regard the atonal elements here as contrasting aspects of a basically tonal structure within the context of a resonant and Romantic symphonic sound. Extreme though some of these advanced aspects are, equally advanced effects can be found in the horror film scores of composers such as James Bernard and Harry Robinson, neither of whom allied themselves with serialism or even modernism, specializing as they did in film rather than concert music — an irony to which we will return in chapter six.

Searle was one of Elisabeth Lutyens' champions at a time in the 1950s when, as Anthony Payne puts it, "her use of 12-note technique seems to have been considered almost morally reprehensible by some in England."[3] Serialism was indeed anathema to traditionalists such as Ralph Vaughan Williams, whose typically pastoral musical style Lutyens once famously referred to as of the "cowpat" school. Vaughan Williams himself confessed that "Schoenberg meant nothing to me — but as he apparently meant a lot to a lot of other people I daresay it is all my own fault"[4]; while that other musical traditionalist, Benjamin Britten, confessed to his protégé James Bernard that he found serialism "terribly inhibiting and academic."[5] Searle had written to Schoenberg in 1948 after Eric Blom had asked him to write an article on the inventor of serialism for the *Grove Dictionary of Music and Musicians*. Searle had also suggested to Schoenberg the idea of forming a twelve-tone composers association, and he eventually received a reply from Schoenberg in which the composer said he was "very glad to hear of Miss Lutyens. It is very interesting that also a lady participates in these aims."[6]

Born in London in 1906, Lutyens was the daughter of the celebrated architect Sir Edwin Lutyens. She studied music in Paris and later at the Royal College of Music, rapidly attracting the not very respectful nickname of "twelve-note Lizzie" from her critics; but her music for film, though highly effective, was rather more conservative than her concert work. There are several possible reasons for this. The demands of the studios for one, but her own understanding of film audiences was perhaps even more important. In her autobiography, *A Goldfish Bowl*, she explained that "films and radio music must be written not only quickly but with the presumption that it will only be heard once. Its impact must be immediate. One does not grow gradually to love or understand a film score like a string quartet."[7]

Having said that, an appreciation of film music, like any other kind of music, benefits tremendously from an exploration of its structure and technique. This is particularly the case with Frankel's score for *The Curse of the Werewolf*. Lutyens' compositional approach to film work was not hidebound to any one particular stylistic theory. Significantly, around the time of her scores for Amicus horror films in the mid–1960s her concert style also changed direction. As Anthony Payne points out, "a widening vocabulary admitted more repetitive and simply patterned ideas; pictorial and atmospheric writing came to coexist with more abstract music."[8] These elements are also very much a part of her approach to film scoring in general. However, this is not to deny that her film music has other modernist elements. The

Horror Queen. Elisabeth Lutyens (unknown photographer and date; courtesy University of York Music Press, Ltd.).

instrumentation of her music for *Paranoiac*, for example, is typical of her film output in general with regard to its predominantly chamber-orchestra textures. This is in marked contrast to the full-blooded Romantic orchestrations of composers such as James Bernard, to say nothing of the orchestral opulence of David Whitaker, whose scores for Hammer's *Dr. Jekyll and Sister Hyde* and *Vampire Circus* (dir. Robert Young, 1972) contain some of the most resonant symphonic music to grace any horror film. (Frankel and Searle were also much more orchestrally resonant than Lutyens.) However, Lutyens' understated approach to *Paranoiac* provides a perfect complement to the stylish black and white photography of Freddie Francis' psychological thriller, and, indeed, the use of the soundtrack as a whole here anticipated the now central role of the sound designer. As Lutyens herself pointed out:

> Dialogue, commentary, music and sound effects should all work together. It is ideal — though not always done — to work in closest cooperation with the sound effects department. I do not think sufficient care is taken by the composer, scriptwriter and the effects department to obtain a properly integrated sound-track — more's the pity; music and dialogue often compete uncomfortably to the detriment of both.[9]

Sound effects sometimes take on the emotional role of the music in *Paranoiac*, as they had done to brilliant effect in *The Innocents*, Jack Clayton's 1961 adaptation of Henry James' story "The Turn of the Screw," but the way in which the music of Georges Auric in Clayton's film interacted with conventional and electronic sound effects had actually been anticipated in Hammer's science fiction film *X — The Unknown* (dir. Leslie Norman, 1956). In *X — The Unknown*, after James Bernard's opening flourish that leads up to the main title, the music abruptly ceases, and the remainder of the main title sequence is played out against the sound effect of a desolate curlew call. In *The Innocents*, the end title is also ironically accompanied by the sound of birdsong, signifying the dawn that the child, Miles, will never see. Similarly, in *Paranoiac*, Oliver Reed's character, Simon, murders his lover, the French nurse (played by Liliane Brusse), without any musical accompaniment. All we hear are the sounds of waterfowl on the lake where the murder takes place. In the earlier scene, when the car that is being driven by Janette Scott's Eleanor falls over a cliff, Lutyens' music is mixed with (and almost obliterated by) the sound of screeching seagulls in a manner that is almost as powerful as the electronically manipulated bird calls of Bernard Herrmann and Oskar Sala for Hitchcock's *The Birds*. (*The Birds* was released in 1963, the year before *Paranoiac*, though *Paranoiac* was actually completed in August 1962). Source music also plays an important part in the soundtrack of *Paranoiac*. Mendelssohn's song "Hear My Prayer," the accompaniment of which Simon plays on the organ (in the manner of the Phantom of the Opera), is sung by the recorded voice of his dead brother, Tony. An earlier scene features the same Chopin Nocturne (played on a gramophone) that Barry

Four: Modified Modernism (Searle and Lutyens)

Maurice Denham (left) and Oliver Reed attempting to come to terms in *Paranoiac* (dir. Freddie Francis, 1963).

Warren's Carl Ravna plays on the piano after the dinner party to which Edward de Souza and Jennifer Daniel's Mr. and Mrs. Harcourt have been invited in *The Kiss of the Vampire* (dir. Don Sharp, 1964).

The musical supervisor on *Paranoiac* was John Hollingsworth, whom Lutyens had first encountered in 1944 while working for Basil Wright's Crown Film Unit, and it was Hollingsworth who conducted her music for Wright's 1944 documentary *Jungle Mariners*:

> John Hollingsworth gave me a "reference" that I thought would lead to better things and better days: "I think it was a fine score and puts you right in the top class.... It *does* mean we should be looking for something first class for you in the feature world and I don't mean just any old commercial film...."
>
> These letters show that I had good reason to believe that I "had made it"; that with good feature films on the horizon I could expect to help keep and educate my family as they deserved. I have never had the chance of "something first class in the feature world," nor ever will. I am, however, as deeply grateful to the film world as to, later, the world of radio, in that they gave me invaluable experience of writing and hearing during the twenty-odd years that I was practically excluded from the musical world. The faith and

trust given to my work by film, radio and theatre producers supported me morally and economically over those years, as well as giving me many life-long friends.[10]

The overall sparseness of Lutyens' music for *Paranoiac* fitted in well with the belief of Hammer's later musical supervisor, Philip Martell, that films generally use too much music, which, in his view, was "a mark of bad acting and bad directing."[11] It was an approach she continued in her other score for Hammer, *Never Take Sweets from a Stranger* (dir. Cyril Frankel, 1960). Indeed, the most significant aspect of Lutyens' horror film scores is their spare, anti–Romantic texture, which derives from her even more experimental concert music; and this emphasis on clarity and simplicity can be felt with particular effectiveness in two of the films Lutyens scored for Hammer's greatest competitor at the time, Amicus.

Amicus was set up by two film producers, Milton Subotsky and Max Rosenberg, who launched their new company with the musical *It's Trad, Dad!* (dir. Richard Lester, 1962), but soon moved into horror films to capitalize on the global success of Hammer horror. The first of these to be scored by Lutyens was *Dr. Terror's House of Horrors*, which was released in February 1965. With its stars Peter Cushing and Christopher Lee, direction by Freddie Francis, and makeup by Roy Ashton, one could be forgiven for thinking that this is a Hammer production in all but name; but it differs in the episodic structure that Amicus favored, in which four or five separate stories are framed by a central narrative. In this case, five train passengers find themselves sharing a compartment with the sinister Dr. Schreck (the German word for "Terror," and no doubt a nod in the direction of the German actor Max Schreck, who had played the role of Count Orlok [Dracula] in F.W. Murnau's 1921 film *Nosferatu*). Dr. Schreck helps his fellow passengers pass the time by telling their fortunes with Tarot cards, and this leads to the presentation of the individual tales. In each case Dr. Schreck predicts death, and in the end the Doctor reveals himself to be none other than Death itself, the travelers gradually realizing that they have all, in fact, died in a train crash. Lutyens' music for this film is certainly "spooky" (or "Eerie weirdie," as she wrote on one of the pages of her score for the obscure Dutch soft-porn film *My Nights with Susan, Sandra, Olga and Julie*, aka *Secrets of Naughty Susan* [dir. Pim de la Parra, 1975]), but in a modern manner. It was in the sparse textures and almost minimalist nature of the musical material that a new, modernist element made its presence known to popular British cinema audiences. Admittedly, there was almost certainly an economic reason for these spare orchestral forces. The producer, Milton Subotsky, had very little money, and Amicus films are nothing if not object lessons in how to make interesting features on very low budgets; but Lutyens took advantage of her limited musical resources to craft scores that were not only appropriate to them but that would also reflect a different musical aesthetic.

Four: Modified Modernism (Searle and Lutyens) 61

Lutyens explained her approach to film music in her autobiography, *A Goldfish Bowl*. At music-spotting sessions she always preferred to watch the film as though she was just a member of the audience, and try to forget that she was going to compose the music. She always reserved judgment until she had heard the views of the producer, director, editor and musical director (who, in the case of her horror films, was usually Philip Martell). Significantly, she was keen to point out that the most difficult question to answer was when and how the music should be stopped, and she prided herself on being able to write a fifty-minute orchestral score in five days. Her greatest problem was the arithmetic involved, at which she confessed to being "notoriously inadequate."[12]

During her childhood, Lutyens was dragooned by her theosophist mother into a very reluctant worship of the guru Krishnamurti, in whose company she spent many uncomfortable and dreary hours; but this no doubt gave her a good grounding in the occult goings-on of her first Amicus film. The score of *Dr. Terrors' House of Horrors* is an astonishing example of Lutyens' ability to create atmosphere out of very little basic material. She frequently employs solo wind instruments in a rather *pointillist* manner, often coloring a single line with contrasting timbres. (For example, when the train journey begins, a solo flute alternates with an oboe.) Everything in this pared-down music is similarly based on the most insignificant of material: the two notes, in fact, that span a minor third. The main title (after the brash studio fanfare of Regal Films, not composed by her) introduces the main theme on a bassoon, with understated percussion accompaniment. It consists of three minor thirds. The notes of the first minor third descend in pitch and are repeated, then, beginning a semitone lower, the next minor third rises in pitch. Lutyens makes this a little more interesting by putting a rest between the second and third notes of the complete phrase, and giving a dotted rhythm to the repeat of the first minor third, but that is all. What could be simpler? And yet, Lutyens bases everything upon these opening notes. With the appearance of Peter Cushing's name alongside the name of the character he plays, "Dr. Schreck," an electric guitar (a still novel sound in a 1960s horror film) oscillates the minor third, thus cementing the relationship of this interval with Dr. Terror himself.

When the first story ("Werewolf") starts, we are transported to a remote Hebridean island, and in order to create the appropriate atmosphere, Lutyens presents us with a cheerful little Scottish air that closer analysis reveals to be related to the minor thirds of the "Dr. Terror" motif. Using a typically Scottish "snap" rhythm (a semiquaver followed by a dotted quaver), the Scottish air moves first down through a major third, then returns to the note it began with and goes up through a minor third. Two crotchets finish the tune off, the first rising up a tone, the second falling back a tone. It's all that's needed to suggest the location. (The film's budget certainly didn't stretch any further on the visual side.)

A young woman called Valda is killed halfway through this first story. She is played by Katy Wild, who had been the beggar girl in Freddie Francis' *Evil of Frankenstein* in 1964, and her presence, along with that of Peter Madden, who had played Bruno, the innkeeper in *The Kiss of the Vampire*, further gives the impression that *Dr. Terror's House of Horrors* is a Hammer film. As Neil McCallum's hero follows a trail of blood back into the house, the strings intone an *ostinato* (based on the simple rhythm of a dotted crotchet followed by three quavers), transforming the minor third of "Dr. Schreck" into a major second. This *ostinato* then forms the principle motif of the story.

The second story ("Creeping Vine") begins with the return from holiday of one Bill Rogers (played by the popular British disc-jockey Alan Freeman). Lutyens creates a cheerfully pastoral melody to set the mood, this time in major thirds. Unfortunately, the cheerful mood doesn't last long, for, while the family has been on holiday, a murderous plant has taken up residence in their garden, and it has developed a decided taste for animal and human flesh. The family dog is its first victim, which it strangles. Lutyens accompanies this outrage with a chord featuring an augmented fourth (the tritone, or "*diabolus in musica*," which few horror films can do without); but, interestingly, Lutyens refrains from music altogether when Jeremy Kemp's botanist, who has come to investigate the strange plant, is strangled by the plant's creeping tendrils. Even when the botanist's body is discovered by the horrified Mrs. Rogers—a moment most composers couldn't resist covering with music—Lutyens remains firmly silent. This highly restrained approach obviously had nothing to do with financial pressures. Lutyens could so easily have provided a simple string *tremolo* for this scene (as she had very effectively done for the title card of the film). On the contrary, the silence here is a purely aesthetic decision—and one that flies in the face of convention; but such silences, which are so characteristic of her modern approach to film scoring, were also, as we shall see, part of a much wider movement in British cinema during the 1960s.

The third story ("Voodoo") gave Lutyens a break, as the music for this section was entirely provided by others. Featuring Roy Castle as a jazz trumpeter, the diegetic music in this sequence was composed by the celebrated jazz musician Tubby Hayes, whom we see playing flute and saxophone alongside Castle. Hayes would go on to perform the sublime sax solos in Mario Nascimbene's score for Hammer's *The Vengeance of She* (dir. Cliff Owen, 1968), as well as the sax solos in Malcolm Williamson's score for *Crescendo* (dir. Alan Gibson, 1970). Indeed, a now very rare vinyl single was actually released featuring the numbers that Hayes and Castle perform in this segment of the film. The Russ Henderson Steel Band also creates an effective Caribbean mood.

The fourth story ("Disembodied Hand") was surely based on W. F. Harvey's tale "The Beast with Five Fingers," or, at least, the Hollywood film of that name. In it, Michael Gough (who had played Arthur Holmwood in Hammer's original *Dracula*) confronts, as the artist Eric Landor, Christopher Lee's pompous art critic, Franklin March. March, infuriated by Landor's humiliation of him

Four: Modified Modernism (Searle and Lutyens)

at a private viewing, deliberately runs down the artist in his car; but Landor's severed hand eventually takes its revenge. Again Lutyens bases everything on the opening two-note theme, but, as in "Creeping Vine," she refrains from any music at all during the most significant scene, in which Landor's severed hand attacks March in his car. All we hear are the tires screeching. The final car crash, in which March is blinded, again has no music; and a very quiet string chord, which fades into silence, brings us back to the train carriage and Dr. Schreck.

The fifth and final story ("Vampire") contains an example of Lutyens' attempt at what is known as "radio music"—in other words, diegetic, or background music that is also meant to be heard by the characters themselves. In a light jazz style, Lutyens creates a relaxed mood as Donald Sutherland's Dr. Bob Carrol takes dinner with his wife, whom he doesn't yet realize is actually a vampire. He soon finds out, however. True to form, there are thirds even in this music cue, but the music is again kept to a minimum. During the extended staircase sequence in which Bob Carrol's medical colleague (played by Max Adrian) is pursued by the female vampire, all we hear are footsteps. Music returns for the scene in which Adrian sits by the bedside of the boy who had been vampirized, and again Lutyens bases her accompanying lullaby on the film's main two-note theme. The melody is no more than a repeated descending major second on a flute, accompanied by a rising major second on a clarinet. In the end, Adrian persuades Sutherland to drive a stake through his wife's heart, only to reveal himself to have been a vampire all the time. Adrian's punchline brings the story to a close: "This town isn't big enough for two doctors—or two vampires!" All that remains is for Dr. Schreck to reveal his true identity and for the assembled passengers to realize their dreadful fate.

The end titles are no less unorthodox, bringing the film to a very understated conclusion, with a mournfully indeterminate motif on the flute, again based on the opening two-note theme. Here the flute descends through a major third and then rises up a perfect fifth, implying a cadence, but the overall mood suggests a desolate drifting away rather than a definite conclusion.

Lutyens' music for her second Amicus film, *The Skull* (1965), plays a vital role in director Freddie Francis' noteworthy attempt at pure cinema. As Jonathan Rigby points out, "The final 25 minutes are almost entirely without dialogue, Francis turning them instead into a visual tour de force."[13] Of all her film scores, this one was apparently Lutyens' own favorite.[14] The story is simple. A nineteenth-century phrenologist disinters the skull of the Marquis de Sade, which is still haunted by the spirit of its infamous owner. In the twentieth century, the skull is sold to a collector of occult artifacts and curios, played by Peter Cushing. Cushing's Professor Maitland is then terrorized by the Skull, which induces him to hallucinate, steal four statues of demons, and ultimately murder the former owner of both the Skull and the statues, his friend Sir Matthew Philips (played by Christopher Lee). In the end, the Skull itself dispatches Maitland.

Once more, despite the presence of Cushing and Lee, and Francis' direction, the texture of Lutyens score for *The Skull*—indeed the whole approach to the soundtrack in general—makes this film very different from a typical Hammer horror film. For a start, the prologue, in which the phrenologist (played by Maurice Good) exhumes the skull of the Marquis de Sade, takes place without any music at all, and, until quite late on in the proceedings, no dialogue either. When the main title appears on screen, superimposed over a shot of the Skull itself, Lutyens' orchestral forces are revealed to be rather more colorful than her palette for *Dr. Terror's House of Horrors* had been, emphasizing predominantly solo wind instruments (particularly two bass clarinets), a string section (without violins) and percussion. Along with an organ and a piano (useful for filling in the texture), she incorporates the distinctive (and, in 1965, when the film was released, quite unfamiliar) timbre of the cimbalom. This instrument is immediately associated with the Skull itself. Indeed, the cimbalom returns throughout the film whenever the Skull takes center stage, with particular effectiveness in the final scenes, as it floats eerily through Professor Maitland's study.

Famed James Bond composer John Barry is often credited with having introduced the cimbalom to the British cinema soundtrack with his score for *The Ipcress File* (Sidney J. Furie, 1965), which was released in the same year as *The Skull*. Of course, given the low status of horror films by comparison with a Michael Caine spy drama, Barry's cimbalom was bound to receive a great deal more publicity at the time. Suddenly, according to Barry's orchestra-booker, Sid Margo, everyone wanted to have a cimbalom in their films.[15] In fact, Barry had first employed the cimbalom for another film that same year, called *King Rat* (dir. Bryan Forbes, 1965). Eddi Fiegel, Barry's biographer, is of the opinion that "Until John's discovery of it on *King Rat* [...] it [the cimbalom] had remained unused in either pop, or film music. But that would change with *The Ipcress File*."[16] However, *The Skull* received its UK premiere on June 9, 1965. *King Rat* didn't appear in the UK until January 24, 1966 (it opened in the USA on October 27, 1965), and *The Ipcress File* was first released on July 2, 1965 (the USA release date wasn't until August 2). While it is certainly true that Barry's use of the cimbalom propelled that instrument to fame, Lutyens' use of it in *The Skull* actually beat both *King Rat* and *The Ipcress File* to the British film soundtrack. Fiegel, however, is quite right when she describes the cimbalom's ability to create "an eerie, sinister mood."[17] Its unusual timbre no doubt signified the fear of something foreign and unidentifiable, and therefore unnerving. Traditionally a Hungarian folk instrument, the cimbalom didn't enter the Western art music tradition until Franz Liszt (with the help of the Polish composer Franz Döppler) included it in the 1874 orchestral version of his Hungarian Rhapsody No. 6 in D-flat Major. Liszt scholar Humphrey Searle also included the cimbalom in his Fourth Symphony in 1962, and, as we shall see later, Harry Robinson exploited the cimbalom's Hungarian and "sinister" connotations in his score for Hammer's *Countess Dracula* (dir. Peter Sasdy, 1971).

In *The Skull*, as with *Dr. Terror's House of Horrors*, Lutyens often creates a powerful atmosphere by the simplest of means. For instance, in the opening scenes, Michael Gough's auctioneer gives a description of the four statues of demons that are about to be sold. A flute quietly plays a single, mid-range note for the statue of Lucifer. This is repeated for Beelzebub, before falling a major third and then a further tone. This sequence of three notes is repeated for Leviathan; and finally, to emphasize the even more sinister character of Belbereth, who incites to murder, Lutyens subtly brings in percussion and an uncomfortable cushion of strings. Nothing could be simpler, but neither could anything be more dramatically effective.

Lutyens also excels in the use of *ostinati*, which contribute a great deal to this film's mounting sense of dread and expectation. These *ostinati*, based on simple rhythmic patterns and small motivic cells, brought minimalism to the soundtrack years in advance of composers such as Philip Glass, who would make minimalist aesthetic very popular in films such as *Koyaanisqatsi* (dir. Geoffrey Reggio, 1983), *Hamburger Hill* (dir. John Irvin, 1987), and, more esoterically, in his 1999 string quartet score for *Dracula* (dir. Tod Browning, 1931).

When Patrick Wymark's grubby, snuff-taking antiques dealer, Marco, makes his way to Professor Maitland's home with a copy of a biography of the Marquis de Sade bound in human skin, Lutyens accompanies his journey with another simple motif that will also feature throughout the score. (I'll refer to it as Motif A.) It consists merely of a rising and falling semitone. This motif is reprised when Marco returns the following night to tempt Maitland into purchasing the actual Skull. The rhythm of Motif A is equally important as, if not more important than, its actual pitches here. Lutyens usually avoids big themes, and their absence demonstrates that her approach, despite its more traditional harmonic language, goes against the prevailing popular–Romanticism of Hammer's musical style. (James Bernard favored quite expansive themes, due, in part, to his habit of basing his material on the syllable stresses of Hammer's increasingly lengthy titles). The dry *col legno* timbre of the strings that play this ostinato also adds to the anti–Romantic texture.

Silence is also of paramount importance to the soundtrack of *The Skull*. Not only are large sections played without music (and, as already mentioned, without dialogue as well), but silence also effectively punctuates the music cues themselves. Lutyens is fond of building up a *crescendo* to suggest an overwhelming event, only for the music to break off suddenly, creating an anticlimax. A notable example of this happens when, at one point, Maitland walks along a corridor to open a door. As soon as he opens it, the expected climax in the music is indeed cut short.

Lutyens also emphasizes the trance-like behavior of Maitland when he is playing billiards with Sir Matthew. A string chord is sustained as Maitland stares vacantly beneath the color-draining lamp above the billiard table, and then, as he bends down to play his shot, Lutyens swiftly changes the harmony to restore a sense of normality.

Just before the two policemen arrive in Maitland's study to take him away to confront his nightmare ordeal in the middle of the film, Lutyens again relies on *ostinati*. As Maitland reads the biography of de Sade, Motif A returns, and to accompany the camera's tracking shot of the bizarre collection of objects in the room, the strings fall through a semitone before the music is interrupted by the entrance of the policemen. The following journey to the "police station" is again hypnotically accompanied by another ostinato based around a semitone. Its rhythm differentiates it from Motif A, consisting, as it does, of a dotted crotchet, followed by three quavers and a final crochet. It is interspersed with an *ostinato* on equal beats in which a tritone is implied between the second and fifth notes, but it's not so much the actual notes as their insistent repetition that creates the hypnotic effect.

Notably, the sequence in which Maitland is forced to play Russian roulette contains no music — a temptation that a less restrained composer might have been unable to resist. Sound effects are all that is required to aid the images here, though Lutyens does subject a dissonant string chord to a *crescendo* when Maitland finds himself in a smoke-filled room, the walls of which begin to move towards him after the manner of Edgar Allan Poe's story "The Pit and the Pendulum."

Maitland then finds himself outside Marco's flat. The nightmare seems to have been just that: an hallucination. On Maitland's return to Marco's, having collected money to pay for the Skull, which he now simply cannot resist, Lutyens employs yet another *ostinato*, rhythmically characterized by two quavers, followed by a crotchet, a dotted crotchet and a final quaver. Again a tritone relationship is implied between the first and third notes of this *ostinato*.

Lutyens makes conventional use of the organ at her disposal to symbolize the forces of good, particularly when Sir Mark gives Maitland a crucifix with which to protect himself from the forces of evil. Borrowing the idiom of a chorale, Lutyens relies on a very traditional frame of musical reference here; but she can also make the most basic of musical intervals (such as a major third) sound unnerving by instructing the strings that play it to slide from one note to another when a light begins to pulsate over the Skull in the final section of the film. Unaccompanied motifs are also very typical of Lutyens' approach: strings, in particular, often play in unison, demonstrating her courage to create unorthodox, spare and hollow sonorities.

Lutyens' musical simplicity in *The Skull* and to a lesser extent in *Paranoiac* was an approach shared by other British films in the mid–1960s. John Dankworth's spare, jazz-inspired score for Joseph Losey's *Accident*, for example, appeared in 1967. Dankworth's restrained use of harp and saxophone throughout his score for this film, particularly during the scenes in which Dirk

Bogarde's sexually repressed Oxford University academic has to contend with Jacqueline Sassard's very seductive legs beside him in a punt, was also part of the British cinema's movement away from sonorously Romantic orchestral soundtracks towards more modern understatement. Freddie Francis' reliance on sound effects rather than music in *The Skull* was also echoed by Losey. As David Caute mentioned in his biography of the American director:

> Michel Ciment noted the striking use of sound in *Accident* — the noise of oars (a punt pole, surely?) in water, the hissing of a kettle. Losey was using both sound booms and telescopic "rifle" microphones. The Oxford of *Accident*, and the neighbouring countryside, is sonically expressive: bells, planes, cows.[18]

Perhaps even more significant is the way in which the sustained silences of *The Skull* anticipated the silences of Michelangelo Antonioni's seminal comment on the 1960s in *Blow Up* (1966), in which David Hemmings' photographer spies on Vanessa Redgrave's mysterious assignation with an unidentified man in a London park. The most celebrated scene in this film has no music and no dialogue. All we hear is the sound of the wind in the trees as an accompaniment to the enigmatic events. (Hemmings later blows up a photo he has taken in the park [hence the title of the film], which reveals a dead body in the bushes. He returns to the park without his camera and indeed finds the body, but on his subsequent return, the corpse has vanished. Thus does Antonioni set up his basic argument about how we perceive the world and what exactly "reality" *is*.) *Blow Up*, however, was released one year after *The Skull*, and so, once again, we see that it was a popular horror film that anticipated the novel soundtrack effects of a film that was much more critically acclaimed at the time — and since. (Having said that, Roberto Gerhard's highly unusual atonal score for *This Sporting Life* [dir. Lindsay Anderson, 1963] is mixed with, and then replaced by, the sound of a crowd at a rugby match half way through the title sequence. Though not Gerhard's original intention, Anderson's editing of the original score in this manner is a masterstroke of sound design.)

Lutyens' score for *The Theatre of Death*, directed by Sam Gallu for Pennea Productions, followed in 1966. Gallu was, unusually for a film director, musically minded, having sung tenor roles in operas under the direction of Toscanini, no less. Indeed, Christopher Lee, who starred in the film, and had always wanted to be an opera singer himself, recalled singing snatches of operatic arias with him in-between takes.[19] Lee's role, however, was that of the strictly non-singing theatrical martinet Phillipe Darvas, who presides over a Parisian theater specializing in *grand guignol* entertainment. We are led to believe that Darvas is a vampire, but, in fact, the murders in the film are committed by one of the young actresses in his company. This actress isn't a vampire either, but she does suffer a craving for human blood, having been forced to turn cannibal while escaping with her family from the Nazis during World

War Two. Darvas intends to turn her life story into a sketch for the theater, but the actress puts a stop to this by killing him halfway through the film.

Bernard Herrmann was originally to have been the composer for this film, but it was Lutyens who got the job in the end. Her fee was obviously less than Herrmann's would have been, and consequently far more appropriate for a low-budget horror film. Though she never rated her commercial work very highly, Lutyens largely depended on it financially, and, as we have seen, it provided her with a circle of professional colleagues that she lacked among the British musical establishment of the time. For *Theatre of Death* she took a similar approach to the other horror films discussed in this chapter, making effective use of *ostinato* patterns and percussion effects (such as the use of *glissandi* on timpani that accompany our first sight of Christopher Lee lurking behind the walls of his home during the theater company's first-night party). What makes this score different from Lutyens' two Amicus horrors, however, is the rather larger orchestral sound. Vibrant brass fanfares open the film, and there is also a larger string section, with extra sonority provided by harps. Perhaps because of this, the main title music is in a much more traditional "horror film" style, which is ironic, really, as this film is, in fact, a backstage mystery thriller rather than a horror film proper. Christopher Lee's character turns out to be a red herring and not at all the vampire he is made out to be. At the end of the main title, when a skull's jaw drops open, Lutyens indulges in a perhaps conscious imitation of John Barry's famous high-pitched trumpets with "plunger" mutes that made their first appearance in the third James Bond film, *Goldfinger*. (This effect is called a "plunger" because the trumpets are actually muted with the rubber bell of an everyday drain plunger.)

Lutyens' first sustained *ostinato* in *Theatre of Death* is more of a repeated dance motif during the first-night party. It consists of a very simple melody based on semitones. During the first beat, two notes rise through a semitone, and after one beat's rest, the process is repeated. The two notes return again, then the melody rises a minor third and falls another semitone before the opening two notes complete the process. According to the original script, Darvas' flat was originally to have been furnished in medieval style, but a later amendment crossed this out, adding the words: "Darvas' salon will be completely modern in decor." (It is appropriate, I think, that, with the exception of the prologue to *The Skull*, all of Lutyens' horror film scores were for modern-dress productions.) The script also calls for a "Darvas theme" to play during the shots of Christopher Lee's eyes moving behind the portrait of Phillipe Darvas Senior, but Lutyens saves her Darvas theme for later. When we do hear it, it appropriately conforms to the syllables of Darvas' full name, consisting as it does of four notes (i.e. F-sharp, rising to G-natural, then down to E-sharp and finally falling to D-sharp).

Darvas' theme is loosely related to the party theme (being restricted to within the same range of pitches—i.e. D-sharp to G-natural). Again typically,

Lutyens distorts the party theme harmonically during the subsequent scene in which Darvas hypnotizes Nicole Chapel (played by Jenny Till), prior to the open rehearsal of the Salem Witches sketch that is put on to entertain the party guests. When Nicole, under Darvas' sinister influence, and holding a red-hot poker, advances threateningly towards her fellow actress and flatmate, Dani (played by Lelia Goldoni), Lutyens builds up the tension with an *ostinato* that also has a constrained pitch range. Again, Lutyens is brave enough to rely on very simple means to create maximum tension, all achieved through relentless repetition. Later, to cover the first murder, all she requires is the steady pulse of a bass drum (over some "French" accordion music) to set the pulse racing.

The rest of the score continues in this vein. For the second murder, Lutyens simply calls for a roll on the suspended cymbal, and many of the subsequent ostinato patterns are derived from either major or minor seconds (what one might call "two-noters"). Similarly, the "Dance" and "Darvas" motifs begin with a rising minor second, while the "Hypnosis" motif begins with rising major seconds.

The third murder mostly dispenses with music altogether, relying instead on sound effects to help create atmosphere (such as foghorns and an outboard motor, as this murder presumably takes place by the river Seine), but Lutyens brings back a "two-noter" for the wielding of the knife.

The fourth murder is based on the Darvas theme to suggest that it is Darvas who is committing the murder (which, of course, he is not). When the body of the murdered victim is discovered by two lovers in a boat on the river the next day, the pitch contour of the Darvas motif is expanded so as to remove its sinister semitone and compressed seconds, thus humanizing his character by making the notes fit into a major key.

The final stages of the film rely on the Tony Scott Drummers, who, as in the "Voodoo" segment of *Dr. Terror's House of Horrors,* set up a driving rhythm to lead up to the moment when Nicole is accidentally stabbed by a spear that penetrates the floor of the stage at the end of the sketch.

In conclusion, then, though Lutyens harmonic language in these popular horror film scores isn't as radical as her serial-inspired concert works, her scores nonetheless modernized the soundtrack with both their motivic and instrumental minimalism. In this respect her challenge to the conventional wisdom about how film music in general—and horror films in particular—should be composed was perhaps even more radical than Frankel's ground-breaking serial score for *The Curse of the Werewolf.* Though the use of serialism was a new departure for British film music in the early 1960s, Frankel's vibrant orchestration and the elements of tonality in his score perhaps disguise its significance from a technical point of view. Humphrey Searle really scored only one horror film, *The Haunting* (*The Abominable Snowman,* as director Val Guest always insisted, is actually an adventure story), but despite atonal elements in Searle's score, these, too, are contrasted by traditionally tonal writing, the whole thing orchestrated in a traditionally resonant manner. Of these three British avant-garde composers, Lutyens perhaps presents the most immediately recognizable contrast, in terms of general mood, to the way in which horror films had been scored before; but she was not alone, and her fervent admirer Richard Rodney Bennett would continue to modernize the soundtrack in the scores he wrote for Hammer around the same time.

Notes

1. Elisabeth Lutyens, *A Goldfish Bowl* (London: Cassell, 1972), pp. 232–233.
2. Humphrey Searle, *Quadrille with a Raven — Memoirs by Humphrey Searle*, Chapter 12, "Breakthrough," www.musicweb-international.com/searle.
3. Anthony Payne's entry for Elisabeth Lutyens in Stanley Sadie (ed.), *The Grove Dictionary of Music and Musicians* (London: MacMillan, 1980), vol. 11, p. 375.
4. Michael Kennedy, *The Works of Ralph Vaughan Williams* (Oxford: Oxford University Press, 1992), p. 376.
5. David Huckvale, *James Bernard, Composer to Count Dracula: A Critical Biography* (Jefferson: McFarland, 2006), p. 114.
6. Humphrey Searle, *Quadrille with a Raven* (Note 2), Chapter 11, "Leslie and Rosie's Pub."
7. Elisabeth Lutyens, *A Goldfish Bowl* (Note 1), p. 171.
8. Stanley Sadie (ed.), *The New Grove Dictionary of Music and Musicians* (Note 3), pp. 375–6.
9. Elisabeth Lutyens quoted in Roger Manvell and John Huntley, *The Technique of Film Music* (London and New York: Focal Press, 1975), p. 229.
10. Elisabeth Lutyens, *A Goldfish Bowl* (Note 1), p. 151.
11. Philip Martell, in conversation with the author, August 24,1988.
12. Elisabeth Lutyens, *A Goldfish Bowl* (Note 1), pp. 169–70).
13. Jonathan Rigby, *English Gothic* (Richmond: Reynolds & Hearn, 2000), p. 121.
14. Meirion and Susan Harries, *Elisabeth Lutyens: A Pilgrim Soul* (London: Michael Joseph, 1989), p. 227.
15. Eddi Fiegel, *John Barry — A Sixties Theme* (London: Boxtree/Pan-MacMillan, 2001), p. 171.
16. Ibid.
17. Ibid.
18. David Caute, *Joseph Losey, A Revenge on Life* (London: Faber and Faber, 1994), p. 190.
19. Christopher Lee, *Tall, Dark and Gruesome* (London: Victor Gollancz, 1997), p. 232.

Five

The Uncanny

Richard Rodney Bennett

One year before it unleashed Benjamin Frankel's serial score on an unsuspecting public, Hammer had secured the services of an up-and-coming young composer for its 1959 film *The Man Who Could Cheat Death* (dir. Terence Fisher). The name of the composer was Richard Rodney Bennett, and he would go on to score two more films for the company. Bennett's approach to horror film scoring was similar to Lutyens in that he favored smaller ensembles over the resonant orchestral *tuttis* of James Bernard, and his writing also demonstrated how it was possible to score horror films and psychological thrillers like this without losing any dramatic impact. Like Lutyens, he, too, had been writing twelve-tone music in the early 1950s—since he was sixteen, in fact. Born in Broadstairs, Kent, in 1936, Bennett went on to study at the Royal Academy of Music, and later spent a year in Paris with Pierre Boulez, whose highly cerebral approach to serialism he did not find personally congenial, and which encouraged him towards a somewhat less rigid approach to Schoenberg's system, following the example of Berg. Recalling his experience of performing with Boulez, Bennett significantly explained: "He snaps the whip. Then you do it. The performance gets tensions and vitality, but not the vitality from being happy."[1] If Bennett's own music and career went in a rather different direction, he nonetheless demonstrated his gratitude to and admiration of Boulez by translating Boulez' own writings, in collaboration with Susan Bradshaw. He was also the percussionist in early British performances of Boulez' *Marteau sans Maître*, as well as being a sophisticated jazz and classical pianist. Able to write in any style, the cinema was a natural place for him to demonstrate his astonishingly versatile talent, but despite his great success in the field of film music, Bennett has always compartmentalized it:

> I think of doing film music as journalism. I happen to love it because I'm a great movie person. But it's journalism: one is using a very small part of one's creative ability, and it has to be done very fast. And it's a collabora-

tion. I think composers find it difficult to accept that a lot of the time in film music they are just the servant of the film, and if you go in thinking you are going to write important music which everybody's going to listen to and admire, you're wrong.[2]

The irony with this point of view, of course, is that actually far more people have heard Bennett's film music than have heard his concert works.

Bennett also enjoyed the unusual orchestral possibilities that film offered. When scoring Ken Russell's *Billion Dollar Brain* in 1967, for example, he wanted to create a hard, inhuman sound to complement this Harry Palmer adventure about an American megalomaniac who has plans for world domination and uses a supercomputer to attain his ends. Bennett's orchestra included eleven brass instruments, three pianos, the electronic ondes martenot, and a body of percussion — a line-up that would have been quite impractical for a concert piece. Bennett was also fully aware that film music was changing in response to the changes that were happening in the world of avant-garde music:

> I started writing movies in the mid–1950s and it was a time when I think the old traditions of film music — the symphonic 1930s/1940s style — were starting to fade, and styles of film-making and acting were changing, and similarly styles of music were changing. And I remember between when I was about sixteen and eighteen I heard some very important film scores — for example, *A Streetcar Named Desire* by Alex North, *On the Waterfront* by Leonard Bernstein, and particularly *East of Eden* by Leonard Rosenman, and they were all scores where there was some awareness shown in the music of what was going on in contemporary music. Not bang-up-to-the-minute avant-garde music, but it sounded as though the composers had heard Bartók and Berg and Stravinsky, as opposed to just Rakhamaninov and Tchaikovsky and Debussy, which was the tradition in film music earlier.[3]

The Man Who Could Cheat Death, which was based on Barré Lyndon's stage play *The Man in Half Moon Street,* concerns a scientist called Geroges Bonnet (played in the Hammer film version by Anton Diffring), who has discovered the secret of eternal life; but, unfortunately, his elixir can only be made from a particular human gland. Inevitably, Bonnet resorts to murder to procure his vital ingredient, and then, when an operation on himself becomes necessary, he blackmails a doctor (played by Christopher Lee) to perform it for him. However, the doctor tricks him, and Bonnet dies a horrible death as his age finally catches up with him.

The play had been filmed before, under the same title, by Paramount in 1944, with Nils Asther in the leading role; and the same sort of story, but with a flamboyant decadence about it that successfully caught the tone of the original Oscar Wilde tale on which it was based, followed a year later with the film adaptation, starring Hurd Hatfield, of *The Picture of Dorian Gray* (dir. Albert Lewin, 1945). All these films, about men who have managed to acquire immortality, are related, of course, to vampire stories, a genealogy that, predictably, was not lost on Hammer. Released the year after the company's first *Dracula* film (though actually filmed in the same year, 1958), Hammer's treatment of Jimmy Sangster's screenplay is characterized by all the qualities one might expect from one of that studio's Gothic horror films. Director Terence Fisher emphasizes vivid reds and greens. Bernard Robinson provides lush period decors, with an impressive eighteen-step staircase that, re-dressed, would be briefly displayed in Hammer's next production, *The Mummy* (dir. Terence Fisher, 1959). (The studded green-baize door in Bonnet's hall had previously appeared in *The Curse of Frankenstein* [dir. Terence Fisher, 1957], while Hazel Court's Janine even owns a piano similar to the one Carl Ravna will play in *The Kiss of the Vampire*.) Christopher Lee stars (though in a benign "Van Helsing" type of role: he is quite determined to prevent Anton Diffring's immortal — and immoral — anti-hero from getting away with his crimes). Immortality is, of course, central to the plot, as is Bonnet's desperate need for an elixir of life (not blood, in this instance, but rather a green liquid distilled from the human gland). There are several murders and finally an immolation scene comparable to Count Dracula's various disintegrations. The major difference from the studio's previous vampire film, apart from the obvious lack of an actual vampire, is the relative absence of music, which also emphasizes the rather stage-bound quality of the whole production. As Jimmy Sangster has explained:

Richard Rodney Bennett around 2003 (photograph by Katie van Dyke, courtesy Chester Music/Novello & Co.).

> it was based on a play, and therefore turned out to be very static. In fact, the whole movie really takes place on two sets, Bonnet's house and the cellar where the climax takes place. Certainly there are a few other small sets, the inn where Bonnet picks up the hooker and a couple of small street scenes, but these were designed merely to open the piece up, which, in my opinion, they fail to do.[4]

However, musically speaking, the film opens in a very unusual way, for this is the only main title sequence of any Hammer film in which there is no musical theme. True, *X— The Unknown* had dispensed with music altogether during its opening titles, but Bennett's score is unique for a Hammer film in that there is music but no theme. Instead, Bennett relies on a rhythm, played by timpani. The effect is indeed similar to the kind of thing that James Bernard would attempt with four timpani in the courtroom scene of *Frankenstein Created Woman* (dir. Terence Fisher, 1967). Over Bennett's timpani rhythm, exotic, *arpeggiated* chords on vibraphone and celesta are played with each successive title card. Each chord is different, but there isn't a hint of melody here. The approach is radical, and perfectly complements the expectation and mystery created by the fogbound scene in which an as yet unidentified Georges Bonnet is hard at work removing the gland he needs from the unfortunate pedestrian he has just murdered. (Indeed, this is similar territory to the murders of *Theatre of Death* that lay a few years in the future.) Bennett's debut in the world of Hammer horror consequently demonstrated, from the very first bars of his score, that his approach was quite different from the style of James Bernard (and also Benjamin Frankel). Having said that, there are one or two things Bennett's music does share with Bernard's score for *The Quatermass Experiment*. For a start, Bernard was restricted to just strings and percussion in his first score for Hammer, and this is a combination that Bennett also exploited (particularly in *The Nanny*, as we shall see later). Bernard's emphasis on rhythm rather than melody in *The Quatermass Experiment* is also comparable to Bennett's approach in *The Man Who Could Cheat Death*, but the volume and texture of Bernard's music is vastly different. (*Quatermass* also has a motif—even if only based on two notes.) Intriguingly, Bernard and Bennett actually met during the recording of the score for *The Quatermass Experiment*. Bernard himself recalled:

> John [Hollingsworth] took me down to the recording because I didn't have a car in those days. He used to pick me up in his little red MG and drive very fast to the Anvil Studios, and he said to me, "Oh, Jimmy, I hope you don't mind, I've asked a bright young composer to come to the recording because I think he's going to be very good in films. He's still at the Royal Academy. He's extremely bright and his name is Richard Bennett." And there was this lanky young man who was extremely nice and I was extremely interested because without looking at the score he analyzed what I was doing.[5]

Little did either of them know that many years later Bennett would go on to score *Murder on the Orient Express*, the screenplay of which would be written by Paul Dehn, Bernard's partner.

After the novel opening title music, Bennett's music for *The Man Who Could Cheat Death* becomes much more conventional, with a straightforward waltz that accompanies the little cocktail party Bonnet has thrown to celebrate the unveiling of his latest sculpture. (Obviously, this is not intended to be diegetic music, as there's hardly room in Bonnet's atelier for the cast, let alone a small chamber orchestra, but, like the way the film in general has been made, the music gives the illusion of greater opulence and space than there actually is on set.) After the waltz comes to a conclusion there's no music for quite a while. Indeed, it isn't until Bonnet murders his model, Margot (played by Delphi Lawrence), that it returns. When it does, Bennett creates a characteristic chord out of fourths, though not quite in the complex way of the Russian composer Alexander Scriabin, who mixed augmented and perfect fourths in his famous mystic chord.

Alexander Scriabin, "Mystic chord."

Bennett prefers more straightforward constructs of perfect fourths, the angular effect of which does indeed create an atmosphere of anxiety. Fourths are a more "modern" interval than the thirds that have dominated Western harmony for over two centuries. By using fourths, Bennett is able to create both a more unnerving and more up-to-date harmony than the diminished seventh chords (themselves built up of minor thirds) that a more conventional composer might have been tempted to use for such a scene of violence or horror. The motif Bennett writes to symbolize the elixir that Bonnet preserves under a beam of sinister green light in his safe is also a construct of four rising fourths. It's a very simple but highly effective idea that exploits the hard-edged timbre of the xylophone, and the music is vital here to highlight the significance (and intended horror) of this key scene. In fact, there's very little to frighten an audience from a visual point of view. These elixir scenes desperately need music, for the elixir itself is, after all, the equivalent of the blood upon which a vampire similarly depends, so it is the job of the music here to invest what is no more than a humble glass beaker containing green liquid with sinister significance. Fisher does what he can with the green lighting, and he also up-lights Diffring's face, but it is the music that brings these effects to life. Fourths occur throughout the rest of the score: when Bonnet shouts "It's too late!" before attacking Margot, and also when he starts to age in front of his former colleague and assistant, Ludwig (played by Arnold Marle). On this latter occasion the fourths occur over a timpani beat that echoes the prologue scene. Fourths also make an appearance when Bonnet eventually strangles Ludwig.

For Bonnet's murder of a prostitute, Bennett tries a different approach, scoring the scene with single, low-register notes on a piano. There are no *tremolo* strings here, as one might have expected. Instead, Bennett creates a spare, understated sound, which is all the more unnerving. As we shall see in chapter nine, John Cacavas uses a similar effect for the scene in which Joanna Lumley discovers a cellar full of female vampires in *The Satanic Rites of Dracula* (dir. Alan Gibson, 1973).

However, *The Man Who Could Cheat Death* gave Bennett very little opportunity to flex his musical muscles. Most of the cues are short, and the film itself gave little real inspiration for musical experimentation. All that was to change, however, with his next score for Hammer. This was for *The Nanny* (dir. by Seth Holt, 1965), starring Bette Davis in the title role. She accidentally kills the little girl whom she is meant to be looking after by unwittingly drowning her in the bath after returning from the deathbed of her own abandoned daughter. The girl's brother, Joey (played brilliantly by William Dix), knows what's happened, but no one will believe him when he claims that Nanny wants to kill him too, to stop him from talking. Such a subject is much closer to the world of Alfred Hitchcock than traditional Gothic horror, and the more realistic, psychological drama of the film coaxed much more genuinely disturbing music from Bennett than had *The Man Who Could Cheat Death*. Indeed, Bennett's music for *The Nanny* does occasionally resemble the approach of Hitchcock's most characteristic composer, Bernard Herrmann (particularly in the way they both use strings, as we shall see later).

The Nanny begins unnervingly without any music at all. Not even the Associated British-Pathé logo has an accompanying fanfare. The opening shot

Anton Diffring (at right) as Dr. Georges Bonnet quenching his deadly thirst and Arnold Marle as Dr. Ludwig Weiss in **The Man Who Could Cheat Death** (dir. Terence Fisher, 1959).

is of children playing in a park, but still there is no music. The title of the film now appears on screen, again without music. This, in itself, is disorienting, as we're left unsure as to what kind of genre the film inhabits. We know that this is a Hammer film, so there are certain expectations, but these aren't in any way confirmed. Director Seth Holt opts for crisp black-and-white photography, with none of the operatic reds and greens for which Hammer films had previously been so well-known. Completely inverting any expectations we may have had, we are shown a straightforward sunny afternoon in Regent's Park. What could appear more normal? Holt does, however, suggest something potentially troubling by focusing at one point on the *shadow* of the roundabout on which the children are playing, and this might well indicate that the shadows of secrets also lie in the light. Perhaps all is not as it seems.

Starting a film like this was still novel for a popular entertainment with no intellectual pretensions in 1965, and it certainly flew in the face of Hollywood tradition (despite the presence of the film's American star). Though *The Nanny* was not alone, it did appear before several other British-based films of the 1960s that took a similar approach. As we have already seen, this was the era of Joseph Losey's *Accident*, that triumph of '60s style over narrative substance. *Accident* also eschews music during its opening shots. Instead, we hear the sound of a jet plane, a screech-owl and then a car crash, all of which take place while the camera stares implacably at the front of a house at night. One might indeed be forgiven for thinking that this is the introduction to a Hammer shocker, for such a surreal opening shot is actually quite disturbing, unnervingly reminiscent, as it is, of Magritte's painting *The Empire of Lights*. Of course, *Accident* is not a thriller, still less a horror film, but it is intriguing to contemplate what Jimmy Sangster would have made of the sexual philandering and academic jealousy of Harold Pinter's plot. The film could easily have gone in the less self-consciously cerebral direction of Hammer's *Paranoiac* or *Nightmare* (dir. Freddie Frances, 1964). The basic ingredients of Pinter's story are hardly more than one would find in a soap opera; but Losey, with the help of Pinter's characteristically pregnant pauses and meaningful silences, transforms them into something apparently more significant by means of his sensational cinematic style. After all, the dialogue between Bogarde and Delphine Seyrig in the middle of *Accident* is banality itself, but the inspired decision to play the dialogue over scenes in which both characters are not actually speaking makes it seem more significant than it is, while, as already mentioned, John Dankworth's restrained harp and sax jazz score further removes the film from cinematic convention.

The black magic occult thriller *Eye of the Devil* (dir. J. Lee-Thompson, 1967), starring David Niven, also abandons main title music. Instead, it uses the muffled announcements of a railway station to create a mood that Tanya Krzywinska describes as a "sense of languid trance [...] in which the sounds of the train and the station noises appear as if underwater."[6] But such experiments with opening sequences can actually be traced back to the beginnings of sound cinema itself, when, released from the convention of continual, live musical accompaniment, more imaginative directors chose to concentrate on sound effects and silence rather than music. The rhythm of the musical introduction that begins Fritz Lang's *The Testament of Dr. Mabuse* (1933) is soon replaced and replicated by the deafening printing presses that thunder throughout the first scene; and, famously, Tod Browning's 1931 *Dracula* plays without a note of music (with the exception of an extract from Tchaikovsky's *Swan Lake* during the main titles). The scenes in Dracula's vault in that film, which James Bernard would no doubt have covered with an array of tremolos and tritones, rely instead solely on the sound of howling wolves, scuttling armadillos and creaking coffin lids. The effect of all this on the film's first audiences, accustomed as they were to the reassuring conventions of live music, would have been considerable.

As Bennett has already observed, the 1960s, particularly in Britain, witnessed a move away from the dominant style of the Hollywood "Golden Age" composers; and though the minimalist style of Philip Glass would take a while longer to infiltrate the soundtracks of feature films, British film composers in the mid–1960s were nonetheless responding to a general desire for clarity, simplicity and modernity.

Of course, since the development of "sound design," the soundtrack has become far more complex and hybrid in the techniques it uses; but like all that eventually becomes commonplace, such developments depend on their pioneers. An astonishing example of experimental sound design in a British Gothic film from the 1960s can be found in *The Innocents*. Towards the end of this film, the governess, played by Deborah Kerr (who is almost as crazed as Bette Davis' Nanny) tries to wrestle the truth from the boy Miles, who is in her charge. She has become convinced that he has been consorting with the ghost of the evil and corrupt Peter Quint, but the film's (and the story's) great strength lies in never making this explicit. After an argument between the governess and the boy, which takes place in a conservatory, the boy runs out into the garden and falls to the ground. As he does so, Georges Auric's agitated music comes to an abrupt halt. Instead, we hear only birdsong, which makes a very significant contribution to the film's general atmosphere — what Sigmund Freud would have called *unheimlich* — or, as we would say in English, though not in a literal translation, "uncanny." In his 1919 essay on the subject, Freud explained that an *unheimlich* atmosphere occurs

> ... when the distinction between imagination and reality is effaced, as when something that we have hitherto regarded as imaginary appears before us in reality.[...] As soon as something *actually happens* in our lives which seems to confirm the old, discarded beliefs we get a feeling of the uncanny; it is as though we were making a judgment something like this: "So, after all, it is *true* that one can kill a person by the mere wish!" or, "So, the dead *do* live on and appear on the scene of their former activities!" and so on.[7]

This is precisely what happens in *The Innocents* (and also, as we shall see later, in Hammer's *The Witches* [dir. Cyril Frankel, 1966]). The birdsong that replaces Auric's music is unnerving in its effect because, after all, most birds don't sing at night, and the one that famously does, the nightingale, has connotations of tranquility that seem out of place in a ghost story. Miles struggles with the increasingly hysterical governess and tries to escape from a hedge-encircled enclosure in the garden that is interspersed with statues, all lit to sinister effect in the darkness. As the camera pans around the circle, electronic sounds now take over the function of conventional music, their impact made more extreme by Miles' high-pitched screaming. Then the ghost of Peter Quint appears, though we are still not sure if Miles can see him or not. To a strangely unnerving sound effect that suggests both heavy breathing and a slab of stone sliding off a tomb, the ghost of Peter Quint raises its hand, displaying long fingernails. Miles collapses, and the birdsong returns, to even more uncanny effect. The governess eventually realizes that Miles is dead and unnervingly bends down to kiss him passionately on the lips. This guilt over the death of innocence (though, again, we're not entirely sure of the boy's innocence) relates this scene thematically to the bathroom scenes in *The Nanny*, when the guilt-stricken Nanny bathes the corpse of the little girl, pretending that she is still alive. Deborah Kerr's governess then prays, while birdsong, not music, brings the film to its disquieting conclusion.

Like *The Innocents*, *The Nanny* was very much a part of the then contemporary wave of experimentation in both popular and more esoteric cinema, and a powerful part of *The Nanny*'s success at the time (and since) is due to the contribution of its soundtrack as a whole. Bennett proved himself to be a master of the uncanny, for he, too, invests the ordinary with an unnerving oddness. In the case of *The Nanny*, he exploits tunes in the style of nursery rhymes, using conventional harmonies and straightforward orchestral forces. If we take tonality as what the German academic and horror film historian S. S. Prawer calls the "world of your normal experience," Bennett is able to make that normality "not quite safe to trust to, mysterious, weird, uncomfortable strange or unfamiliar." Prawer continues:

> the "un-secret" [is] that which should have remained hidden but has somehow failed to do so. "Unheimlich"— so runs the well-known definition from Schelling's *Philosophy of Mythology*—"nennt man alles, was in Geheimnis, im Verborgnen, in der Latenz bleiben sollte und hervorgetreten ist" ("Uncanny is a term for everything which should remain mysterious, hidden, latent and has come to light"). To be *unheimlich*, a work need not provide shocks of horror: the uncanny may be diffused over the whole as an atmosphere like the fogs that blanket London in the more macabre pages of Dickens, like the eerie light that illuminates the "white nights" of Gogol's or Dostoevsky's St. Petersburg.[8]

Freud himself put it like this:

this uncanny is in reality nothing new or alien, but something which is familiar and old-established in the mind and which has become alienated from it only through the process of repression. This reference to the factor of repression enables us, furthermore, to understand Schelling's definition of the uncanny as something which ought to have remained hidden but has come to light.[9]

The music for *The Nanny* begins only as the camera pulls focus on Bette Davis, who appears walking in the distance behind the children in the playground; but, again, we are left uncertain as to what to expect from her because the music expresses nothing sinister at all. Instead, we hear a tune that is indeed rather like a nursery rhyme. There is, however, a potentially troubling element within this melody, for it starts off with a rising fourth, and then opens out on the third beat to climb up to yet another fourth. Given the signification of fourths that we have already discussed, one could say that within this seemingly benign tune lie the seeds of something much more disturbing. They will indeed evolve into the unnerving chords based on layered fourths, familiar from *The Man Who Could Cheat Death* and which we will hear again in *The Witches*. (There is, incidentally, another theme in *The Nanny* that Bennett reuses for *The Witches*. It begins with a descending semitone and then drops a perfect fourth [or, in other variants, a major sixth], before repeating the initial semitone. Bennett also varies the rhythm of the motif. In some versions, the first three notes form a triplet, in others a dotted crotchet followed by two semiquavers. Usually the last two notes are a single beat each. But of that theme, more later.)

The Nanny's nursery rhyme theme is first heard on a harpsichord, with a solo cello quietly playing the bass line beneath. Again, this is unusual in the context of a psychological shocker, though it was also part of a musical fashion of the time. As we have seen in the case of Elisabeth Lutyens, 1960s film music was keen to exploit unusual timbres to increase its impact. Just as Lutyens and John Barry had brought the cimbalom to the British film soundtrack, so Bennett's use of a harpsichord was also part of a revival of interest in this particular keyboard instrument at the time, in both commercial and classical music. The pioneering classical harpsichordist George Malcolm brought the instrument back into the limelight during the 1960s, along with the simultaneous revival of interest in so-called early music (i.e. pre–J.S. Bach). By contrast, in the world of popular music, the old-fashioned harpsichord suddenly sounded new, unusual, even "hip"— perfect, in fact, for the swinging sixties, a period that loved raiding the past to make statements about the present. In a host of 1960s British television themes harpsichords often found themselves up against swinging brass and percussion. Edwin Astley's theme for *Dangerman* ("High Wire"), Laurie Johnson's theme for the cult T.V. series *The Avengers*, and Cyril Stapleton's theme for the once phenomenally successful series *Department S* all used this very old keyboard instrument to give their seemingly obligatory "spy" *ostinati* a contemporary timbre. Like colors in clothing and interior design, instrumental timbres are also subject to fashion. Just as orange and brown became *the* colors of the 1970s, and indeed seem to have returned in the first decade of the twenty-first century, so the harpsichord was a curiously fashionable timbre for popular entertainment in the 1960s.

While it's part of this fashion, Bennett's harpsichord also denotes the old-fashioned dignity of the Nanny herself. In addition, it echoes the sound of a musical box — a sound strongly associated with the nursery and innocence. Of course, the Nanny is not innocent, but we need to think that she is at this stage, so the harpsichord has been recruited to help persuade us. However, its novelty is also somewhat unnerving, and coupled with the fourths that lie within the nursery rhyme tune it plays, we are left with a wholly ambivalent feeling. As the main title sequence continues, *pizzicato* upper strings lightly join in the accompaniment, and as Bette Davis stands by a railing to admire a view of the park, the strings take over from the harpsichord and develop the fourths of the nursery tune, making a chain of fourths out of them. The strings then reprise the nursery rhyme theme with contrapuntal decoration. A harp sweeps in, and all now seems romantic, pleasant and untroubled. The absence of wind and

Bette Davis feeding the ducks in the opening scenes of *The Nanny* (dir. Seth Holt, 1965).

brass also aids the music's fresh, uncluttered texture, in marked contrast to the score (by Bernard) of Hammer's next offering, *Dracula Prince of Darkness* (dir. Terence Fisher, 1966), which was filmed at roughly the same time as *The Nanny*. A glockenspiel adds to the cheerful mood as Nanny buys some flowers from a street vendor; but as we approach the building in which the bulk of the action is to take place, the chain of fourths return, there is a *ritardando* and the harpsichord returns. We soon cut from the imposing neo-classical columns of the apartment block to the doors of the elevator shaft inside, and as the doors open Bennett creates a slight *crescendo* in a sustained string chord to help frame Davis, not only to emphasize that she is the star of the film but also to create an undercurrent of anxiety about the character of the Nanny. The *crescendo* also serves as an iconic symbol of the opening doors themselves, of course.

Immediately on entering the flat we hear that all is not well. Wendy Craig's Virgie Vane is in tears, and her husband (played by James Villiers) is growing increasingly impatient with her. The Nanny's seeming unconcern about this emphasizes the sense of disorientation that, so far, has been suggested solely by the music. The next music cue screws the tension even more. We follow Nanny into her bedroom, where a series of silver-framed photographs of children are arranged on a chest of drawers. As the camera pans meaningfully across these, the music informs us that all is not quite as it seems—that the apparent innocence of these photographs is somehow tainted. Bennett scores this section for quiet solo strings to emphasize the intimacy of this environment—not only the privacy of a bedroom but also the secret to which the bedroom is privy. The strings express a hidden truth, and the intervals they play create the equivalent of a musical question mark. The first interval rises a fifth (the mirror image of a fourth, for a fifth is merely its inversion). Such an interval is known as an open fifth because it lacks the all-important third that defines whether or not we are in a major or minor key. The resulting hollow sound aptly suggests the absence of the little girl in the photo, who is now dead, and also the absence of the truth, for we do not yet know why this photograph is significant. These two notes are held to form a chord, which is soon joined by another solo string playing a third above the fifth. We therefore now have an overall span of a major seventh, which is almost, but not quite, an octave. The harmonic tension resulting from this again suggests a question. We want the augmented seventh to resolve onto the octave above, but it doesn't.

All this is really quite basic in harmonic terms, but its very simplicity is what makes Bennett's approach so modern. There isn't a tritone in sight, there are no diminished sevenths, no tremolo strings, nothing obvious, no old *clichés*. Understatement is the secret of Bennett's success here, his ability to make the ordinary unnerving. By these means he is able to create a powerfully uncanny atmosphere. He continues this approach in the next musical cue, when Virgie Vane gets up off the bed after Nanny agrees to go in her place with Mr. Vane to fetch Joey from the school at which he's been boarding for the past two years.

As Virgie stands up, Bennett introduces the theme that he will use again in *The Witches*. The cue begins with a solo flute that is soon joined by two solo strings below, out of which the "Witches" theme emerges. As mentioned above, the key harmonic element here is the initial falling semitone, which returns at the end of the motif; but even more significant is Bennett's emphasis on a solo instrument (in fact, the vulnerable timbre of the oboe, which we hear as tearstained Virgie wanders into the kitchen). As with Lutyens and Dankworth, such sparsity of texture is another of the elements that make Bennett's approach to scoring so modern.

As Virgie contemplates the photographs of her dead daughter in Nanny's bedroom, a flashback of when the girl was alive is accompanied by desolate string writing strongly reminiscent of Bernard Herrmann's non-vibrato string textures in *Psycho* (dir. Alfred Hitchcock, 1960). Herrmann's score is famed for having inverted the traditionally Romantic signification of the string orchestra (though James Bernard's *Quatermass* music actually anticipated this), and Bennett is certainly in tune with Herrmann's anti–Romantic approach. Consequently, when Joey is found pretending to be hanged in his school bedroom, Bennett covers this very disturbing image with high-pitched strings very much in the style of Herrmann's music for the shower scene in *Psycho*. Bennett also avoids brass, which, again, a more conventional composer might have been tempted to use. A tam-tam provides a frightening shiver of sound, and a brief flurry of notes for harpsichord concludes the cue, suggesting that this instrument is not as innocent as we might have thought it was during the main title music. Also, the wind instruments that we might have expected to support the strings here are instead replaced by various kinds of tuned percussion, creating a drier, less expressive, and consequently much more contemporary sound.

The following scene, in which Nanny brushes Virgie's hair, is the first of many reprises of the "Witches" theme to which I referred earlier. This time it is played by a solo violin. The violin is followed by a solo flute, which plays the third phrase of the nursery rhyme theme with accompanying *pizzicato* strings. After this, the solo violin plays the "Witches" theme once more, and finally the flute hesitantly starts the nursery theme from the beginning, with more *pizzicato* strings beneath. This emphasis on solo textures creates the sense of intimacy here, which the semitones of the "Witches" theme also make disturbing. The use of solo violin and the close-ups of Nanny brushing Virgie's hair are, indeed, reminiscent of the use of strings in Franz Waxman's score for Hitchcock's *Rebecca* (1940). The equivalent of Nanny in that film is the possessive, jealous and probably lesbian housekeeper Mrs. Danvers (played by Judith Anderson). In one scene in the middle of the film, Mrs. Danvers invites the new bride of Laurence Olivier's Maxime de Winter (played by Joan Fontaine) to sit at the dead Rebecca's dressing table. There, Mrs. Danvers goes through the motions of brushing her hair — a nightly ritual when Rebecca was alive. For this scene, Waxman's solo violin is muted as it plays a falling semitone, the first note of which is accented to emphasize the hesitancy of Fontaine's character. As in Bennett's music for *The Nanny,* the solo timbre similarly creates a sense of intimacy, and the semitone again makes it unnerving. However, Waxman, of an older generation, then brings back the main body of strings, creating a much more traditionally Romantic quality, an effect that Bennett is careful to avoid.

Bennett's emphasis on solo timbres and understated combinations of two or three solo timbres continues throughout the score, though he does create thicker textures for certain key shock scenes. Not all of them, however. Even during the death scene of Aunt Peg (played by Jill Bennett), he again restricts himself to strings (echoing the haunting sea interludes of Benjamin Britten's opera *Peter Grimes*). Bennett holds back as often as he can. For example, in a subsequent flashback that shows the Vane's daughter accidentally falling into the bath, Bennett avoids all temptation to add music. The thud of her body against the enamel sides of the bath is all that's needed here. Similarly, when Nanny later advances on Joey in his bedroom, with a pillow under her arm and the chilling line, "You mustn't make it difficult for Nanny, Master Joey," the entire scene is also played without music. Music returns, to devastating effect, only when Nanny carries the unconscious Joey down a corridor prior to her attempt to drown him in the bath. Here, Bennett again demonstrates his debt to Herrmann, scoring the growing tension with screeching *glissandi* in the strings, which grow ever louder, leading up to an explosive tam-tam and the now totally corrupted harpsichord, which stutters alongside the tuned percussion as Joey splashes into the water.

Bennett's last score for Hammer was for *The Witches,* a tale of rural witchcraft which, to a large extent, prepared the ground for *The Wicker Man* (dir. Robin Hardy, 1973). Like the prologue to *The Man Who Could Cheat Death,* Bennett's score for *The Witches* begins with percussion as it accompanies the scenes in which Miss Mayfield prepares to leave an African village school that is in the midst of a native uprising. (Miss Mayfield was played by Joan Fontaine twenty-six years after her role in *Rebecca*). Instead of the timpani, celesta and vibraphone that accompanied the title cards of *The Man Who Could Cheat Death,* Bennett here combines tribal drumming with a piano (a percussion instrument itself, after all), and again demonstrates that films often begin more effectively with understated music. With the frightening appearance of a giant African mask in the doorway of Miss Mayfield's school, the main titles start. Quiet *col legno* strings set up an eerily insistent rhythm over which an *ostinato* chord on the piano, and *tremolos* on xylophone lead to the solo flute's statement of the main "Witches" theme, which we have already encountered in *The Nanny*. Again, it is the understated instrumentation of this cue (along with a relatively quiet dynamic throughout) that marks it out. Chords built up of layered fourths also feature in this main title section, lending "modernity" to a film that was set in the time of its original release.

The apparent normality of the opening shots of the English village in which the action largely takes place is emphasized by the tonal optimism of Bennett's next cue; but when Michelle Dotrice's character, Valerie, later responds ambivalently to Miss Mayfield's enquiry about the Rectory where her new employers live, Bennett brings back the main "Witches" theme. It is introduced, once more, by the layered fourths first heard in the main title. A black cat, called Vesper, also makes his first appearance in this early scene, and he, too, has a *leitmotiv*—a mysterious, oriental melody played on a solo cor anglais. Again, Bennett demonstrates restraint here by restricting himself to such a spare texture. He also exploits contemporary note cluster harmonies for strings when, outside the Post Office a little while later, the two children, Ronnie and Linda, are observed furtively conversing together. The ambivalence of these harmonies is, of course, ideal for supporting the general sense of ambivalence that pervades the entire film. Are Ronnie and Linda involved with witchcraft? Is Alec McCowen's Alan, who wears a dog collar but is not actually a priest, a force for good or evil? Is his sister, Stephanie, benevolent or dangerous? Is anyone

Teacher's pet? Joan Fontaine gets a nasty surprise in *The Witches* (dir. Cyril Frankel, 1966).

in this story who they seem to be? Note clusters are a particularly effective way of emphasizing such ambivalence. To increase the ambiguity here, Bennett also alters the intervals in the "Witches" theme. This theme is already unnerving because it begins with the ambivalent interval of a semitone, but, as mentioned earlier with regard to its appearance in *The Nanny*, Bennett often changes the interval between the second and third notes. In *The Witches*, this interval is sometimes a perfect, sometimes an augmented, fourth, and fourths often appear at key moments of suspense. A chord of layered perfect fourths, for example, accompanies the scene in which Ronnie explains the message Miss Mayfield reads in a school exercise book: "Linda's Granny Treat her something Crool." After clever Ronnie takes Miss Mayfield's intelligence test, and the decision is made to let him remain in the village to further his studies rather than go to boarding school, Alan sullenly responds that it would have been better if Ronnie had gone away. Again, to underline this ambiguous statement, Bennett brings in more layered fourths, and, as with *The Nanny*, he again exploits the apparent innocence of a nursery rhyme style for the scene in which Ronny and Linda are observed shopping together. Things seems perfectly innocent, but we can't be sure....

Bennett does resort to more conventional means occasionally, such as the use of a tam-tam and vibraphones, the blurring sonorities of which create a musical equivalent of the out-of-focus light bulb to which Miss Mayfield wakes up in a hospital bed. This occurs after her ordeal in the Rectory when she fainted after having seen the giant African mask that had terrorized her in the film's prologue. Such writing, however, is combined with much more contemporary high-pitched string textures, again in the manner of *Psycho*. On Miss Mayfield's return to the Rectory after her ordeal in the nursing home, Bennett again echoes the strings of *Psycho* during Stephanie's concerned questioning about what happened on the night of Miss Mayfield's collapse: "Ever since that night. Do you remember? Alan found you." We then cut to a sinister shot of Alan, up-lit, staring back.

Alan, however, is a red herring, and actually quite innocent. It is his sister, Stephanie, who is behind all the sinister goings-on in the village, and it is she who is preparing a magical ceremony to gain a "skin for dancing in" in order to transfer her own knowledge and intellectual power to the young body of Linda. (The plot is indeed very similar to *Nothing but the Night* [dir. Peter Sasdy, 1972], the only film to emerge from Christopher Lee's ill-fated production company, Charlemagne.) Alan, whose sole ambition to be a priest has been unsuccessful, spends his time listening to recordings of organ music. In one scene he is found listening to a recording of Liszt's *Missa Choralis* for both organ and choir (a rather esoteric piece of Liszt for the 1960s when Liszt's more obscure works were yet to be revived). Amidst the ambiguous fourths and tone clusters that pepper Bennett's score, Liszt's ecclesiastical work (itself modeled on the style of Palestrina) seems positively antique, especially in comparison to the music of the orgy during the final ceremony.

For these climactic scenes, Bennett's atonal strings quietly ruminate on another *ostinato* figure. Again, their sparsity and understated insistence is far more successful in creating a truly weird atmosphere than the much more flamboyant and operatic bacchanal composed by James Bernard for the orgy scenes in *The Devil Rides Out,* directed by Terence Fisher two years later. The screenwriter of *The Witches,* Nigel Kneale, was disappointed by director Cyril Frankel's handling of this scene. "There's nothing as funny as people imagining they're witches," he observed. "It's naturally comic. I think a cleverer director would have faced that possibility of it all turning into laughs and he would have managed to make it really horrible, creepy and threatening."[10] As it stands, it might have been considerably more laughable than Kneale found it had it not been for Bennett's vital musical contribution.

The final end title music is also unusual, not in itself but because of its context within the overall score. This triumphal concert piece is based on a rhythmic pattern that divides up its four crotchet beats into a "modern" percussive arrangement of two groups of three quavers each, followed by two more quavers to make up the required eight, but the harmonic language here is tonal and conventional, giving Bennett an opportunity to write a fully developed cue that brings normality, optimism and modernity back to the soundtrack — just as it has been brought back to the village itself.

Notes

1. Bennett quoted in Joan Peyser, *Boulez, Composer, Conductor, Enigma* (London: Cassell, 1976), p. 162.
2. Michael Oliver (ed.), *Settling the Score—A Journey through the Music of the 20th Century* (London: Faber and Faber, 1999), p. 152. Bennett is quoted from an interview on BBC Radio in 1974.
3. Ibid., p. 155.
4. Jimmy Sangster, *Inside Hammer* (Richmond: Reynolds & Hearn, 2001), p. 54.
5. David Huckvale, *James Bernard, Composer to Count Dracula* (Jefferson: McFarland, 2006), p. 52.
6. Tanya Krzywinska, *A Skin for Dancing In* (Trowbridge: Flicks Books, 2000), p. 101.
7. Sigmund Freud, "The Uncanny," in *Art and Literature* (Harmondsworth: Penguin, 1985), pp. 367–371.
8. S.S. Prawer, *Caligari's Children* (Oxford: Oxford University Press, 1980), p. 111.
9. Sigmund Freud, "The Uncanny" (Note 7), pp. 363–4.
10. Marcus Hearn & Alan Barnes, *The Hammer Story* (London: Titan Books, 1997), p. 109.

Six

Romantics

Harry Robinson and James Bernard

The composers discussed so far in this book all had active concert careers, and film music to them was a lucrative and challenging sideline. Harry Robinson, however, worked exclusively in popular and film music. Born in Elgin, Scotland, in 1932, he started life with the rather grand name of Henry MacLeod Robertson, and began his career in music the same year that Hammer films launched their first color Gothic horror film, *The Curse of Frankenstein* (1957). However, Robertson, as he was then known, was working in the very different world of television pop shows, such as the BBC's *Six-Five Special*. His name changed when a check arrived from his record company, Decca, in payment for his work on a string orchestra arrangement of Van Morrison's skiffle hit "Don't You Rock Me, Daddio."

> I was stoney broke. They paid cash for the performers, but a check for the composer, and it was made out for Harry Robinson — not Harry Robertson. So I rushed down to the bank and said, "There's been a terrible mistake." That night I thought I was going to be as rich as Creosus — Chinese meals and West End food here I come! The other thing I completely forgot to do was check with the Decca record company what they were doing. They put the record out, and there was my name emblazoned as "Harry Robinson." It became a hit record, and I was then known, so I stuck with it.[1]

Under another name, he had another hit record in 1958, the year of Hammer's *Dracula*. Entitled "Hoots Mon," it was performed by Lord Rockingham's XI, which was actually Robinson himself singing alongside session musicians. Going on to work with Lionel Bart, Tommy Steele, Judy Garland, Liza Minnelli, and the Beatles, he entered the film business by scoring films for the Children's Film Foundation, but, of course, it is for his Hammer horror films that he's remembered today.

Soon after arranging and conducting a recording of Ronnie Hilton singing

Harry Robinson conducting session musicians in the 1960s (photograph courtesy Lesley Reid).

"The Ugly Bug Ball" and "A Windmill in Old Amsterdam" for EMI in 1970, Robinson began work on the music for Hammer's so-called "Karnstein Trilogy" (which comprises *The Vampire Lovers* [dir. Roy Ward Baker, 1970], *Lust for a Vampire* [dir. Jimmy Sangster, 1971] and *Twins of Evil* [dir. John Hough, 1971]). He went on to score the company's Gothic historical epic *Countess Dracula*, the psychological Gothic romance *Demons of the Mind* [dir. Peter Sykes, 1972], and even began work on *Dr. Jekyll and Sister Hyde* but withdrew from the project after an early conversation with the film's producer, Albert Fennell:

> I stopped working on *Dr. Jekyll and Sister Hyde*. I'd done all the barrel organ music and songs and various other stuff, and then the guy said, "OK, the way I work with Laurie Johnson — and I wish he was doing the score — is to fill the entire picture. Ninety minutes of music ; and then I'll throw it all out." I said, "No. I'm not going to do that — write ninety minutes of music and get paid for sixty minutes. No, damn it, I'm not going to do it." So I told Philip [Martell] and said, "Count me out on that one."[2]

All Robinson's scores for Hammer operate unashamedly within the context of popular Romanticism, but they are nonetheless full of surprises. Indeed,

Robinson himself was happy to acknowledge his approach as a highly eclectic one:

> There was a man, Puccini, who liberally thieved — and made no bones about it. The rest of us steal, in fact, but pretend we don't. I don't think there's a composer living who's not stolen.
>
> I heard a sound in I think it was Lutosławsky; and what he'd got was the woodwind to make a sort of a yelp; and it sounded to me to be so much like a knife cutting that the next time I saw a knife being used in a film — and it was a film called *The Oblong Box* [dir. Gordon Hessler, 1969], and poor old Christopher Lee gets his throat cut in that — I remembered this Lutosławsky sound and I wrote it in. Pinched it completely. Unfortunately, against the scene it was a little bit like a cartoon, and instead of coming out as horrific and cold, it was far too funny, in fact, because it sounded like a squeak. So I was paid back for stealing.
>
> Sometimes I got into serial music, but I find it a bit soulless. It's terribly easy in Hammer films and horror music to go into serial music because you can go on mathematically page after page. There's a hell of a lot of modern music that sounds like it's taken from a horror film score.[3]

Twins of Evil and *Countess Dracula* are both good examples of how Robinson incorporates more adventurous orchestral and harmonic effects into a predominantly Romantic tonal idiom. Loosely based on J. Sheridan Le Fanu's short story "Carmilla," *Twins of Evil* concerns the further adventures of the aristocratic vampire family of Karnstein and its provocatively lesbian vampire daughter, Carmilla. Hammer had first brought this character to the screen in *The Vampire Lovers,* the film that launched Ingrid Pitt's cult status as one of Hammer's most famous leading ladies. Robinson was working on *Twins of Evil* simultaneously with Ingrid Pitt's other Hammer film, *Countess Dracula*, with the consequence, as he put it, that "themes kept winging into one another." Indeed, both film scores share certain effects in common. After seeing *Twins of Evil* for the first time, Robinson realized that this was his opportunity to write what he had always wanted to write: "a cowboy score." The film, with its horse-riding Puritan witch-hunters, is indeed a form of Gothic cowboys and Indians story, and the music certainly echoes the classic "Western" style of Jerome Morross, as well as the classic "Spaghetti" Western idiom of Ennio Morricone, as we shall see later. Robinson calls for a moderately large orchestra, consisting of two flutes, one alto flute, three oboes, one cor-anglais, two bassoons, one double bassoon, four horns, three trumpets, two tenor trombones, one bass trombone, timpani, snare drum, bass drum, vibraphone, electric harpsichord, piano and strings (violins, violas, cellos, double basses).

The music for the prologue and main title of *Twins of Evil* provides us with an excellent example of Robinson's approach in general. As with all film music, accurate timing of the material was of paramount importance, but Robinson never regarded such restrictions as a problem:

Six: Romantics (Robinson and Bernard)

Harry Robinson at a recording session in the 1970s (photograph courtesy Lesley Reid).

If it's a good editor, there's no problem. If it's a bad editor [you do have problems]. A bad editor is somebody who has no sense of rhythm — he has no innate rhythm. There are certain techniques that some composers use: Laurie Johnson, for example, uses a very simple technique which is the pause chord. In other words, you get a hanging diminished chord on the horns, and then you wait [until the moment of suspense is resolved]. Now that used to be the technique of the old film composers, like [Max] Steiner. The first thing I did was a children's serial: a nine-parter with about an hour-and-a-half's music called *The Valley of the Kings* [dir. Frederic Goode, 1964], and I actually sat with a stopwatch as I wrote the music because I didn't have any idea how I should actually shape the music in time. It was only when I conducted that score that I realized how stupid I'd been and how to work it out. In fact, you just sit there with a cue-sheet and you figure out the basic pulse of the sequence. I'd have said you only need three tempos in film music: crotchet = 60, which will fit everything because when you double the tempo you've got what I would call a fairly breezy chase but not too much pressure. Then if you go up to crotchet=144 you're getting tremendous pressure—chase. And the other one is maybe somewhere round about crotchet = 96, and that will give you what I would call "romantic-indeterminate." So really, when you've decided which one of those pulses is right for the sequence, you then write in whatever measure you're going to use. The less multiple measures you use the better, because, as a rule, you've only got a couple of rehearsals and it's got to be in the can. Muir Mathieson conducted one of the first scores I did, and I had multiple beats like flash 11/8s. He was a very cruel man, Muir Mathieson. He could pull you out before the orchestra and say, "Gentlemen, we are indebted to the qualities of our composer here but, by Christ, it's impossible to play. Next time write in 4/4 or 3/4!" But in a curious way this actually is an aid to a composer. We've all tried to write music just for the sake of writing music, and the difficulty is actually getting started and then trying to plot it all out. Somewhere around that time you might just actually give up. At least with a film you've got a cue-sheet and the actual film itself, and the fact that it's got to be written that day. So the important thing is that your tempo is nearly set for you—the film will give you the tempo. There's a feeling you must convey, and music is the strongest element in a film to convey that.

Philip Martell is of the old school. He really likes sonority. So do I. I'm pretty old fashioned in that way—as opposed to what I'd call spidery writing. Philip would always say that after doing a Liz Lutyens score the next one would have to be sonorous! The producers of Hammer films just wanted a big symphonic score. Now, the only problem was they never had the money for a symphony orchestra. I've always been very adaptable with orchestras. In the record industry you were working with very weird line-ups. Philip would say, "OK, I've got this number of musicians for you. What do you want to do with this one?" I've certain predilections. The thing is, I've never been very keen on trumpets. I don't like saxophones at all. I've been forced to do two or three what I call jazz scores, and I hate them because I'm not a jazz musician at all. I can't be bothered with jazz. I can't bear listening to it. So I would go for combinations that would maybe give you as much difference in tonal quality as possible. If you tilted too much into the "kitchen" [i.e. percussion] or into the woodwind it meant that you maybe had to lose something in the strings, so sometimes

I'd write a score with no violas. I've never tended to use woodwind in the normal pattern because sometimes I haven't had enough woodwind, and if you haven't got the full complement of woodwind you've got to think of them as different animals entirely. The same with the horn section. Instead of them being really a second chunk of strings, you might actually use them in a different way that will allow the strings to do something different.

The problem with *Twins of Evil* was that I had no idea when it was day, when it was night. Was it the night before or was it the morning afterwards? If you've got a sequence where you're bridging all that and you're attempting to help the time change it's very difficult. There was one bit where I thought it was the same sequence, and when I saw the picture I suddenly realized afterwards that it was supposed to be three days later![4]

The action in the prologue of *Twins of Evil* is straightforward: Puritan witch-hunters, led by Peter Cushing's fanatical Gustav Weil, advance through a dark forest on horseback. A woodman in his cottage (Inigo Jackson) assures his daughter (Judy Matheson) that there is no one outside; but the girl nonetheless insists that she can hear something. The woodman goes out to investigate and is assaulted by one of the Puritans in the doorway. Gustav Weil enters. The girl screams and protests that she is not a witch. Weil prays for the girl, who is now tied to a stake in the forest. The pyre is ignited, the girl is burnt alive and the main title credits are superimposed over the flames.

Such a prologue immediately identifies the activities of the Puritan witch-hunters. It also introduces and establishes Peter Cushing as the "star" around which the film is constructed, and helps to establish the genre of the film. The function of the music is to bind together five scenes that compress the unity of time, to aid dramatic tension, and to indicate the genre (though this is complicated by the references to the "Western," which are made explicit in the main title music).

The music begins as the film opens with a unison A-natural, played *fp<*, in the manner of what musicologist Philip Tagg has called a "reveille" function, alerting the audience that the action has begun.[5] (We will return to Tagg's classifications of the functions of main title music later.) The *martellato* snare drum, brass and horns also bring appropriate military connotations. The first theme we hear is actually an embryonic form of the main title "cowboy" theme, the triplet figure being marked *tenuto* to emphasize the stridency of the accompanying action ("the feeling you must convey," as Robinson put it). The motif is really no more than a decoration of a single note (a sustained A-natural, followed by a triplet, which rises through a semitone to B-flat, falls back down to the A-natural, and then below to a G-natural before a return of the A-natural). The musical tension here is created by our interest in finding out how the A-natural will develop. The electric harpsichord helps to create a sense of period (the film being set in an approximation of the seventeenth century), and the fact that it's a synthesized imitation of a harpsichord also fits in well with the film's stylized period setting. The piano, as is often the case in film scores, helps create a thicker texture.

This opening section ends with the first line of dialogue, as Weil shouts, "Halt!" His paramilitary role is enforced by another *martellato* figure from the snare drum just before he shouts. A horse snorts at the end of the first section, providing the equivalent of a full-stop. Frequently, sound effects obscure the intentions of composers, a fact of which Philip Martell was all too aware: "The big problem is when you get tremendous sound effects like sea-storms; then even if you have a seventy-five piece orchestra you can't get through it."[6] However, the sound effects in this section are carefully incorporated into the musical structure and actually help to delineate the divisions of the dramatic structure.

In the second section of the prologue we move from the explicit menace of the witch-hunters outside to the implicit menace felt by the characters inside the woodman's hut. To reflect this change of atmosphere and environment, Robinson reduces his orchestral texture, rejecting all the brass. Muted, divided strings play a *pianissimo* tone cluster, in marked contrast to the diatonic opening bars, and the resulting harmonic ambiguity, along with the muffled quality of the mutes, creates the sense of unease. Further ambiguity is provided by the strange and unexpected timbre of a bowed vibraphone (an effect created by drawing a violin bow across one of the vibraphone's bars).

The string tone cluster is held for four bars with the instruction *"diminuendo* to nothing," thus providing an eerie cushion of sound over which embryonic statements of the main "cowboy" theme are introduced in the woodwind, first on the cor anglais, which is instructed to play in a "distant" manner. The cor anglais has a traditionally melancholy, but sometimes also rather macabre, signification, which is appropriate here to suggest the presence of the Puritans outside. The girl whispers "Listen!"—and immediately afterwards, we hear a melodic fragment on alto flute that is based on an augmented triad (i.e. a major chord in which the fifth note has been sharpened). Augmented triads have often been employed to signify distress of some sort (Brünnhilde's battle cries in Wagner's *Die Walküre,* for example, are also based on them). While this chord is presented, the woodman assures his daughter that she's worrying unnecessarily, but the girl insists that she can hear something.

The first half of this interior scene is once more punctuated by the sound effect of a horse whinnying. Again, Robinson treats the sound effect as a structural element of the music. The woodman now walks across the room to the door in order to investigate, while the tone cluster in the strings continues. The "cowboy" motif is played again, this time quietly by the "feminine" timbre of the oboe; and by combining the motif of oppression (the "cowboy" motif) with the timbre of the oboe, Robinson is able to suggest that it is the girl who is now in imminent danger from the Puritans outside. The next device again increases the tonal ambiguity. Over the omnipresent cluster in the strings, the piano (with sustaining pedal down) plays a series of minor seconds (F-sharp — G-natural). This blurring effect is further obscured by *pianissimo* E-flats on the vibraphone; but the music also reflects the actor's movements (the woodman moving towards the door).

An agitated semiquaver figure on oboes and cor anglais (D-sharp, up to E-natural, back to D-sharp, then up to F-sharp) now forms a short *ostinato*, suggesting imminent action. Here the musical carries very traditional physiological correlations: the *staccato* marking suggests nervousness, while a *crescendo* suggests an increase in the intensity of this feeling. It is also significant that the agitated figure is played on oboes, thus suggesting that it is the girl who is the most frightened. However, it is the woodman who is attacked first. For his assassination, the traditionally diabolic connotations of tritones are emphasized by being scored for trumpets and horns.

More interestingly, Robinson uses dynamics to introduce Peter Cushing's close-up. Cushing is first introduced in shadow. After the loud dynamic of the assassination, the brass tritones undergo a *diminuendo* to provide a metaphor for the on-screen shadow. The following *crescendo* up to a *fp* chord acoustically "frames" Cushing's move into the light. A brief hiatus follows as he stares at the girl, and tension is created by the uncertainty of the exact nature of his assault on her. This finds its musical correlation by a musical retreat "back into the shadows" once more (i.e. a sudden quietness) that is followed by a *crescendo*. Weil advances upon the girl, and a snare drum announces a fragment of the triplet rhythm that will eventually run throughout the main title music. Following, as it does, a tritone that is cut off after a *crescendo*, the effect is disorienting, especially as the rest of the orchestra remains silent. Not only the timbre but also the dynamic of the snare drum suggests violence. The *crescendo* markings of each triplet group suggest Weil's movement towards the girl (sound, after all, gets louder the nearer the sound-producing object advances towards the listener). The "cowboy" theme is now transferred to the horns and then, in counterpoint, to the trumpets. The gradual increase in brilliance of tone and dynamic reflects the increasingly aggressive behavior of Weil and his men to the girl, who now pleads with them that she is not a witch.

An incantation follows, following a well-established operatic convention. It begins with a string *tremolo*, but the *tremolo* also serves to help us move from the interior of the woodman's hut back outside into the forest. The girl is now discovered tied to a stake. Weil raises his arms and intones, "Oh God, have mercy on this poor unfortunate creature. She is a child of the Devil...." Beneath this first part of the incantation, two bars of semitonally shifting and increasingly loud lines for cellos and bassoons lead us into the music of the incantation proper, in which the brass and electric harpsichord intone a motif that resembles the medieval chant of the *Dies Irae*. Robinson actually quotes the *Dies Irae* in *Lust for a Vampire*, but here he merely suggests this ancient melody and the connotations it brings with it. As the pyre is ignited, Robinson employs scalic passages to suggest the leaping flames, much in the manner of Wagner's music for the fire-god Loge in the *Ring* cycle. A discordant outburst of minor seconds scored for full orchestra then brings this section to a climax and is largely responsible for the horrific effect. The images are far less explicit than the music at this point because the writhing girl is obscured by flames. Indeed, this is an excellent example of how music can monumentalize what we see on screen, investing images with a grandeur they often don't possess by themselves.

At the beginning of the main title sequence another framing device is used. The *fortissimo* outburst is suddenly followed by *pianissimo* strings, as a snare drum instigates the rhythm that will continue throughout the main title. This sudden change of dynamic again "frames" Peter Cushing, accompanying his face in close-up, with his name in purple lettering superimposed over the image.

The music of the main title proper is based on a conventional AABA song form, but, less conventionally, Robinson blends his references to "Western" music with more straightforward "Horror" conventions. The joke went down well during the original recording session. According to Robinson himself, "when the producers heard it they ran around shooting guns, and they were highly delighted."[7] A galloping rhythm on timpani is combined with a full statement of the "cowboy" theme on solo horn. This theme is based on balanced phrases that operate along the lines of a question and answer, and it is this structure that creates the music's "cowboy" connotations, for it is exactly the same phrase structure that Ennio Morricone had made synonymous with "Spaghetti" Westerns in his famous theme for *The Good, the Bad and the Ugly* (dir. Sergio Leone, 1966). Robinson's theme is repeated on trumpets, flutes and oboes, with a chromatically descending figure on violins that confirms the film's true genre of Gothic horror; but this doesn't stop Robinson from using other "Western" clichés, in particular a strident countermelody for horns, which rises heroically through broken major chords.

As this analysis shows, Robinson is able to incorporate novelties of timbre and harmony within the context of a predominantly popular Romantic idiom. Later in the film he introduces other adventurous elements, such as harmonic string *glissandi*, Scriabinesque chords constructed from fourths, and flutter-tongue *glissandi* on wind instruments. It has to be said, however, that none of these more extreme effects ever undermine the essentially Romantic language of the score.

Robinson's approach was even more Romantic in *Countess Dracula*, though, again, the wonderfully resonant music he composed for this film contains certain elements that were derived from more contemporary idioms. *Countess Dracula* was released in 1971, by which time Hammer had reached its peak production period, with ten films completed within ten months. It had, however, slightly different aims (if not necessarily results) from a typical

Hammer horror film. It was produced by Alexander Paal and directed by Peter Sasdy, who were both Hungarians and so had a vested interest in this episode from Hungarian history. Based on the historical figure of Elizabeth Bathory, the fourteenth-century "Blood Countess," *Countess Dracula* was an attempt to make an historical costume drama. Although Jeremy Paul's script inevitably distorted a good deal of historical fact in favor of a supernatural explanation of Bathory's blood lust, several of the characters are confirmed as being based on historical personages by the historian Raymond T. McNally.[8] Robinson found working on this film more of a challenge from a stylistic point of view:

> Of all the Hammer pictures, they [the producer and director] were the ones who actually asked for very authentic-sounding music. They said, "We do not want a Hammer score. It's a historical picture we're making." I thought that was great — and they showed me all these pictures of Countess Bathory — this incredible story! We had lunch down at Pinewood. Philip and I started to get very hilarious after a couple of glasses of wine, and we were rolling with laughter. This guy, Alexander Paal, spoke with Philip afterwards and said [in a thick Hungarian accent], "I'm not sure about this composer, because composers do not laugh."[9]

Paal even gave Robinson a recording of Romanian folk music played on the panpipes by George Zamphir, the Hungarian performer who was relatively unknown in Britain in the early 1970s. Robinson's first idea was to exploit this instrument, but, unfortunately, no panpipe players could be found, so that idea had to be rejected. Instead, Robinson listened to recordings of Romanian folk music and studied scores by the two most famous twentieth-century Hungarian composers, Zoltán Kodály and Béla Bartók. From these sources, along with the nineteenth-century Hungarian music of Franz Liszt, he eventually created a very successful pastiche of "Hungarian" music:

> The main theme is very close to an Hungarian theme, which Kodály used himself. I went backwards from

Harry Robinson in 1994 (photograph courtesy Lesley Reid).

Kodály to find out where he got some of his material. A lot of the themes that you find in these Eastern European countries come down to nearly two-bar phrases. It's also typical of Scottish pipe music. What I eventually found in the library was a book of things for violin, and I also took out of that a little phrase that I used for the circus music as well. That's more Romanian than Hungarian. The only other thing was that we had to have a reel, and I could not find anything at all. I had a record which was all Hungarian pieces, but I couldn't take the risk that they weren't in copyright. You think that you're lifting a folk piece and it's been written last year by somebody! So what I did was listen to it and got the general drift of it. One of them sounded remarkably like a Scottish reel, so I then went to the Scottish reel, slightly changed the shape of it and brought it into the Hungarian mode and used that.

What a lot of composers do is sit and listen to a lot of music, let it drain into them and then by spitting it back out it comes out slightly different — one hopes! The plagiarism is there because you're using the same material as other people. Philip Martell helped me by giving me certain books that he had on gypsy fiddle music, and I went through all of those; but the trouble is that most of the gypsy fiddle music is well known. What you always want to achieve is a sense of originality.[10]

Before the main titles are presented there is a prologue featuring a burial scene, and this serves to introduce the major characters. There is no music, but a bell tolls as the funeral service is read out in Latin by a priest. The main title then breaks away completely and presents luridly tinted details of István Csók's late–nineteenth-century painting *The Blood Countess*, which depicts Countess Bathory surrounded by naked female victims, howling instructions from a throne-like chair. The incorporation of this picture into the main title sequence already begins to suggest the quasi-historical approach that is matched by the score.

In his study of the theme music for the T.V. detective series *Kojak*, Philip Tagg identified three functions at work. He calls these "reveille," "preparatory" and "mnemonic identification." The "reveille," which we've already encountered in the opening bars of *Twins of Evil*, takes the form of a call to attention. The "preparatory," as its name suggests, prepares us for the mood of the main part of the music. "Mnemonic identification" refers to the audience's recognition of the theme of the title music. We remember the theme and immediately prepare a frame of expectations with which to decode its musical signs. "Mnemonic identification," however, can also be interpreted in a more complex way. Instead of involving only the recognition of a particular theme tune, it could also refer to a broader recognition of a particular style of music. This is, of course, implicit in the *Kojak* theme, which carries with it many connotations that are broadly appropriate for such a subject (synthesized sound, jazz-related rhythms, and strident fanfare-like motifs played by brass — all of which are connotative of twentieth-century urban America). The "mnemonic identification" function of the main theme for *Countess Dracula* operates on this more complex level. On hearing the Hungarian idiom and certain other elements that are connotative of horror films, we are able to identify the genre and setting immediately. The Hungarian folk idiom lets us know that this film will be set in Hungary, while the large orchestra promises the portrayal of important and impressive events. The chromatic element in the strings indicates the Gothic aspect, and the cimbalom, as well as reinforcing the Hungarian connotations, also suggests the strange nature of the story (the latter element also being the case in Lutyens' score for *The Skull*—and, for that matter, Barry's score for *The Ipcress File*).

It is now possible to apply all three of these functions to an analysis of the main title music of *Countess Dracula*. The "reveille" function of the main title differs in detail from Tagg's *Kojak* example (*Kojak* begins with an octave *glissando* for horn), but it is still a "call to attention." The soundtrack music of *Countess Dracula* begins with a *sforzando* tremolo, but, interestingly, the *sforzando* is not actually indicated in the original score, where the string *tremolos* and a flute arabesque are actually marked *piano*. In its original form this was obviously not considered a striking enough "reveille" with which to emphasize the Gothic lettering of "Countess Dracula" that it accompanies. Consequently, this dynamic was changed for the recording. (Alexander Paal also insisted during the recording that a figure for the flutes, later in the film, be amplified far in excess of its original dynamic in order to emphasize a glittering jewel on screen. The result was a distortion not at all as the composer had originally intended.)

The "preparatory" function that follows lasts for only one-and-a-half beats. The duration of this could, however, be extended by one more beat if the *diminuendo* of the "reveille" chord is included. A quaver rest provides a sense of anticipation after the shock of the "reveille." Then an *arpeggiated* chord for violins, piano and two harps firmly establishes the key of A-minor. Although this key was implicit in the opening bar, it was distorted by the crushed F-natural and D-natural in the tremolo strings. The sudden change in dynamic to *pianissimo* also aids the sense that this is a new beginning. The fact that the "preparatory" chord is scored for harp and piano (in addition to violins) again draws attention to the rhetorical connotations of those instruments. Many of Liszt's piano works begin with a similarly rhetorical gesture. In Romantic pieces, the "preparatory" function is often associated with the harp, presumably due to this instrument's bardic associations (for example, the harp introduction to "Dir töne Lob" in Wagner's *Tannhäuser*, or the harp writing that introduces "The Waltz of the Flowers" in Tchaikovsky's *Nutcracker* ballet).

There are several elements that characterize the main theme as "Hungarian." The tritone interval implicit within it has dual connotations. Not only is its reputation as the devil in music appropriate here, it is also a natural part of the Hungarian "gypsy" scale that was frequently employed by Liszt in his

Hungarian Rhapsodies (e.g. C-natural, D-natural, E-flat, F-sharp, G-natural, A-flat, B-natural, where the tritone relationship is implied between the first and fourth notes of this scale). We should also consider the so-called acoustic octave (with its major third and sixth, augmented fourth and minor seventh), which both Kodály and Bartók pointed out were central to authentic Hungarian folk music. Liszt was actually mistaken in his belief that he had rediscovered genuine Hungarian folk music. What he had actually been inspired by was a type of middle-class, urban music that had been adopted by the gypsies but not actually created by them. As we shall see, it was this Romantic concept of folk music rather than authentic folk style on which Kodály and Bartók based much of their music, which provided the real model used in Robinson's score for *Countess Dracula*.

Robinson's use of the cimbalom is also indebted to Liszt's example. As we have seen, Liszt supervised Franz Döppler's orchestration of the Hungarian Rhapsody No. 6, known in its orchestral version as No. 3. In the *Lassan* section of this orchestral Rhapsody the cimbalom made its first major appearance in Western symphonic music. A further Romantic folk idiom is Robinson's use of a two-chord accompaniment to the melody. In *Countess Dracula* this consists of the alternating chords of a D-major chord with an added seventh, and an E-flat major chord. This two chord harmonic scheme corresponds in principle to that found in the introductory section of Liszt's second Hungarian Rhapsody, and it also appears in all the folk dance sequences that occur throughout the film (as, indeed, does the cimbalom). With regard to the rest of the orchestration, Robinson had this to say:

> *Countess Dracula* has no brass. It's only got four horns. It doesn't have any trumpets or trombones or tuba.... I used a lot of percussion—and the cimbalom, obviously. I also tried to put in other atmospheric percussion instruments, like tuned sleigh-bells. To make one job different from the next you might get one idea or you hear a sound in somebody's work and you extrapolate it and then build on it. It's exactly the same with *glissando* strings in harmonics. You hear that sound and you say, "That's wonderful! Where can I use it?!" And in movies there are lots of times in which you can use atmospheric sounds. With the bowed vibraphone in *Countess Dracula*, what I wanted was *only* the bowed vibraphone, but I put on the harmonic strings as well. That was chickening out. The main reason for that was that the percussionist on that was Tristan Fry, and Tristan said, "The only drag about bowed vibes is that you've got to give me a long time, and sometimes it's not a very clear note"—because you don't have time at those recordings to go into the niceties of sound. It's a hit or miss affair. For example, I once got a wonderful sound off a large bowed cymbal. The next time I tried it the percussionist couldn't do it. Perhaps the cymbal wasn't a really good cymbal. The tuned sleigh-bells in *Countess Dracula* were not on everyone's list of percussion. What I did was to go down to Tristan Fry's place and had a look through all the percussion he

Six: Romantics (Robinson and Bernard)

had. He had peculiar tubaphones, Greek instruments, Turkish things. The amount of finger cymbals there are is quite incredible. Often I'd use finger cymbals like castanets.

The standard string section for a Hammer picture at that time? You traded off certain things. In other words, if I had to have violas it meant that I had to trade down the violins and cellos. Now, I believe the violins would have been twelve violins, four violas, four cellos and two basses. That would have been the string compliment.

I don't know what other composers were doing at that time but there were always eyebrows raised if you came in without brass, because the typical Hammer sound was maybe something like six woodwind, two horns, two trumpets, three trombones, one percussion, one keyboard (either harp or keyboard), and the rest strings. I very seldom came in with what was a typical woodwind line-up, so on *Countess Dracula* I think I had five woodwind; but I wanted two harps, because there were certain sounds I wanted to get (whispering harps), and also I was heavily into pedal *portamentos* at that time [i.e. moving the pedal of the harp after the string is plucked]. It was a rather strange sound and I liked it, so it went in. And I also wanted double percussion and a keyboard player as well. That took away from the woodwind section, and it took away from the string section.

Ingrid Pitt and Sandor Elès working out certain problems in their relationship in *Countess Dracula* (dir. Peter Sasdy, 1971).

The first bell-tree I saw was not very long before *Countess Dracula,* and I'd used it in pop-records. It had very limited effect because you could only use it like a harp *glissando,* but it's wonderful. Again, it depends on the quality of the bell-tree, because I've had some which sounded like somebody rolling tin cans down the road.[11]

The bell-tree (an arrangement of miniature tubular bells) makes a particularly effective decoration of the scene in which the rejuvenated Countess (played by Ingrid Pitt) goes riding with Imre Toth (played by Sandor Elès). They dismount by the side of a lake, and the bell-tree accentuates the glittering light on the ripples of the water.

We hear the bowed vibraphone and tuned sleigh bells on several occasions, most notably in the scene when the Countess unsuccessfully tries to regain her youth via the blood of the murdered prostitute Ziza (played by Andrea Lawrence). The *bisbigliando* (or "whispering") harps of which Robinson was so fond also add to the disturbing effect of this scene, which is introduced by tone clusters in the strings (Robinson instructs the string players to "CRUSH ALL NOTES IN BETWEEN" the pitches he indicates).

Unfortunately, Ziza's blood doesn't have rejuvenate qualities. So far, the Countess' victims have all been suitably virtuous, but she hasn't yet realized that the virtue of her victims is a prerequisite for her murderous transformations. A Gypsy girl (played by Niké Arrigi) proved suitably chaste earlier in the film, and a swift stab with an elaborate hairpin into the girl's neck had brought the Countess temporary relief. Immediately after this murder, Robinson responds to the confusion of the visual imagery with various blurring devices in the music. A minor ninth chord built on C-natural is clouded by an added F-flat, and the blurring effect of this is increased by the use of the vibraphone *glissandi* over it, which Robinson was careful to mark with the specific instruction "BLUR." Such deliberate blurring of tonality and timbre does indeed correlate to the disorientating dissolve on the screen which these two bars accompany.

However, as with *Twins of Evil,* these more experimental elements in Robinson's score don't really affect his overall popular–Romantic style. In many ways one could regard this film (and its music) as a lexicon of the various categories of an aesthetic that were central to much nineteenth-century Romantic art, and which were identified as early as the mid–eighteenth century by Edmund Burke in his *Philosophical Enquiry into the Origin of Our Ideas of the Sublime and the Beautiful,* first published in 1757, when the *Sturm und Drang* movement held sway over Europe. Among Burke's various categories of sublime effects, fear and horror were particularly important, and he placed great emphasis on them in the *Philosophical Enquiry*'s most famous passage:

> Whatever is fitted in any sort to excite the ideas of pain, and danger, that is to say, whatever is in any sort terrible, or is conversant about terrible

objects, or operates in a manner analogous to terror, is a source of the *sublime*: that is, it is productive of the strongest emotion which the mind is capable of feeling.[...] When danger or pain press too nearly, they are incapable of giving any delight, and are simply terrible; but at certain distances, and with certain modifications, they may be and they are delightful, as we every day experience.[12]

Burke's definition of the sublime could apply equally well to the "delightful danger" of the horror film in general. Burke gives many examples of how the Sublime may be manifested, but insists that the underlying qualities inherent in all these manifestations share the same attributes:

The passions which belong to self-preservation, turn on pain and danger; they are simply painful when their causes immediately affect us; they are delightful when we have an idea of pain and danger, without being actually in such circumstances; this delight I have not called pleasure, because it turns on pain, and because it is different enough from any idea of positive pleasure. Whatever excites this delight I call *sublime*.[13]

Burke divides his analysis of sublime effects into categories such as "Terror," "Obscurity," "Vastness," "Infinity," "Difficulty," "Magnificence," "Light," "Color," "Sound and Loudness" and "Suddenness," which it is possible to apply to the film in question.

Following the murder of the Gypsy girl, we follow Imre Toth and the rejuvenated Countess to a sunlit forest where the main title music, in slightly modified form, is reprised. This forest scene encapsulates many of Burke's categories and is one of Hammer's most successful evocations of the sublime in nature. The music here grows out of the previous love scene between Imre and the Countess, where the languorous love theme was supported by tritone harmonies in the bass line, reminding us that their love affair is actually founded on death and decay. As the music reaches its climax (along, presumably, with that of the lovers), the Countess grabs hold of the now phallic hairpin, with which she had killed the gypsy girl, in a rather obvious, but nonetheless highly appropriate, gesture. This was the moment that Alexander Paal insisted should be emphasized in a way that Robinson, rather more tastefully, didn't intend in his original score.

As the scene cuts to the forest, the flute motif that we first heard in the main title appears in its true context as a signifier of nature. Indeed, the music is largely responsible for the sublime effect of this scene, the categories of Burke's theory that are most in evidence here being "Vastness" and "Magnificence." Burke writes: "The passion caused by the great and sublime in nature, when those causes operate most powerfully, is Astonishment."[14]

Here we are "astonished" mainly by the *arpeggiated* C-sharp minor chord that follows the flutes' "nature" motif. The transition from the love scene to the forest is covered by a perfect cadence (G-sharp to C-sharp), accompanied by a string *tremolo* on A-natural and G-sharp). The "nature" motif appears on the tonic resolution of the cadence, but the *tremolo* continues, and the slight tonal ambiguity it causes isn't resolved until the second bar of the new key of C-sharp minor. This tonality is emphasized by the two harps and piano, which play a wide and richly *arpeggiated* C-sharp major chord. The "astonishing" effect of this chord is partly due to our delayed gratification, but it is made more so by its "astonishingly" wide range, along with the glittering effect of the combined timbres of piano and harps in a hushed *pianissimo*. Such a clear statement of a diatonic chord is also "astonishing" because of the contrast it makes with the chromaticism and tritone harmonies of the preceding scene. Robinson is able, therefore, to make a platitude — the humble perfect cadence — into a "sublime" effect.

With the entry of the Countess and Imre Toth, the main cimbalom theme helps reinforce the illusion that this is a Hungarian forest, rather than the more prosaic reality of Black Park in Buckinghamshire where the scene was actually filmed. The next five bars are a repeat of the corresponding section of the main title music, but another "astonishing" perfect cadence occurs a little later on when we move from C-sharp major to F-sharp major. The cimbalom, in its *concertante* role, now rhythmically decorates the main melody, and is joined by the tuned sleigh-bells. It is here that the bell-tree emphasizes the glittering ripples of the lake, and the rising countermelody for violins again helps to monumentalize the images and make them conform to Burke's categories of "Vastness" and "Magnificence":

> Greatness of dimension is a powerful cause of the sublime.... A great profusion of things which are splendid or valuable in themselves, is *magnificent*. The starry heaven ... never fails to excite an idea of grandeur.[15]

The scene closes with Imre and the Countess sitting next to each other beside the lake. Suddenly afraid that she has reverted to an old woman, the Countess lifts her hand to her face and gasps. The score responds to this action with the musical equivalent of an intake of breath: the tuned sleigh-bells and cimbalom rise to a high C-sharp, instructed to "Let ring," while the harps and piano play a series of repeated minor seconds. Instead of resolving the discord, the music simply stops, quietly and harmonically unresolved, leaving it up to the dialogue to complete the scene.

It is important to point out that Hammer was not always so concerned with depicting genuine horror as classically Burkean sublime effects filtered through the "gothick" aesthetic of late–eighteenth-century literature and nineteenth-century melodrama. The sublime presentation of nature in the popular–Romanticism of a film such as *Countess Dracula* is as central to Hammer's aesthetic as it had been in much late– eighteenth and nineteenth-century Romantic art, and the music of Harry Robinson is vital to its success. However, as we have seen, his predominantly Romantic musical grammar is seasoned with several novel effects that are indebted to developments in contemporary music that derived from avant-garde composers who were very much at odds with Romanticism, whether of the popular variety or not.

The same could be said of the composer most readily associated with Hammer, James Bernard. For a full exploration of his approach, the reader is directed to my own study of his life and work,[16] but I would like to point out here some

Composer to Count Dracula. James Bernard with Hammer's LP vinyl disc of *Dracula with Christopher Lee* in 1998 (photograph by Lionel Cummings).

of the more experimental aspects of his style. As we've already mentioned, Bernard was out of sympathy with atonal and serial styles—indeed, he felt oppressed by them. Having said that, he was capable of some very adventurous writing when required. He was composing note clusters long before he had even heard of Penderecki. Indeed, some of his other novel effects wouldn't have been out of place (if taken out of context of the rest of the scores) in an avant-garde concert piece of the time.

Bernard was born in India in 1925, the second son of Col. Ronald Playfair St. Vincent Bernard and his wife Katherine. It was while he was a boy at Wellington College in 1943 that young James first met Benjamin Britten, who was visiting the school to discuss the set designs of his opera *Peter Grimes* with Kenneth Green, Wellington College's art master. Taking an interest in an inter-house music competition, Britten assisted the budding composer with a piece called *Spur of the Moment*, and the friendship lasted through the Second World War and well into Bernard's successful career as the principal composer of Hammer's classic Gothic horror films. This illustrious position had originally come about through his early work on radio drama. Bernard's music for a radio production of John Webster's Elizabethan revenge tragedy, *The Duchess of Malfi*, had come to the attention of Hammer producer Anthony Hinds, and it led to Bernard's first film score, *The Quatermass Experiment*, in 1955. In fact, Bernard laid out much of his subsequent musical menu in his early science fiction films for Hammer.

The tritone was central to Bernard's musical vocabulary, and this interval was an integral part of his famous theme for *Dracula* (dir. Terence Fisher, 1958). Tritones appear in virtually every score he wrote. Sometimes his use of them approximates the way in which they were incorporated into the so-called "mystic chord" of Scriabin, which we have already encountered. This is particularly the case in his score for *The Hound of the Baskervilles* (dir. Terence Fisher, 1959). More of an harmonic than a melodic idea, the main theme is indeed based on a collection of perfect and augmented fourths. We've already seen how much of Bernard's score for *The Quatermass Experiment* anticipated the approach of Bernard Herrmann's score for *Psycho*. String *glissandi* and note clusters also featured in his next Hammer score, for *X— the Unknown*. Indeed, it is hard to think of a British film composer from the mid–1950s who was using such extreme effects. In an interview piece in *The Star* newspaper on August 22, 1955, the journalist who interviewed Bernard reported:

> James Bernard told me today that he had just finished one of the oddest musical tasks of the year. Twenty-nine-year-old Mr. Bernard, former personal assistant to Benjamin Britten, has been writing music for a monster—a giant Thing, half-man, half-cactus, of *The Quatermass Experiment*, TV science-fiction serial of a couple of years ago.
>
> Mr. Bernard has done the music for the film version. There are about 20 minutes of it and, says the composer proudly, "not a single tune from beginning to end."

Six: Romantics (Robinson and Bernard)

MONDAY 18 JUNE: RECITAL: TWENTIETH CENTURY MUSIC

II. MERMAID'S VESPER-HYMN
James Bernard (b. 1925)

Troop home to silent grots and caves,
    Troop home and mimic as you go
The mournful winding of the waves,
    Which to their dark abysses flow.

At this sweet hour all things beside
    In amorous pairs to covert creep;
The swans that brush the evening tide
    Homewards in snowy couples keep.

In his green den the murmuring seal
    Close by his sleek companion lies,
While singly we to bedward steal,
    And close in fruitless sleep our eyes.

In bowers of love men take their rest,
    In loveless bowers we sigh alone;
With bosom-friends are others blest,
    But we have none—but we have none.

        George Darley

III. VIRTUE *James Butt (b. 1929)*

Sweet day, so cool, so calm, so bright!
    The bridal of the earth and sky—
The dew shall weep thy fall tonight;
    For thou must die.

Sweet rose, whose hue angry and brave
    Bids the rash gazer wipe his eye,
Thy root is ever in its grave,
    And thou must die.

Sweet spring, full of sweet days and roses,
    A box where sweets compacted lie,
My music shows ye have your closes,
    And all must die.

Only a sweet and virtuous soul,
    Like season'd timber, never gives;
But though the whole world turn to coal,
    Then chiefly lives.

        George Herbert

3. SONATA FOR PIANO *Malcolm Williamson (b. 1931)*

This work was written in 1954–5. There are three movements, *Allegro, Andante* and *Allegro Misurato*.

The music is entirely contrapuntal in a straight-forward tonal framework. The structure of the two flanking movements varies from traditional sonata and rondo forms, only in that key relationships are governed by the thematic germs rather than by proximate tonalities. The slow middle movement is much more concentrated, and is symmetrical in design.

The work is mono-thematic.   M. W.

4. FIVE FRENCH FOLK SONGS arranged by *Richard Bennett (b. 1936)*
   for soprano and harp

These songs were written in 1954–5 at the request of Sophie Wyss.

I. A LA CLAIRE FONTAINE
II. LA QUENONILLE
III. LA BELLE AU PIED DE LA TOUR
IV. LA FILLE DU LABOUREUR
V. LE NID

44

Rising Stars. Program of a concert featuring works by Malcolm Williamson, James Bernard and Richard Rodney Bennett, given in the Jubilie Hall, London, on June 18, 1956 (photograph by the author, courtesy the J.M. Bernard Will Trust).

It was recorded for the picture by the strings of the Royal Opera House orchestra who produced one of the more bizarre effects by drawing their bows across taut strings on the wrong side of the bridge of their violins. "An absolutely terrible noise" is the composer's description of the result.[17]

One could also argue that Bernard anticipated, in the furious whirring effect of a section in the prologue of *Quatermass II*, the "ghostly rustle and buzz" of the Transylvanian composer György Ligeti's 1968 harpsichord piece *Continuum* ("ghostly rustle and buzz" was exactly how Ligeti himself described his own piece).[18] As a young couple drive along a country road at the beginning of the film, they narrowly avoid colliding with a man who has been infected by the alien force that we later discover is intent on taking over the Earth. Bernard accompanies this with a simple four-note chromatic motif. Its minimalist style and furious energy to some extent resembles that of Ligeti's obsessively repeating scalic passages in *Continuum*, and, again, Bernard's music here also anticipates the frenetically obsessive energy of Herrmann's *Psycho* score.

Aliens are discovered to be guarding a mysterious government research plant in *Quatermass II*, and when they arrest Quatermass' assistant, Bernard creates an appropriately brutal accompaniment with a chord that is again constructed from perfect and augmented fourths. (Yet again, Herrmann was to take a similar approach when Janet Leigh is tailed by a patrol car in *Psycho*). In fact, Stravinsky beat both Herrmann and Bernard to this effect in "The Dance of the Young Girls" from *The Rite of Spring* (first performed in 1913), where the same chord is repeated insistently for many bars. When we finally get to see the alien monster itself, which is revealed towards the end of the film as Quatermass infiltrates the "food" dome, Bernard creates an astonishing effect by means of *glissandi* in the strings, which slide through the discordant (and, for him, highly characteristic) interval of major seconds.

In 1957, the same year that Hammer released *The Curse of Frankenstein*, Pierre Boulez revised his notorious example of integral serialism, *Le Marteau sans Maître*. At the time, it would have seemed that the triumphant progress of Hammer films was taking place not so much in a different country as on a different planet, far from the self-consciously intellectual world of Boulez' total serialism, but we can now place both once apparently opposing camps in a shared perspective. Even in the work of so overtly Romantic a composer as James Bernard, there is much that reflects the spirit of the time. In *The Plague of the Zombies* (dir. John Gilling, 1965), for example, when Alice (played by Jacqueline Pearce) is decapitated in the middle of the film and the famous dream sequence begins, the strings are again instructed to play on the wrong side of the bridge "to make a grotesque squealing noise throughout." Bernard often instructs the strings to play *sul ponticello*—i.e. on or near the bridge. A particularly effective example of this effect of timbre occurs in *The Devil Rides Out* (dir. Terence Fisher, 1968) when a giant spider appears during the film's

Front cover of Sigurd Rascher's concert program, July 27, 1961, which included Bernard's *Passacaglia* in 1961 (photograph by the author, courtesy the J.M. Bernard Will Trust).

central scene set inside the magic circle that has been drawn on the living-room floor of Richard and Marie Eaton (played by Paul Eddington and Sarah Lawson). The spider is an illusion conjured by the black magician Mocata (Charles Gray), who hopes, unsuccessfully, to lure the Duc de Richleau (Christopher Lee) and his friends out of the protection of the circle. The spider also threatens a similarly illusory manifestation of the Eaton's daughter, Peggy (Rosalyn Landor). Eventually, de Richleau destroys the spider with holy water, and as it disintegrates Bernard brings in his grotesquely shrieking *sul ponticello* strings to astonishing effect.

```
*Passacaglia, Theme and Variations. . . . . . . . . . .Bernard
    Andante
      Feroce
        Con tenerezza          World premier
          Appasionata
            Volante
              Scherzoso
                Piu mosso
                  Tempo primo
                    Tempo di valse
                      Molto energico
                        Molto agile
                          Furioso
                            Tempo primo
```

```
*Solo Cantata for Soprano, Saxophone and Piano. . . . . .Jacobi
    (American Premier)

*Nature Suite for Saxophone Solo. . . . . . . . . . . . .Swain

*Elegie et Rondeau . . . . . . . . . . . . . . . . . . . Husa
    Quasi improvisando
      Allegretto          US premier
```

* Dedicated to the Soloist

Program of Sigurd Rascher's concert that included the world premiere of James Bernard's *Passacaglia* in 1961 (photograph by the author, courtesy the J.M. Bernard Will Trust).

Another section from this score is also comparable to the mystical style of Boulez' teacher, Olivier Messiaen. When Peggy is abducted by Mocata in the middle of the film, de Richleau performs a magical ceremony in order to gain contact with the spirit of Tanith, who has already fallen victim to Mocata's wrath and died. De Richleau hopes that Tanith's spirit can help him find where Mocata has taken Peggy. As de Richleau intones, "The sign of Osiris slain; the sign of Osiris risen," trills on the strings are accompanied by an effect unique in Bernard's music to suggest the shimmering descent of Tanith's spirit into the body of Marie, who is acting as Tanith's medium. The effect is created by a quartet of hand-bells playing a simple E-major chord, accompanied by trills on celesta and high-pitched violins. The violin trills give the impression of there being an

Baron Frankenstein

dares you to meet the Creature

at the

Warner Theatre, Leicester Square, w.c.2

on Thursday, May 2nd, 1957

at 8.30 for 9.0 p.m.

Dress : Funeral   *R.S.V.P.*

*Top: **Did I request thee, Maker...?** The Promethean vulture on the reverse of the Frankenstein invitation card (photograph by the author, courtesy the J. M. Bernard Will Trust). Bottom: **Monster bash.** The rare invitation card issued for the premiere of* The Curse of Frankenstein, *May 2, 1957 (photograph by the author, courtesy the J.M. Bernard Will Trust).*

added sixth (C-sharp) on top of the E-major triad, connoting the kind of mystical atmosphere so often conjured by Messiaen, whose harmonic style is also characterized by chords of the added sixth.

In 1967, one year before the devil rode out, Bernard had scored *Frankenstein Created Woman* (dir. Terence Fisher), and for this film he achieved one of his most spectacularly avant-garde effects. This film's story is remarkably similar to the nineteenth-century symbolist novel *The Future Eve*, by Villiers de L'Isle Adam, first published in 1886. In Villiers' astonishing story, an inventor, based on the real-life Thomas Alva Edison, places a disembodied female soul into a very realistic but entirely mechanical "Andraiad" (or android), and thus creates the perfect woman. Interestingly, this Andraiad carries a dagger to defend herself (very like Christina in the film), and the inventor's laboratory, as described by Villiers, is also a virtual blueprint for a Hammer set:

> On his right was a high window opening toward the flaming west — the glowing sunset casting on all objects a red-gold mist. In the room were moulds of various shapes, instruments of precision, piles of blue prints, strange wheelwork, electrical apparatus, telescopes, reflectors, enormous magnets, bottles full of peculiar substances, slates covered with quotations.[19]

In *Frankenstein Created Woman*, Peter Cushing's Frankenstein brings the body of deformed and crippled Christina (played by Susan Denberg) back to life after her own suicide. He then transfers the soul of his unfortunately executed assistant, Hans (played by Robert Morris), into Christina's now repaired and perfected body. Bernard's musical evocation of Hans' glowing soul is achieved by combining high-pitched vibraphone oscillations with equally high-pitched strings that not only play harmonics but also execute *glissandi* from one note to the next. Combined, the vibraphones and strings create a complex tone-cluster, fully the equal, in effect, of the kind of thing one so often encounters in the works of Penderecki and Lutosławski. Bernard himself was never sure quite how such effects would sound when he conceived them, and he often had to wait until the recording session before he found out. Certainly, no mere analysis can give an adequate account of this strange and, indeed, very contemporary sound.

In the same year that *Frankenstein Created Woman* was released (actually in the same month of that year, May 1967), György Ligeti completed one of his most characteristic pieces for string orchestra, called *Lontano*, which is entirely devoid of traditional melodic motifs. Instead, clusters of harmony gather and diffuse to create a sensation of drifting and spatial depth ("Lontano," in fact, means "distance"), and the overall effect is very similar to Bernard's music for the glowing soul — though much longer in duration and, of course, far more complex. Ligeti also seems to have felt the same way about the compositional process as Bernard: "Music is for me something intuitive. Afterwards, though,

I have to work in a speculative manner, when I make concrete what had been a purely acoustic or musical vision."[20]

One might call the whole of Ligeti's *Lontano* a musical sound effect, in much the same way that Thomas Mann called Richard Wagner's Prelude to *Das Rheingold* an "acoustic idea" rather than conventional music.[21] (The *Rheingold* prelude is, after all, "merely" a coloration and rhythmic rumination of the chord of E-flat.) Bernard's great strength as a film composer was his ability to create acoustic ideas out of very simple material. In the introductory section of his music for the LP vinyl disc of *The Legend of the Seven Golden Vampires*, to quote yet another example, he elaborates a simple semiquaver pattern, consisting only of an oscillating semitone, by means of orchestration and a *crescendo*, building it up to

At home with Oscar. James Bernard in 1999 with the Academy Award he shared with his partner Paul Dehn for the story of *Seven Days to Noon* (dir. John Boulting, 1950; photograph by the author).

a searing climax that, again, would not be out of place in a concert work by one of his avant-garde contemporaries.

As with Harry Robinson's approach, we see in the Hammer scores of James Bernard a variety of "modern" effects operating within an overall Romantic musical idiom; and their significance cannot be fully understood outside the context of the times in which they were written, when avant-garde experimentation by composers such as Ligeti, Stockhausen, Boulez, Lutosławski and Penderecki was at its height.

Notes

1. Harry Robinson, in conversation with the author, August 24, 1988.
2. Ibid.
3. Ibid.
4. Ibid.
5. Philip Tagg, *Kojak — 50 Minutes of Television Music* (Gothenburg: Gothenburg University Press, 1979), p. 84.
6. Philip Martell quoted in Edward Buscombe, *Making "Legend of the Werewolf"* (London: British Film Institute, 1976), p. 103.
7. Harry Robinson, in conversation with the author (Note 1).
8. Raymond T. McNally, *Dracula Was a Woman* (London: Robert Hale, 1983), *passim*.
9. Harry Robinson, in conversation with the author (Note 1).
10. Ibid.
11. Ibid.
12. Edmund Burke, *A Philosophical Enquiry into the Origin of our Ideas of the Sublime and the Beautiful* (Oxford: Oxford University Press, 1990), p. 36–7.
13. Ibid., p. 47.
14. Ibid., p. 53.
15. Ibid., p. 66–71.
16. David Huckvale, *James Bernard, Composer to Count Dracula: A Critical Biography* (Jefferson: McFarland, 2006).
17. *The Star*, August 22, 1955.
18. Paul Griffiths, *György Ligeti* (London: Robson Books, 1983), p. 63.
19. Villiers de l'Isle Adam, "The Future Eve," in *The Frankenstein Omnibus* (ed. Peter Haining) (London: Orion, 1994), pp. 84–5.
20. Paul Griffiths, *György Ligeti* (Note 2), p. 59.
21. Thomas Mann, "The Sorrows and Grandeur of Richard Wagner," in *Pro and Contra Wagner* (trans. Allan Blunden) (London: Faber and Faber, 1985), p. 108.

Seven

Prehistoric Modernism

Mario Nascimbene and Tristram Cary

In 1965 Hammer proudly announced their one-hundredth film (a designation that rather depends on which film one begins the company's history with). This was to be a remake of the 1940 Hollywood prehistoric adventure *One Million B.C.* (dir. Hal Roach). Re-titled *One Million Years B.C.*, and directed by Don Chaffey, Hammer's version would appropriately run for one hundred minutes as well. Capitalizing on the phenomenal success of *She* (dir. Robert Day, 1965), the producers of *One Million Years B.C.* were nonetheless unable to secure the services of *She*'s star, Ursula Andress, and turned instead to former weather girl Raquel Welch, who would be forever afterwards identified with her role as the scantily clad, fair-haired, stone-age pinup Loana. The film was a gigantic commercial success, grossing, according to Hammer archivist Marcus Hearn, around $8,000,000 worldwide.[1] Not only did this film bring audiences the delights of ample cleavage in fur bikinis and the stop-motion dinosaurs of Ray Harryhausen, but also the music of Italian composer Mario Nascimbene. Whatever audiences made of Nascimbene's novel approach to this film score, it was not, alas, admired by Hammer's music supervisor, Philip Martell, who recalled his experience of working with the composer as follows:

> Mario Nascimbene was discovered, so to speak, by Val Guest. Now, I did my first film with Val, so I owe him something, so at least I'll be absolutely truthful. Having done my first film with Val, he phoned up one day and said, "I have just finished a picture [*Where the Spies Are*, 1965] with a most marvellous composer — dance music — and we're running it tonight and I'd like you to come and have a look." So I went down there, and that music was *unbelievably* bad. There are no words to describe it. It was senseless — particularly as dance music, which has a form and a pattern, so I got away before anyone could drag me into a group who were going to discuss the merits of the film. If they'd asked me the next day I'd have said I'd got a car or a taxi or whatever and that I'd got an appointment; but it was awful. Well, that was Mario Nascimbene. I learnt afterwards that he didn't know

the first thing about dance music, that's for sure. So, Val then told Michael Carreras about this "great genius" called Mario Nascimbene, you see. Well, I'd heard his dance music, but we were going to do *One Million Years B.C.*, and Michael had said he'd engaged him. So, I went to Rome. (This was the other thing that used to be with Hammer. It isn't any more because Roy [Skeggs] is a different cup of tea; but Michael let me do whatever I wanted — no question of money.) So I went to Rome and met Mario Nascimbene, and he started telling me that he was going to do the music in his own recording studio (he'd got a recording studio at the bottom of his house) where he was making tapes; and they were all being made with mechanical devices. Well, I sort of swallowed it up to a point because it was prehistoric and there weren't any musical instruments then, so OK. Well, he made the tracks, but we couldn't do a whole picture like that. We'd have to get some orchestral music somehow, so he said he would write the music — and he turned out three of four pictures before I finally managed to get rid of him for good. Everything he wrote was written at something like seven seconds a bar. Now, I don't mind seven seconds a bar if you've got one-hundred notes in the bar, but he didn't. He put two. It was all slow and dragged, and it was bloody awful.

One big scene gave me the fright of my life — the scene where they were going to initiate a girl into the tribe, and all the populace there were banging things to set up a rhythm for her to dance to and run around to.[2] Mario then phoned up and said he'd completed the whole thing and was coming over. What date could I book the orchestra for? I did all those things, and then Michael said to me, "Go and meet him at the airport." They were impressed by him. He was a great actor — a terrific actor! He was very good-looking, and he was beautifully dressed, as the Italians can be, and elegant and a great talker — a

Raquel Welch almost revealing all in *One Million Years B.C.* (dir. Don Chaffey, 1966).

terrific talker. I think one of the first things he said after the recording was over was, "This Martell! Where did you get him? He's absolutely marvellous!" (because I could usually get everything in on take one; you train yourself to do that). That was Mario's way.

Well, when we'd finished the recording he said he was going home the next morning, and I said to Michael, "You can't let him go, because we haven't checked the track for the initiation." The customs had held that up, and we'd got to clear it through customs. Mario started saying he had to go—he'd got this to do and the other to do—so Michael said in the end, "Well, let him go. If he said he's made it, he's made it!" So we let him go, and we got the can of tape out of customs—and nothing was in synch. People were banging, and the soundtrack didn't marry the banging! So I and one editor had to remake the whole track. It took hours.

Now that's the man they tried to sell to me—and they did, because he came and he did another picture, and I complained. Another thing was he didn't care if he'd got his synchronization points in the right place or the wrong place. I used to ring him up and tell him. He'd say, "Ah, Phil," with his Italian accent, "Phil, you so clever! You put it right! Don't worry. As long as I know you're there I know it's going to be all right!" And that went through the second film, and then I think on the third film we had a long chase of seven or seven-and-a-half minutes, and he did the whole thing with jawbones. So I said to Michael afterwards, "That's it. You can't do that. You've got to put some music in there somehow. If you do another one I want to be there while he's writing. I want to see exactly what he's doing." He didn't orchestrate. He had "ideas."[3]

Regardless of Martell's opinion, however, and, indeed, any argument about the relative merits or faults of Nascimbene's music, there's no denying that Nascimbene's approach to scoring this film was radically different from any other Hammer film that Martell had worked on before. This in itself is significant, for Hammer's beautifully photographed but inevitably absurd prehistoric adventure film was seen by more people than any other film released by the company. Nascimbene's approach, therefore, was experienced by an extremely large audience, and certain aspects of his score for *One Million Years B.C.* did indeed put that audience into contact with some of the developments that were occurring in the musical avant-garde during the 1960s. Nascimbene's connection with these was his adoption of the trend for so-called *musique concrète,* which had first emerged in Paris in the late 1940s. As Hubert S. Howe, Jr., puts it, the practitioners of this style "intended to denote both their use of natural, or 'concrete' sound sources and their manner of composing 'concretely' on tape rather than 'abstractly' through notation and performance."[4] The most celebrated practitioner of *musique concrète* was the French composer Pierre Schaeffer, whose approach to composition was to base everything on sounds that exist naturally, avoiding anything that was electronically generated. The *Groupe de Recherches Musicales,* with whom Schaeffer worked, also took a firm line with regard to this approach to *musique concrète*; but other composers were less rigid. Since his first major work, *Symphonie pour un homme seul*, in 1949, Schaeffer went on to collaborate with such illustrious names as Messiaen, Boulez, Karlheinz Stockhausen, Edgar Varèse, Luciano Berio and Iannis Xenakis, who had all at some time or another visited Schaeffer in his Paris studio. By the 1970s *musique concrète* had begun to influence the world of popular music when the rock group Pink Floyd incorporated some of its techniques in their 1972 best-selling album *Dark Side of the Moon*. Film music, however, bridged the gap between art and popular culture some time before that, and Nascimbene's score for *One Million Years B.C.* played a significant role.

Reginald Smith-Brindle has usefully explained how *musique concrète* is created by means of changing the speed of a tape, reversing the direction of a tape, tape cutting and editing, tape loops, superposition of sounds, multitrack recording, stereo and quadraphony, the electronic modification of sounds by means of electronic filters (which can make any sound "seem smooth, hollow, brittle, bright, metallic, or mellow"), reverberation and ring modulation, during which processes sounds "can be distorted out of all recognition and rendered extremely complex [... though] ring modulation [...] belongs more legitimately to the field of electronic music."[5]

> Pieces have been written using only the sounds of scissors or drops of water falling into a bucket. The manipulation of vocal sounds can produce a very rich effect. Stockhausen's *Gesang der Jünglinge* (1955–6) is a very extensive piece made up substantially of the spoken and sung voice of one boy, so manipulated and multiplied that at times there seems to be a vast multitude.[6]

Tristram Cary, who provided electronic effects for Hammer's *Quatermass and the Pit* (dir. Roy Ward Baker, 1967), had this to say about the aims of *musique concrète* in a magazine article he wrote on electronic music in 1971:

> The aims of musique concrète were to liberate *l'objet sonore*, as Pierre Schaeffer calls it, and to regard any "sound object" as a possible artistic unit in its own right — not to think of some sounds as "musical" and others as "unmusical." The composer's art lies in what he does with the sound, and although some sounds are naturally much more interesting than others, there is no sound which is positively inadmissible as musical material.[...]
> Over the years the Groupe de Recherches Musicales of the ORTF in Paris, under Schaeffer's supervision, has researched "l'objet sonore" very thoroughly, and the Paris school has held firmly over twenty years of development to the idea of the complex, interesting sound as raw material for music, rather than the notion of electronic synthesis from basic generated sources.[...]
> In musique concrète the composer takes a sound and pulls it apart, exploring the various possibilities of its internal structure. The original

identity of the sound may be left as a literary reference, or removed. But it should not be necessary to ask yourself "what is that sound?"—it must be regarded as a musical phenomenon itself.[7]

Even after only this brief overview of *musique concrète*, the context in which Nascimbene was working should now become clear; but his approach was, of course, far more eclectic and commercial than any member of the *Groupe de Recherches Musicales* would have countenanced. A degree of elitism and a rejection of popularity certainly informed the attitude of such avant-garde composers. As Smith-Brindle says, with regard to popular applications of one of the most popular developments in electronic music, the synthesizer, "To reproduce instrumental music on the synthesizer is highly entertaining in the short term, but to the serious musician the real potentialities of this miracle box only begin where imitation of any kind leaves off."[8] Nascimbene's use of the esoteric ideas of *musique concrète* in *One Million Years B.C.* was therefore a radical one, and, it could be argued, one which brought these musical ideas and approaches to its largest ever audience at the time. Philip Martell was clearly out of sympathy with this style, but one could also argue that the likes of Schaeffer and Stockhausen would also have been equally out of sympathy with highly commercial prehistoric adventure films. In Nascimbene's work we find another significant interface between the exclusive world of the esoteric avant-garde and the commercial world of popular entertainment at a time when those two worlds were much more divided than they are now. In itself, regardless of the role played by the music, the film is highly unusual in the fact that it contains no real dialogue. The role of music, sound effects and musical sound effects was therefore crucial to its success.

Mario Nascimbene was born in Milan on November 28, 1913, and studied at the Giuseppe Verdi Conservatory. It was a screening of *The Jazz Singer* with Al Jolson that made him want to become a composer specifically of film music. Among his many scores for epic films are *Alexander the Great* (dir. Robert Rossen, 1956, in which Peter Cushing appeared as Memnon), *The Vikings* (dir. Richard Fleischer, 1958), *Solomon and Sheba* (dir. King Vidor, 1959), *Barabbas* (dir. Richard Fleischer, 1962), and, of course, Hammer's various prehistoric dinosaur adventures. Nascimbene's Meridiana Recording Studio, to which Martell referred above, housed what the composer himself called his "Mixerama": a console that controlled twelve tape decks, which Nascimbene had built to his own specifications and on which he mixed conventional musical sounds with voices and sound effects. It was on this console that he created, with the help of assistant Gianni Mazzarini, what he called the opening "cosmic sequenza" of *One Million Years B.C.*, which accompanies the film's depiction of the creation of the world. For this track he mixed sixty-seven effects, twelve at a time, and it took four days to complete. The final product is similar in effect to the purely orchestral tone-cluster that opens John Williams' score for *Close*

Encounters of the Third Kind (dir. Steven Spielberg, 1977). The cluster effects in both these films gradually rise in pitch, but whereas Williams' orchestrally generated cluster ends in a diatonic chord, Nascimbene's cluster, created by means of *musique concrète*, changes texture midway through. The swirling clouds that fill the screen for the first section of this sequence are replaced by a vortex of rapidly moving stars, and Nascimbene responds to this visual change with electronically manipulated string sounds. When a spinning disc appears (presumably the Earth in embryo form), Nascimbene slows down the tape to dramatic effect, and then brings in naturalistic sound effects of explosions to accompany stock footage of volcanoes erupting.

Two years after the release of *One Million Years B.C.*, popular audiences were directly confronted with an avant-garde cluster-style that had no original cinematic intention at all. It appeared in the soundtrack of Stanley Kubrick's *2001— A Space Odyssey* (1968), and Philip Martell recalled being summoned by Kubrick to assist with the music for this film:

> I was the first person to be asked by Stanley Kubrick. We had a long talk. I got on very nicely with him about what he thought the music ought to say, and the only problem with him was he could never express what he really wanted. What he imagined, what he heard, he couldn't put into words, and he couldn't get over to whoever was going to work with him. So I tried to figure out what he was after, and then I began to give him music to listen to; and I went to every composer that you could think of who at that time was modern enough. I gave him music of Richard Rodney Bennett and he said, "No." It wasn't "way-out" enough. He didn't *say* that; he didn't say anything. He said, "No, that's not what I'm looking for." That was as far as one could get in actual information out of him. I think I went to almost everybody. Then, in the end, he did what he had done before. He went and got himself a pile of records and finally settled for Richard Strauss.[9]

But that final decision wasn't made until Kubrick had infamously commissioned, and ultimately rejected, Alex North's score for the film. Amidst the heroic Romantic style of Richard Strauss and the nostalgic "Blue Danube" waltz of Johann Strauss, Jr., which replaced what North had composed, Kubrick also chose the vocal note clusters of György Ligeti's *Requiem*. As Ligeti's biographer, Paul Griffiths, put it when describing this work:

> The "Introitus" [of the *Requiem*] begins very slowly and quietly in the extreme bass register, the Latin [...] intoned by a choir of basses in four parts, accompanied by the cavernous lowest instruments of the orchestra.[...] The promised "light perpetual" is, as Ligeti has said, a "black light." The feeling is enormously solemn and awe-inspiring, but also disconcertingly alien, like Egyptian funerary art. It is, too, rather absurd: any attempt by the living to comprehend the dead must be.[...] The "Kyrie" [which we hear in *2001*] [...] is the most overwhelmingly impressive product of Ligeti's cluster style. It is more measured than *Atmosphères*, more monumental,

Seven: Prehistoric Modernism (Nascimbene and Cary)

keeping the Introit's division of the choir into four-part groupings of sopranos, mezzos, contraltos, tenors and basses, and using this twenty-part texture to weave dense patterns of what Ligeti likes to call "micropolyphony."[10]

Being chosen by Kubrick to accompany the psychedelic scenes of *2001* brought Ligeti the largest audience he would ever command—larger, indeed, than he could ever have dreamt of—and what Griffiths described as the "disconcertingly alien" aspects of the music were certainly appropriate for the astronaut's journey to "Jupiter and Beyond" in the latter stages of the film. Other composers, loyal to Alex North, weren't so happy, one of them (who shall remain nameless) referring to the director ever afterwards as Stanley Kuprick.

Nascimbene's score for *One Million Years B.C.*, however, arrived on the scene before either *2001—A Space Odyssey* or *Close Encounters of the Third Kind*, and it should be regarded as the more significantly pioneering film score in its use of cluster effects, particularly as these were generated by means of *musique concrète* principles rather than orchestral or purely electronic ones. The actual main title music of *One Million Years B.C.* reverts to conventional orchestral instrumentation, and Nascimbene also anticipates John Williams' famous *Close Encounters* theme by basing his thematic material on the basic building blocks of Western harmony. His melody begins by moving up a fifth and down a third. Williams also exploited these fundamental intervals in his famous *Close Encounters* theme, which is structured around a third, an octave and a fifth. By so doing, the scientists in that film are able to initiate a musical question to which the aliens of the spacecraft that visits Earth then respond and eventually develop contrapuntally into a musical "conversation." Williams scored the entire *Close Encounters* conversation (and, indeed, the remainder of his score) for a conventional symphony orchestra, though the action of the film implied that the sounds of the "conversation" were being electronically generated. For the main title music of *One Million Years B.C.*, Nascimbene also restricted himself to conventional instruments but avoided any supporting harmony, the large orchestra intoning the theme in unison. Such a monumental unison, along with the "primitive" musical intervals, successfully complements the prehistoric setting. This primitivism is combined with desolation during the opening scenes following the main title, which Nascimbene complements with solo wind instruments. He then dispenses with music altogether until we catch our first glimpse of a caveman who is lying in wait to ambush a wild boar. It is at this moment that Nascimbene introduces the novel instrument percussion with which many later scenes are to be accompanied. He called this a "Rastrophon," and it creates a sound like a whip and rattle combined. His fellow Italian composer Ennio Morricone indeed used similar effects in the same year as *One Million Years B.C.* in his score for *The Good, the Bad and the Ugly*.

One Million Years B.C. was without doubt Nascimbene's most inventive score for Hammer. His music for the sequel, *When Dinosaurs Ruled the Earth* (dir. Val Guest, 1969), followed in the tradition of many a nineteenth-century Italian opera composer by recycling previous material. The main title music, the theme of which recurs many times throughout the film, was originally written for *Solomon and Sheba*, though here it is re-orchestrated and played at a slower pace. *When Dinosaurs Ruled the Earth*, which has little of the visual majesty of its forerunner, similarly lacks musical innovations. It's true that Nascimbene created a compelling effect by means of his Mixerama for the shots of the sun, to which three girls are about to be sacrificed in the opening scenes, but the majority of the score is symphonic, tonal and really quite conventional. The main title, which presents the *Solomon and Sheba* theme, is quietly scored for a choir, but the understated dynamic here creates an inappropriately contemplative mood against the imposing presentation of the title of the film on screen. The musical climax occurs several bars later, with a reprise of the theme for full orchestra, a moment one can't help feeling should have been placed against the main title card instead; and when Victoria Vetri's character, Sanna, later encounters a "cute" infant dinosaur, the comedy music Nascimbene offers to accompany their incongruous fun and frolics would not have been out of place in the soundtrack of a *Carry On* film.

Nascimbene's score for *The Vengeance of She* (dir. Cliff Owen, 1968), Hammer's sequel to their hugely successful epic *She*, was also more conventional, despite the fact that it contrasted some attractive jazz writing, to complement the contemporary scenes, with a much more imposing symphonic style for the world of Kuma, where Kallikrates awaits the return of the reincarnated Ayesha (played this time by Olinka Berova; once again Ursula Andress was not available). Nascimbene did use the Mixerama in *The Vengeance of She* for the so-called "Call of Kuma," which summons Berova's character, Carol, back to the ancient city (it is indeed very similar to the sound we hear in *One Million Years B.C.* when Tumak [played by John Richardson] emerges from a sulphurous cavern inhabited by sinister ape-like creatures), but this was the Mixerama's only contribution to the score.

Despite the uneven contribution of Nascimbene's work for Hammer, his scores undeniably brought a novel approach to the soundtracks of these extremely popular films, and while it's true that there had been more extreme, purely electronic film soundtracks before Nascimbene's Hammer films (notably Louis and Bebe Barron's score for *Forbidden Planet* [dir. Fred M. Wilcox, 1956], and Bernard Herrmann's collaboration with Oskar Sala on Hitchcock's *The Birds* [1963]), Nascimbene's adoption of *musique concrète* principles was indeed unusual in the context of a popular film at that time.

Electronic music had been used in films made before *Forbidden Planet*, however. The theremin, invented by Léon Thérémin in 1920, was made popular by Miklós Rósza in films such as *The Lost Weekend* (dir. Billy Wilder, 1945), *Spellbound* (dir. Alfred Hitchcock, 1945) and *The Red House* (dir. Delmer Daves, 1947); while Dimitri Tiomkin famously exploited the swooping

Seven: Prehistoric Modernism (Nascimbene and Cary)

exoticism of the ondes martenot in his score for *The Thing from Another World* (dir. Christian Nyby, 1951). David Raksin had also experimented with recorded sound in that classic of *film noir, Laura* (dir. Otto Preminger, 1944), creating an effect that he called "Len-a-toning" (after the sound engineer, Harry Leonard, who helped him develop it). In the famous "apartment" scene in *Laura*, the detective (played by Dana Andrews) falls asleep in the lounge of the mysteriously missing Laura, and as he drifts off to sleep we hear Leonard's curious effect, which was created by milling the playback capstan wheel of a tape recorder into an oval shape, thus varying the pressure of the tape against the playback head. Leonard cut off the initial attack of a piano chord and played the decay of the sound through the adapted tape deck. This created a fluctuating timbre that attracted a great deal of attention at the time. However, all these electronic effects operated within the context of traditional tonal structures. It wasn't until Louis and Bebe Barron's groundbreaking score for *Forbidden Planet* that electronic music came of age in the soundtrack. Bebe Barron had studied with American avant-garde composer Henry Cowell, while Louis had always been fascinated by the possibilities of applying the technology of cybernetics to electronic music. For *Forbidden Planet* they created a series of leitmotifs from individual electronic cybernetic circuits, each circuit having its own characteristic pattern and "voice."[11] One of the most significant platforms for the popularization of electronic music in the 1960s was the BBC Radiophonic Workshop, from whose studios in London's Maida Vale many of the iconic effects and music for the long-running BBC T.V. series *Dr. Who* were created. The Radiophonic Workshop differed from more esoteric institutions, such as the *Groupe de Recherches Musicales* or

Tristram Cary in 2007 (photograph copyright the University of Adelaide, Australia; reproduced with permission from the University of Adelaide).

IRCAM (*Institut de Recherche et Coordination Acoustique/Musique*), in that it was called upon to provide popular music for radio and television as well as allowing its staff to experiment freely with sound. Tonality and conventional musical forms were never a problem for the Radiophonic Workshop, and it created a great deal of popular music using innovative timbres and effects. Most famous, of course, was Delia Derbyshire's electronic "realization" (more accurately, a transformation) of the fairly straightforward theme tune by Ron Grainer for *Dr. Who*. One of the team who contributed incidental music and effects to *Dr. Who* was Tristram Cary, who also scored two Hammer films. His second for the company was for *Blood from the Mummy's Tomb*, which concerns the reincarnation of the ancient Egyptian Queen Tera in a contemporary (1970s) setting. It was adapted from Bram Stoker's novel *The Jewel of Seven Stars*, which was first published (and, indeed, set) in 1903. Three other adaptations of the story have been made by other companies: Britain's Thames Television screened *Curse of the Mummy* in the same year as *Blood from the Mummy's Tomb*, starring Isobel Black (who had played Tania in Hammer's *The Kiss of the Vampire*). This was followed by *The Awakening*, directed by Mike Newell, with Charlton Heston and Stephanie Zimbalist in 1980, and finally, to date, *Bram Stoker's Legend of the Mummy*, directed by Jeffrey Obrow in 1997. This latter version also featured Aubrey Morris, who had played Dr. Putnam in Hammer's version, and he reprised the role in Obrow's film (though the name of the character reverted to Stoker's original of Dr. Winchester). Both of the subsequent film versions were indebted to Hammer's adaptation, which had ended ambivalently, leaving the audience unsure if the perfectly preserved Mummy itself had come back to life or if the spirit of Tera had completely possessed Valerie Leon's Margaret Trelawny. In the first edition of the novel, however, Margaret dies at the end, and Stoker suggested that the mummy had indeed been reanimated before mysteriously disappearing. (The ending was considered so shocking at the time that Stoker was forced to replace the dénouement with a happy ending for subsequent editions.) Both *The Awakening* and *Bram Stoker's Legend of the Mummy* followed Hammer's lead and left no doubt that Margaret is finally possessed by the unquestionably evil spirit of Queen Tera. (The novel actually remained ambivalent with regard to the Queen's morality.) *Blood from the Mummy's Tomb* also turned the character of Corbeck (played with delightfully camp malevolence by James Villiers) into a power-crazed villain. This was certainly not the case in the novel, but Hammer's alteration was nonetheless taken up by Obrow's film, where the role of Corbeck was played as a deranged egomaniac by the black actor Louis Gossett Jr., whom we first encounter in a lunatic asylum — yet another nod in the direction of Hammer's film, large portions of which take place in a similar environment. To confuse matters further, *The Awakening* for some reason changed Queen Tera's name to Kara, while giving the Egyptologist, Trelawny, the name of Corbeck. In a more innocent age, Hammer had renamed Trelawny as Professor Fuchs which, by 1980, was perhaps considered too liable to mispronunciation to repeat.

Blood from the Mummy's Tomb is certainly the best of the three film versions, especially as screenwriter Christopher Wicking even went so far as to give Valerie Leon's Margaret Fuchs some of Stoker's original lines[12]; but, as is well known, the spirit of Queen Tera nonetheless seems to have cursed the making of the movie. Peter Cushing, who was originally to have played the role of Professor Fuchs, in fact completed only one day's shooting before his beloved wife, Helen, died from emphysema. Distraught, he asked to be released from his contract, and was replaced by Andrew Keir; the film's director, Seth Holt, died of a heart attack halfway through filming, while Christopher Wicking was actually banned from the set due to disagreements with the film's producer, Howard Brandy. Tera's curse also affected the music. For some reason, Philip Martell was unhappy with certain aspects of Cary's score, and used Cary's cue for the opening temple scenes to accompany several subsequent scenes for which Cary had provided specifically tailored music. This is hard to understand, considering the high quality of Cary's score for this film, which the CD of the original recording session now eloquently reveals in its full glory. Roy Skeggs, who was the production supervisor on *Blood from the Mummy's Tomb*, recalled in his notes for that CD that Martell re-orchestrated a section from Rachmaninoff's Second Piano Concerto for this film, which is nonsense, as all the music in the film is quite definitely Cary's own. The harmonic language is, however, fairly conventional, awash, as it is, with whole-tone and oriental scales, the writing for harp in particular being reminiscent of Ravel's *Introduction and Allegro* (1905). Indeed, the score as a whole is a compendium of those "exotic" effects much prized by early twentieth-century composers, such as Debussy in his Egyptian ballet *Khamma*, which was written in 1912 for the American dancer Maud Allen. Cary's music also resembles some of Debussy's exotically entitled pieces from *Six épigraphs antiques,* as well as some of the effects in André Caplet's *Conte fantastique* (based on "Masque of the Red Death"). Ironically, Skeggs and Martell originally hired Cary because they felt that electronic sounds were needed to complement the eerie atmosphere of the film itself. In fact, *Blood from the Mummy's Tomb* used conventional orchestration throughout. Mystic harp *glissandi*, shuddering tam-tams, dreamy vibraphones, shivering suspended cymbals, mysterious flutes, ethereal strings—they're all there, if not necessarily in the order Cary originally intended; but there's nothing that's electronically generated. However, as we shall see, Cary's music for Hammer's earlier adaptation of Nigel Kneale's *Quatermass and the Pit* did contain some significant electronic effects.

Cary was born in 1925, the third child of novelist Joyce Cary and Gertrude Ogilvie. After serving in the Royal Navy between 1943 and 1946 he specialized in radar and electronics, a training that laid the foundation for his experimentations in electronic music. After taking a degree at Oxford University, he worked part-time in a record shop while creating his first electronic music studio; and since 1954 he has been a professional composer for film, theater, radio, television and the concert hall. In 1967 Cary founded and became professor of the electronic music studio at the Royal College of Music, and also designed and built his own electronic music studio in Suffolk, which he later transported to Australia, where he took up a new post at Adelaide University. He returned to a freelance career in 1986, and remains a passionate yet always sensible advocate of electronic music:

> Let me first of all remove some apparently widespread misconceptions:
>
> 1. That electronic music is very new. Wrong. It's coming was seen in the '20s.[...]
>
> 2. That electronic music is seeking to put musicians out of a job. Wrong, or only right at the crassest and least interesting end of the business. The interpretive musician is the only means by which to realise music written for instruments, or in a style designed for instruments. This is not what electronic music is about.[...]
>
> 3. That electronic music is trying to be iconoclastic. Wrong. The progress of art is by evolutionary change, not by sudden revolutions.[...] The idea that electronic music should seek to supplant established methods and masterpieces is as absurd as it is impossible. Music is a great big art, the biggest of all, and there is plenty of room inside.
>
> 4. That electronic music is [...] cold and technical and therefore inartistic. Wrong again, or at least wrong if it is written by a composer.[...] Creation is ideas, and how the ideas get to an audience is technique.[...] If the ideas are good and truly musical, we should be able to find the right technique to express them, and this may involve oscillators or oboes or both.[...]
>
> Let me make a comparison. Instrumental music, as we have said, depends upon a performer, and the composer reaches his audience at one remove.[...] The first dream of Varèse and others after him was a musical technique by which a composer could himself handle complex material, and himself present it to an audience in as direct a way as a painter hanging a picture on the wall [...] (one parallel in traditional music — virtuoso composer/interpreters like Paganini, Liszt).[13]

Cary's music for Hammer's adaptation of *Quatermass and the Pit* relied on electronic effects to create the unnerving quality of a Martian spaceship that is discovered behind the walls of a London Underground tunnel. This is, of course, a science fiction story, but it is also, like *One Million Years B.C.*, a prehistoric drama, as the Martian spaceship has been hidden in the mud and clay of subterranean London for thousands of years. Cary's use of electronics therefore suggests both the past and the future. Pierre Boulez would have strongly disagreed with this approach:

Seven: Prehistoric Modernism (Nascimbene and Cary) 127

There are always a few electronic *glissandos* in science-fiction films, enough to suggest the "leap into the future." They play, in fact, a pretty stupid role and one that is much too facile to be accepted as a role at all. The point of electronic and electro-acoustic devices is that they will expand our instrumental means.[14]

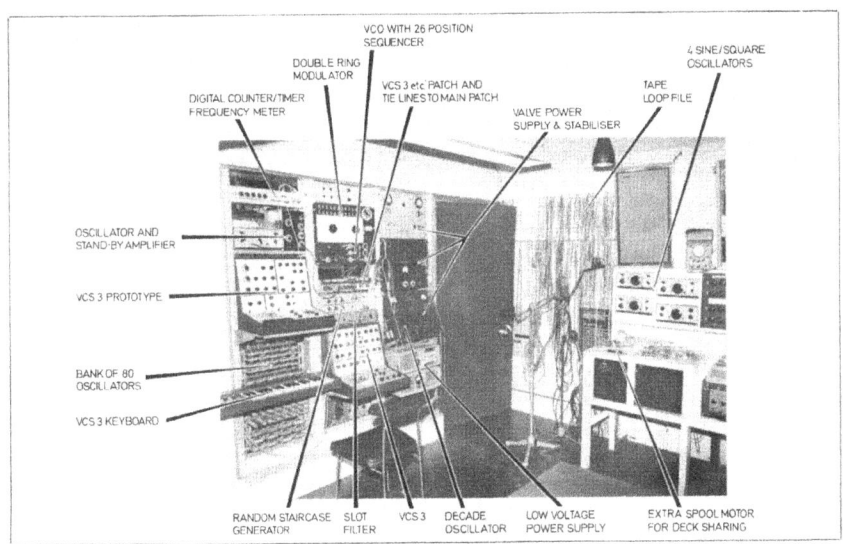

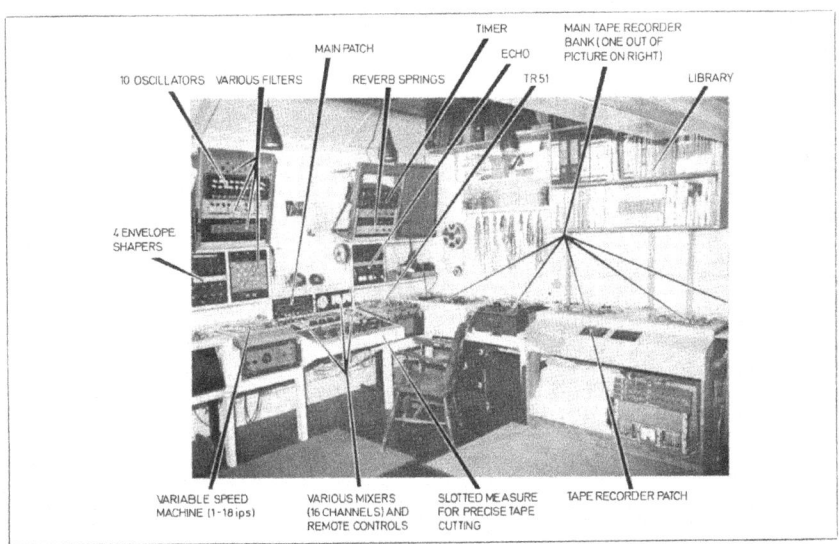

Wired up. Tristram Cary's electronic music studios, circa 1970 (photograph courtesy Tristram Cary).

The irony here is that both the world of avant-garde music and most musical reference books ignore the fact that Bernard Herrmann's theremin-inspired score for the science fiction film *The Day the Earth Stood Still* (dir. Robert Wise, 1951) appeared before the first electronic pieces by Stockhausen (his *Etude* of 1952) and Varèse (his *Déserts* of 1954), both of whom are usually credited with being the pioneers of electronic music.

Cary himself was keen to promote electronic music in any context, regarding film directors and producers as being rather limited in their appreciation of its applicability.[15] However, there's no denying that the predominant use of electronic effects in film has prejudiced the popular reception of such sounds. No composer can hope to avoid completely the accumulation of science fiction connotations electronic music now brings with it. Again, it seems that film music, while bringing many innovations to popular audiences, has also undermined what avant-garde composers initially hoped to achieve. Could it be that popular culture has actually confined rather than expanded our instrumental means—if not quantitatively, at least as far as their reception is concerned?

Aliens on the Underground. Julian Glover as Colonel Breen (with unidentified actors in the background) inspects the alien spacecraft that is discovered on the London Underground in ***Quatermass and the Pit*** (dir. Roy Ward Baker, 1967).

Cary's score is not entirely electronic, however. The majority of it is symphonic, and much more traditional in its approach. The resulting whole is therefore far more eclectic than what an avant-garde composer such as Stockhausen would have countenanced in his own work. Intriguingly, Stockhausen's electronic *Etude* appeared only one year before the original BBC transmission of Kneale's play. It wasn't until 1961, however, that Hammer thought about turning *Quatermass and the Pit* into a feature film, and the project had finally to wait until 1967 to be filmed and released. Cary has explained:

> By 1967 (year of Quatermass) I had been composing electronic music for about 18 years, starting in London and moving to Suffolk in 1963, so it was no innovation to me. My first electronic score for the BBC was in 1955 (*The Japanese Fishermen*). Shortly after that I used electronics for the supernatural elements in Macbeth (instrumental for the cues Shakespeare gives). Some important radio shows in the late 50s I did electronically, and of course from 1963 onwards there was *Dr. Who*, some with electronics, and some with instruments (most of my *Who* music has been released on a double CD). The main use of electronics in Quatermass, I think, was the violent shaking, vibrating sound that the "thing in the tunnel" gave off, successfully writing off that bad actor who played the army fellow [presumably Julian Glover's Colonel Breen]. It was not a terribly challenging sound to do, though I never played it very loud because I didn't want to destroy my speakers—I did have hopes of destroying a few cinema loudspeaker systems, though it never happened. There was nothing special about the scoring of the orchestral stuff. Obviously I scored for the orchestral resources allowed by Martell's budget, and the fact that Hammer employed a music director relieved me of having to book and pay an orchestra myself, which I usually did, as well as the conducting. 1967 was a very busy year—at the start I was in Montreal doing all the sound for the Industrial Section of the British Pavilion, plus a documentary for the Canadian Government and a number of instructional films for the Central Office of Information. Later in the year came *Quatermass* and finally *A Twist of Sand* [dir. Don Chaffey, 1968], with Richard Johnson and Honor Blackman, about a boatload of crooks who manage to kill each other fighting over loot on the Southwest African coast. I made the *Quatermass* music as exciting and high tension as I could, and Phil and the producers seemed to like it at the time, whatever they did to it at the dub. The final piece in the film is not mine—they changed the ending of the film, and my score did not suit the final scene. Too late for me to compose a new piece, so they used a library track.[16]

Electronic music, like so many other aspects of contemporary musical developments, has perhaps been more successful in film and television (where it is also more often used as a signifier of what is alien, troubling or supernatural) than in the concert hall. However, it is perhaps not so much the *medium* as the kind of music that is written by avant-garde composers of electronic concert music that could be held responsible for its failure to find a popular audience. After all, in the field of popular music, electronic sound and the techniques of *musique concrète* were cheerfully exploited by Jean-Jacques Perrey and Gershon Kingsley in their light-hearted 1973 album *The In Sound from Way Out* (1973), as well as in Perrey's solo 1972 album *Moog Indigo*. The express purpose of these recordings was to redress the misconception, strongly held at that time, that electronic music was only for avant-garde intellectuals. Perry and Kingsley's electronic pop tunes were the result of painstaking labor, blending electronic and acoustic instruments with *musique concrète*. Kingsley's experiments also brought electronic music to the pop charts in 1972 when his piece "Popcorn" (which first appeared on his 1969 album *Music to Moog By*) was

LP cover of Douglas Gamley's eccentric recording project with the London Symphony Orchestra with synthesizers in 1976 (photograph by the author).

recorded by the group Hot Butter and became an international hit. Two years later, Douglas Gamley, who scored several horror films himself, conducted the London Philharmonic Orchestra in an eccentric recording of standard orchestral classics, such as Richard Strauss' *Also Sprach Zarathustra,* Mussorgsky's "Great Gate of Kiev" from *Pictures at an Exhibition,* and the finale of Beethoven's Ninth Symphony. The performances themselves weren't eccentric, but the addition of synthesizer accompaniments was, the whole project having been designed to exploit what the sleeve notes proudly announced as "speaker to speaker interplay." (Stereo sound was a new phenomenon at the time.) Called *Sounds Astounding* (the cover was adorned with two silver-painted nude women sporting the latest in headphones), it was yet another example of the craze for the synthesizer, which Robert Moog had been developing since 1964. The synthesizer reached phenomenal levels of popularity in 1969 with the release of Walter Carlos' phenomenally successful electronic album *Switched-on Bach,* which proved that electronic instruments were not in themselves the reason for the relative lack of interest in avant-garde electronic music. Carlos went on to score Stanley Kubrick's adaptation of Anthony Burgess' novel *A Clockwork Orange* in 1971, around the same time that 1970s electronic rock/pop groups such as Kraftwerk and Tangerine Dream were enjoying considerable success. (Significantly, neither of these groups abandoned tonality in their various recordings, and Tangerine Dream also went on to score William Friedkin's film *Sorcerer* in 1977). Smith-Brindle seems at a loss to explain the failure of electronic music to engage large audiences, suggesting, rather lamely, that the reason might be that it's difficult to applaud a loudspeaker.[17] This, however, isn't a very convincing explanation. After all, no one is bothered by loudspeakers in the cinema where there is no need for applause, and electronic music blends effortlessly (when handled sensitively) with the rest of the soundtrack. Perhaps it isn't so hard to explain why the electronic music advocated by avant-garde composers has yet to find a mass audience when one acknowledges the fact that tonality is still the dominant musical force in our culture, despite a century of musical experimentation. Once again, it is tempting to consider the cinema as the place where the electronic experimentation of such composers found its largest audience, and was also responsible for undermining the aesthetic ambitions of the avant-garde to create a new musical language free from conventional associations.

Notes

1. Marcus Hearn, *The Hammer Story* (London: Titan, 1997), p. 105.
2. Martell could be thinking of the sacrificial scene that opens Nascimbene's second prehistoric epic for Hammer, *When Dinosaurs Ruled the Earth,* where synchronization is indeed important, as a very definite rhythm is set up by the characters banging bones

against skulls in this scene. For the initiation scene in *One Million Years B.C.*, in which Martine Beswick's character is surrounded by cacophonous hoards playing erratic rhythms, synchronization is nowhere near as important.

   3. Philip Martell, in conversation with the author, August 24, 1988.

   4. Stanley Sadie (ed.), *The New Grove Dictionary of Music and Musicians* (London: Macmillan, 1980), vol. 6, p. 107.

   5. Reginald Smith-Brindle, *The New Music* (Oxford: Oxford University Press, 1982), pp. 100–102.

   6. Ibid., p. 102.

   7. Tristram Cary, "Electronic Music," in *Audio Annual '71*, 1971, p. 44.

   8. Reginald Smith-Brindle, *The New Music* (Note 5), pp. 110–111.

   9. Philip Martell, in conversation with the author (Note 3).

   10. Paul Griffiths, *György Ligeti* (London: Robson Books, 1983), pp. 50–51.

   11. Barron, Louis and Bebe, album sleeve notes for the *Forbidden Planet* soundtrack LP, Small Planet Records, 1956.

   12. Valerie Leon's Margaret says, "I get a feeling of great loneliness, of her dreaming alone, dreaming of things far different from those around her. A land far away in miles and years, yet close to her heart. No scheming and malignant priesthood. No archaic laws or endless rituals of death. A land where love is the divine position of the soul." Stoker's original is as follows: "I can see her in her loneliness and in the silence of her mighty pride, dreaming her own dreams of things far different from those around her. Of some other land, far, far away under the canopy of the silent night, lit by the cool, beautiful light of the stars. A land under that Northern star, whence blew the sweet winds that cooled the feverish desert air. A land of wholesome greenery, far, far away. Where were no scheming and malignant priesthood; whose ideas were to lead to power through gloomy temples and more gloomy caverns of the dead, through an endless ritual of death! A land where love was not base, but a divine possession of the soul!" (*The Jewel of Seven Stars* [Stroud: Alan Sutton, 1996], p. 128). Despite Wicking's best attempts, the remains of Stoker's heightened prose style do not quite match the contemporary diction of the rest of his screenplay. Stoker's original words also tended to obtrude whenever Christopher Lee valiantly attempted to incorporate them into his portrayals of Count Dracula.

   13. Tristram Cary, "Electronic Music" (Note 7), pp. 42–44.

   14. Pierre Boulez, *Orientations* (trans. Martin Cooper) (London: Faber and Faber, 1986), p. 459.

   15. Roger Manvell and John Huntley, *The Technique of Film Music* (London and New York: Focal Press, 1975), p. 241.

   16. Tristram Cary, in a letter to the author, November 22, 2006.

   17. Reginald Smith-Brindle, *The New Music* (Note 5), p. 119.

Eight

Australian Menace
Don Banks and Malcolm Williamson

Horror and the supernatural might not be what immediately leap to mind when one thinks of Australia, but that country actually has an excellent cinematic track record in that department. The unexplained mystery of disappearing schoolgirls that formed the basis of *Picnic at Hanging Rock* (dir. Peter Weir, 1975) is just one of the more high-profile examples of supernatural Australian cinema; while *Harlequin* (dir. Simon Wincer, 1980), in which Robert Powell plays a faith-healer in a story loosely modeled on that of Rasputin, is a rather less overtly intellectual, though still very effective supernatural chiller. In the realm of Australian composers who worked on British horror films, two names surely dominate the field: Don Banks and Malcolm Williamson, both of whom were very proud to be Australian. Williamson himself was keen to point out:

> Most of my music is Australian. Not the bush or the deserts, but the brashness of the cities. The sort of brashness that makes Australians go through life pushing doors marked pull."[1]

And William S. Mann has described Banks' style as similarly Australian in character:

> Typical of the Australian character in Banks' music, as he admits, are the qualities of uninhibited noisiness [...] and plain, even naive lyricism, the exploration of the simplest musical materials and sound sources for new and striking purposes, the pristine Australian pioneer's persistence in creating something apparently out of nothing and his inherited response to the land of bright light, strong primary colours, lushness and the relentless desert.[2]

Both composers were highly eclectic in their approach to composition, but their film music for Hammer belies their simultaneous interest in serialism and the more experimental tendencies of the European avant-garde.

Born in Sydney in 1931, Williamson enrolled in the Sydney conservatory at the tender age of eleven and came to London for the first time in 1950, where he studied with Elisabeth Lutyens. (Along with Richard Rodney Bennett, Williamson was one of Lutyens' greatest fans: both composers knew all her music virtually by heart.) Thanks to Lutyens, Williamson came into contact with the music of Schoenberg, Boulez and Stravinsky. Three years later he returned to England for good, eventually becoming the nineteenth Master of the Queen's Musick in 1975, replacing the then recently deceased Sir Arthur Bliss. Sir William Walton was astonished by the appointment, going so far as to say that the post had gone to the wrong Malcolm. He thought Sir Malcolm Arnold should have got the job. He wasn't alone in his disapproval; but Williamson it was, beating Benjamin Britten (later Lord Britten of Aldeburgh) and Sir Michael Tippett. Williamson, unlike these ennobled composers, was never knighted himself, even though it was customary for Master of the Queen's Musick to be so. As a Roman Catholic convert, the music of that extremely devout Catholic musical modernist Olivier Messiaen was perhaps bound to appeal to him, though there is nothing in Williamson's film music to suggest this. (By contrast, Ron Goodwin's fascinating score for the British science fiction film *Children of the Damned* [dir. Anton M. Leader, 1964] contains cues that are very similar indeed to passages in the orchestral version of Messiaen's "Paysages" from *Poèmes pour Mi* [1937].)

Malcolm Williamson (date unknown; photograph used by permission of Josef Weinberger Limited).

Neither is the influence of Messiaen and Boulez particularly strong in Williamson's concert music. True, his 1961 Organ Concerto employs serial techniques, and the spirit of Messiaen informs his solo organ works. Also, his second Piano Sonata suggests the spirit of Boulez, but Williamson was particularly keen to write popular, accessible music. He had worked as a jazz pianist in the 1950s, and jazz rhythms were always important in his work. The Organ Concerto, for example, blended them with serialism; and when using serial techniques he often, like Frankel, arranged things to create traditional harmonic possibilities. This is particularly the case in his first Piano Sonata, written in 1955. He also experimented with creating modal harmonies structured by serial means, a style derived from Williamson's interest in medieval music, along with the influence of Messiaen's own interest in modality. The result was rather different from the cerebral organization of Boulez and the Darmstadt school, and consequently much more immediately appealing to general audiences. Such an eclectic temperament inevitably attracted Williamson to the challenges and rewards of writing film music.

After the amazing success of Hammer's first *Dracula*, the company was keen to consolidate its success with another vampire story. It came up with a Dracula film that didn't feature Dracula. (This would be suggested again when *Taste the Blood of Dracula* was originally proposed, but on that occasion Christopher Lee was eventually persuaded to appear, much against his will, as the vampire Count for the fourth time. As it turned out, he had so little to do he might as well not have bothered.) Anyway, Hammer's second vampire film, *The Brides of Dracula*, which appeared in 1960, starred Peter Cushing once more in the role of Van Helsing. The Dracula substitute was played by David Peel, whose Baron Meinster proved to be one of the more interesting vampires in Hammer's gallery of monsters, as his performance suggested a possibly homoerotic element at work—certainly an Oedipal relationship between the Baron and his hapless mother (played by that mistress of eccentric, Miss Haversham types, Martitia Hunt). Over dinner one evening in the chateau, the Baroness gives the game away by confessing, "We had gay times here." It's true that the word "gay," used in a homosexual sense, is an anachronism for the period in which the film is set, but not for 1960 when it was made. Could it be that the ambivalent Baron attacks women because he doesn't like them? "Come here, mother," he insists with distinctly camp menace before turning her into one of the undead herself. When Peter Cushing finds her wandering the corridors of the chateau later in the film, veiling her fangs along with her shame, she asks him if she knows who she is. "I know who you were," Van Helsing wittily responds, before she willingly submits to his redeeming stake.

Rated by many as one of Hammer's finest first period features, *The Brides of Dracula* certainly has a lot going for it: fantastically elaborate sets by Bernard Robinson, fine performances by Peel, Hunt and Cushing, characteristically atmospheric photography by Jack Asher and plenty of excitement, brilliantly arranged by director Terence Fisher; but the film lacks an important ingredient. Far more than the absence of Christopher Lee, what's missing here is the music of James Bernard. Instead, John Hollingsworth commissioned Malcolm Williamson to write the score — a job the composer did not undertake lightly. Williamson had met Bernard on several occasions, and when they met for the last time at Britten's memorial service in 1976, he expressed his admiration of Bernard's music and how he had tried to write in homage to it.[3] He later described Bernard's music as "faultless."[4] Unfortunately, horror film fans have not awarded the same accolade to Williamson's score. Whereas Bernard could make thirty-six players sound like seventy, the effect of Williamson's orchestration is much less resonant. This was intentional in one sense, for he originally hoped to bring a different approach to the music of this film, and he always claimed he had been prevented from doing what he wanted:

> Hammer was then, and still is, very circumscribed in its ideas of what horror music should be. They accept a certain modernity in the musical language, but, as far as the orchestration is concerned, they tend to be stereotyped and conventional; they like the same sort of use of brass to give a certain sense of shock. I like to do things different ways, but have often been suppressed or stopped by Hammer.[5]

How just Williamson's criticisms of Hammer's music policy are is open to question. Hammer, as we have seen, were remarkably open-minded about new musical approaches to their films, so one begins to suspect the motivation behind such a statement. The fact remains, however, that it was James Bernard who was commissioned to score all of Hammer's subsequent period-dress Dracula films.

One of Williamson's apparent models for *The Brides of Dracula* was Bernard's theme for *The Hound of the Baskervilles*, which, as we have seen, looked to Scriabin's "mystic" chord for its inspiration. Williamson's music indeed places a particular emphasis on perfect and augmented fourths, which are piled up on top of each other at regular intervals throughout. We hear these fourths as a fully formed chord when Marianne and Greta ascend the staircase of Chateau Meinster. This chord recurs when the Baroness walks down the stairs to confront her son; and it also accompanies Greta's soliloquy in front of the dead Baroness (where it punctuates the dialogue). A Bernardian augmented fourth also informs the main "Vampire" theme of the film, first heard when Marianne discovers the Baron in his chambers below her bedroom (i.e. from a D-natural dotted crotchet down through a C-sharp quaver, onto the G-sharp below, then moving back up in quavers to the C-sharp and the D-natural; the implied tritone is, of course, between the D-natural and G-sharp).

The more stable interval of a major third is reserved for the "Love" theme, but the tranquilizing effect of this interval is somewhat undermined by the fact that the "Love" motif shares the same rhythm, and follows a similar pitch contour, as the "Vampire" motif. It also contains two fourths, the combined effect of which suggests the troubled nature of the love interest in this story. The organ also plays an accumulation of fourths for the resurrection of the vampire girl in the graveyard. However, that instrument also intones a chorale-like theme to signify the forces of good over evil, so it apparently has a dual signification. Williamson played both piano and organ, and was particularly fond of composing for these instruments, so it is no surprise to find that both these instruments feature in *Brides of Dracula*. Indeed, this score was contemporary with Williamson's second Piano Concerto from 1960 and his Organ Concerto, composed the following year.

Williamson's last two scores for Hammer were both composed in 1970. A disappointing remake of the company's original Frankenstein film, called *The Horror of Frankenstein* (dir. Jimmy Sangster, 1970), sent up the whole story in dubious taste, demonstrating all too painfully that sarcasm is the lowest form of wit. Williamson's main title music starts off promisingly, reminiscent, in its harp and string writing, of Debussy's *Danse sacrée et danse profane* (1904). Against a filigree harp accompaniment, another harp and the strings intone a series of consecutive triads. (Significantly, this technique was also exploited by Bernard, who admitted to being much influenced by Debussy, a favorite from childhood.) An arabesque pattern for flute then further emphasizes the Debussian flavor. Williamson's original approach was inspired by advice from his friend Richard Rodney Bennett, who suggested he base his orchestration around one particular instrument. Williamson accordingly planned to have eight clarinets, ranging from piccolo clarinet to contrabass clarinet, and no other woodwind at all alongside the rest of the orchestra, but he claims that he was forced to abandon this idea and reinstate the "missing" flutes and oboes.[6] The monster, played by a particularly psychotic Dave Prowse, is characterized by the tuba. Unfortunately, the result, as Randall Larson aptly put it, "sounds like an orchestral warm-up session."[7]

With the appearance of the film's title, Williamson adds a snarl of brass but immediately thereafter returns to the attractively pastoral feeling. This, however, is appropriate, as the shot it accompanies is of the adolescent Frankenstein (played by Ralph Bates) marking up the anatomy of a picturesque shepherdess, a print of which he has pinned to the lid of his school desk. Needless to say, the idiom here is emphatically tonal. Tonality could be defended, of course, as being appropriate to the period setting, but there are rather too many anachronisms in the script (to say nothing of the acting style) to justify such platitudes on these terms. Frankenstein not only attends a co-educational school, but, even more unheard of in the nineteenth century, a co-educational university. Later, Dennis Price's graverobber refers to "the welfare state" and "the government meat inspector." As the original pressbook proudly, if misguidedly, enthused: "The 'Permissive' Society catches up with Frankenstein."[8] So, it would seem, did twentieth-century politics. During the film's wearisome and extremely tame love scenes, Williamson relies on conventionally sweeping string lines in the manner of Max Steiner, while for the scenes in

Frankenstein's laboratory he is reduced to holding not particularly dissonant string chords for bar after bar, with not much happening either above or below. Harps play descending scales, the wind make half-hearted interjections, and by the time of the actual creation sequence itself, Williamson seems to have completely run out of ideas, leaving the job to the sound effects. These, it has to be said, are much more successful in creating the appropriate atmosphere. When the Creature is eventually dispatched, by accident, in a vat of acid at the end of the film, Ralph Bates' Baron Frankenstein doesn't seem particularly bothered, and neither, sadly, does the audience. Williamson himself thought the film a "ludicrous disaster,"[9] and, to be fair, any composer would have struggled to have found musical inspiration under such circumstances, though one suspects that James Bernard would, as ever, have triumphed over this material. After all, Bernard composed one of his most effective scores for the equally uninspired *Scars of Dracula* (dir. Roy Ward Baker, 1970), which was made immediately after *The Horror of Frankenstein* as part of a two-picture deal with EMI.

The Horror of Frankenstein was actually Williamson's last score for Hammer. Earlier in 1970 he had worked on a much more rewarding film for the company, which gave him rather more opportunities to take center stage. This was the suspense thriller *Crescendo*. Its contemporary setting gave Williamson the opportunity to indulge in the jazz style he loved; but despite the plot's several murders and its general air of mystery, there are few examples of his more experimental tendencies. Instead, the lush, sweeping Romanticism of the main "piano concerto" theme informs the majority of the score; but such a Romantic idiom wasn't entirely his choice. Philip Martell recalled working on this music with Williamson, who originally came up with something rather more harmonically challenging. Martell apparently thought this was too highbrow in style, and tore it up. To his surprise, Williamson wrote another piece, but that was still not what Martell had in mind. Eventually, Williamson refused to talk to him. A reception to launch the film and the "concerto" was planned, but in the end they were forced to play a tape of an existing classical concerto instead. Eventually, Williamson reopened the lines of communication, and Martell kept telling him to think more along the lines of Richard Addinsell's "Warsaw Concerto," which is certainly appropriate for this story of a musically talented psychopath, by the name of Jacques Ryman, whose mother, Danielle (played by Margaretta Scott), invites a musicology student, who resembles Jacques' dead girlfriend, to stay at the family villa in France. Danielle hopes that the student and her son will be able to carry on the musical genius of Danielle's dead husband by marrying and conceiving another musical genius. Stephanie Powers, who played the student, wasn't the only one to be confused by what was going on, especially as the psychopath has a paralyzed identical twin, called Georges (both men are played by James Olsen), with whom she falls in love instead. (As screenwriter Jimmy Sangster put it after giving his own synopsis of the plot, "Reading that back, one wonders how some of these films ever got off the drawing board.")[10]

Addinsell's "Warsaw Concerto" was composed for *Dangerous Moonlight* (Brian Desmond Hurst, 1941), in which Anton Walbrook, as a Polish fighter pilot and composer-pianist, loses his memory and consequently his command of his own concerto. In both *Dangerous Moonlight* and *Crescendo* there are scenes in which the deranged composer-pianists attempt to play through their respective concerti only to break down midway through, having grotesquely distorted their masterpieces. "No! No! That's not right!" shouts Danielle Ryman in *Crescendo,* as her deranged son's performance of Henry Ryman's unfinished piano concerto disintegrates into conventionally "disturbing" dissonances. Ultimately these degenerate into the pianist hitting the keyboard at random (and it's actually Williamson's hands we see on screen doing this). Whereas that sort of performance practice was seriously adopted by the American modernist Henry Cowell, the popular Romantic aesthetic at work here categorically marks such sounds as "wrong." (Cowell's own Piano Concerto, which calls for the pianist to attack the keyboard with his fist and sometimes his arm in order to create very advanced tone clusters, led to the apocryphal story of a conscripted pianist being arrested by the military police who thought he was deliberately damaging government property!) Similarly, during the dream sequence that opens the film (one of several throughout the action), Williamson scores his principle theme for Tubby Hayes' boozy saxophone over an impressionistically discordant haze in the strings. These scenes depict Jacques Ryman's murder of Catherine while Catherine lies in the arms of Jacques' brother Georges, and they gave saxophonist Hayes, who only had under three years to live at the time he recorded these cues, an opportunity to fill the soundtrack with his flamboyant and immediately identifiable performance style.

Williamson is given ample opportunity to present his equally flamboyant, if rather perfunctory, main theme during the main titles, in which a *concertante* piano, played by Gershwin specialist Clive Lythgoe, takes over the theme and is pitted against a conventional orchestra that is, unusually, credited on screen for what it is: the London Symphony Orchestra. Williamson already had four full-scale piano concerti behind him by the time of *Crescendo*, one of them a double piano concerto. His first two concerti have more in common with the *Crescendo* "concerto," being similarly *bravura* in style (number three is rather different: a more controlled and spare work, modeled on the example of Stravinsky).

After all the tonal swagger of the main title music, which accompanies shots of Stephanie Powers' character being driven to the Ryman villa by Joss Ackland's sinister butler-cum-chauffeur, Williamson holds back throughout the rest of the film, reserving his non-diegetic music for scenes of violence and the four flashbacks. The rest of the score provides the diegetic music that has supposedly been composed by Henry Ryman. When Georges and Susan listen to a recording of Ryman's Second Symphony after dinner one night, Williamson provides a tonal slow movement in which wind *arpeggios* ripple away in triplets (rather in the manner of the opening bars of the sunrise from Ravel's ballet *Daphnis et Chloë*), over which a dreamy string melody (reminiscent of a Mantovani arrangement) is eventually introduced. This attractively impressionistic piece is indeed similar to the mood of Williamson's own equally dreamy and ruminative single-movement Second Symphony (completed the year before *Crescendo*), which itself resembles the forest music of his opera *The Violins of Saint-Jacques* (1966).

In the second dream sequence, Georges imagines himself in the swimming pool before getting out for another rendezvous with Catherine, thus providing another opportunity for Jacques to attempt murder. To cover this, Williamson brings back the main theme with more drifting strings beneath; and when Jacques raises his shotgun, Williamson exploits the conventionally "disturbing" timbre of string harmonics on more chords built out of piled-up fourths. Perhaps the most unusual sounds in the whole score occur just after the murder of Jane Lapotaire's maid, Lillianne (who, incidentally, has been supplying Georges with heroin, and is blackmailing him into agreeing to marry her). Lillianne takes a midnight swim, unaware that in a few moments psychopathic Jacques will plunge a knife into her body. As she drifts lifeless in the bloody pool, Williamson brings in a genuinely dissonant chord in the strings, followed by truly rootless, atonal harmonies, before the main theme quietly and forlornly drifts back on high woodwind. There's another interesting, though very brief, atonal moment when Carter is also murdered in the pool, but for the most part *Crescendo* is very much a tonal affair. (Obviously the fictional Henry Ryman was far from being a follower of Schoenberg or Webern.)

Tubby Hayes is given another opportunity to make the most of the main theme over another lush string accompaniment during another post-prandial gramophone session between Georges and Susan, which eventually leads to a kiss; so presumably Ryman couldn't make up his mind if his concerto was for saxophone or piano. Of course, the *Crescendo* "concerto" is no more of a genuine concerto than the "Warsaw Concerto" is a concerto. Both are what the American press once used to call "tabloid concertos": single movement *concertante* pieces that give the impression of being an extract from a traditionally structured, three-movement work. Since *Dangerous Moonlight* in 1941, there has been a "Lullaby of the Bells Piano Concerto" by Edward Ward for *The Phantom of the Opera* (dir. Arthur Lubin, 1943); a "Cornish Rhapsody" by Hubert Bath for *Love Story* (dir. Leslie Arliss, 1944); a "Spellbound Concerto," Miklós Rósza's own reworking of themes from his score for Hitchcock's *Spellbound* (1945); "The Dream of Olwen," by Charles Williams, for *While I Live* (dir. John Harlow, 1947); "The Quebec Concerto," by André Mathieu, for *Whispering City* (dir. Fedor Ozep, 1947); a "Legend of the Glass Mountain," by Nino Rota, for *The Glass Mountain* (dir. Henry Cass, 1949); and a piece called "Midnight on the Cliffs," by Leonard Pennario, for the Doris Day–Louis Jordan film *Julie* (dir. Andrew Stone, 1956), in which Jordan's character, who has already murdered his wife's first husband, uses a recording of this piece to terrify her even more. Perhaps the best of all these tabloid concerti is the "Concerto Macabre," by

Bernard Herrmann, for *Hangover Square* (dir. John Brahm, 1945), in which another insane pianist is let loose in the form of Laird Cregar. He plays a kind of musical Jack-the-Ripper who murders pretty women between slaying audiences. And, of course, James Bernard's celebrated "Vampire Rhapsody" from *The Kiss of the Vampire* was another of Addinsell's Gothic descendants. "Something of your own, perhaps, Carl?" suggests Noel Willman's sinister Dr. Ravna, as his even more sinister son starts to hypnotize Jennifer Daniel's hapless Mrs. Harcourt with a Lisztian pastiche. It was a technique that had already been tried out by John Carradine in *House of Dracula* (dir. Erle C. Kenton, 1945), except that in that example it wasn't the vampire who played the piano. This is left to his victim, who is innocently amusing herself by playing Beethoven's "Moonlight" Sonata. "You like it?" she asks. Carradine stares back: "It breathes the spirit of the night." Then the film composer Edgar Fairchild cleverly injects the influence of Debussy into the piece. His intended victim has obviously never played any Debussy before: "I've never heard this music

"*Something of your own, perhaps?*" (Left to right) Jacquie Wallis as Sabena, Noel Willman as Dr. Ravna and Edward de Souza as Gerald Harcourt look on while Jennifer Daniel's Mrs. Harcourt is serenaded at the piano by Barry Warren's Carl Ravna in *The Kiss of the Vampire* (dir. Don Sharp, 1964).

before, yet I'm playing it." "You're creating it. For me," explains the Count. The music sounds increasingly like Scriabin. "It is the music of the world from which I come." So, perhaps Carradine's Dracula wasn't from Transylvania after all? Made the following year, in 1946, Robert Florey's *The Beast with Five Fingers* featured Victor Francen as piano virtuoso Francis Ingram, complete with flowing Lisztian locks. It's not the pianist who is mad in this film, but rather the delightfully deranged Peter Lorre, who is tormented by visions of the virtuoso's severed hand scurrying over the keys with a fluidity most two-handed and fully intact pianists would surely envy.

Perhaps the most unusual variation on this theme can be found in Amicus' *Torture Garden* (dir. Freddie Francis, 1967), in which the girlfriend of a famous pianist (played by Barbara Ewing and John Standing, respectively) experiences the wrath of the pianist's jealous grand piano. The piano goes by the name of Euterpe, after the Greek muse of lyric poetry. While playing Chopin's Funeral March by itself, the piano pushes its rival out of the window. However, there is also jazz in one of the other stories in this film, and this was composed by Malcolm Williamson's compatriot, Don Banks (although James Bernard dealt with the rest of the film's dramatic scoring). *Torture Garden* is, indeed, an excellent example of how film soundtracks frequently blend together different musical styles. Set in a fairground, the Torture Garden itself is a chamber of horrors, borrowing its name from the title of Octave Mirbeau's 1899 novel of *décadence*, *The Torture Garden*, which describes the horrors that take place in a beautiful Chinese garden in the middle of a prison, wherein exquisite tortures are perpetrated on criminals. There, however, the film's resemblance to the book ends, though Burgess Meredith's Dr. Diabolo, who runs the Torture Garden, does cheerfully remark, in true Mirbeau fashion, "There is no end to man's inhumanity to man." In fact, the Torture Garden of the film merely provides a pretext for four more horror tales in the best Amicus tradition. A group of fairground punters are invited by Dr. Diabolo to stare into the Shears of Fate held by a statue of Atropos (played by the statuesque Clytie Jessop) so as to discover the hidden evil about themselves. Bernard's cue for these Atropos sequences actually resembles his music for the scene in *The Kiss of the Vampire* in which Dr. Zimmer performs the occult ritual that dispatches Ravna's vampire acolytes.

Bernard scores the first story in his usual style; but for the second story, set in Hollywood, Banks takes over with what amounts to a miniature jazz suite. There are around twelve short numbers here (some shorter than others), each corresponding to different scenes. The first is set in a flat shared by two would-be-starlets, the second is in a restaurant, the third in a bar; then we go back to the restaurant, to the bar, to the girl's flat, and on to a film studio. Further scenes follow. Banks' natural flare for jazz finds a real opportunity here, which wasn't the case with most of the other horror films he scored. (Hammer's *Hysteria* [dir. Freddie Francis, 1965] proved a notable exception.) For the third story, about the jealous piano Euterpe, only diegetic classical piano music is used, including extracts from Schumann's "Träumerei," Beethoven's "Für Elise" and Chopin's "Marche funèbre." Bernard's music returns for the final story, in which Peter Cushing resurrects Edgar Allan Poe in his own cellar; and, together, the music for these four stories provides a useful, if unorthodox, example of what later became known as "crossover" at a time when classical music was having difficulty maintaining cordial relations with popular music outside the more conciliatory realm of cinema.

The cinema, of course, had been mixing musical genres since the silent days, but in the 1960s barriers began to be broken down elsewhere. This was the period when innovative disc jockeys in the United Kingdom, such as Kenny Everett and Alan Freeman, began to include excerpts of classical music alongside their radio shows' staple diet of pop. By contrast, pop music rarely, if ever, appeared alongside the classical repertoire broadcast on British radio stations, such as the BBC's Third Program — later to be known as Radio 3. Amicus' later compendium films continued to highlight repertoire concert works. *The House That Dripped Blood* (dir. Peter Duffell, 1970) incorporated Schubert's "Death and the Maiden" String Quartet into the proceedings (indeed, Duffell originally wanted to call the film *Death and the Maiden*); while *Tales from the Crypt* used Bach's famous Toccata and Fugue in D Minor to accompany the atmospheric main titles shot in London's Highgate Cemetery; but both these films lacked the jazz element of *Torture Garden* and, as we explored earlier, *Dr. Terror's House of Horrors*.

Don Banks was a great champion of "crossover" and "the third stream." This was partly due, no doubt, to his having been an Australian and immune to the prevailing snobbery of the British and continental musical establishment. Born in South Melbourne in 1923, Banks rapidly became a proficient trombonist, saxophonist, violinist, guitarist and pianist, and his composing career began when he helped to arrange parts for his father's jazz band. After serving his country during the second world war, he attended the Melbourne University conservatorium, and then, in 1950, visited London, studying with the Hungarian composer Mátyás Seiber at Morley College. Seiber had been a pupil of Kodály, and Banks was particularly attracted to him because he not only worked with serial techniques and jazz, but also wrote film music (perhaps his most well-known score is for Halas and Batchelor's animated adaptation of George Orwell's *Animal Farm* in 1955). In 1954, Banks' *Four Pieces for Orchestra* were premiered by Sir Adrian Boult with the London Symphony Orchestra, and, after winning a scholarship, Banks then went to Salzburg to study with the American avant-garde composer Milton Babbitt, who was active in the development of total serialism and its application to electronic music, as well as experimenting with jazz. After a year with Babbitt, Banks then moved to Florence, where he studied with Luigi Dallapiccola, who similarly employed twelve-tone techniques, but in a lyrical Italian style.

Not surprisingly, then, Banks' student works were also often structured along serial lines. His Duo for violin and cello from 1951–2 is actually based on a fourteen-note row, rather than the usual twelve. Other early works were performed with success in I.S.C.M. concerts and broadcasts by the BBC; but such work unfortunately didn't pay, so Banks, now settled in London, turned readily to commercials, film and television scoring to earn a living. He was also a co-founder of the Australian Musical Association, which championed the work and careers of Australian musicians abroad; and for this purpose he composed works specifically for Australian performers, of which his Horn Concerto, written for Barry Tuckwell, is perhaps the most well-known. Banks frequently composed concert works with specific performers in mind. His *Pezzo dramatico* (1956), for example, was composed for the pianist Margaret Kitchin; and the Horn Trio (1962), again, for Barry Tuckwell, along with violinist Brenton Langbein and pianist Maureen Jones. On the death of Seiber in 1960, Banks dedicated his *Sonata da Camera* of 1961 to his teacher's memory. Banks continued to use serial techniques and electronics, as well as jazz and even elements of American soul music, strongly believing in the possibilities of combining different styles in a single work. His piece *Equations*, for jazz players and a chamber orchestra, appeared in 1963, and he went on to collaborate with those other champions of "crossover" style, Cleo Laine and John Dankworth, in *Settings from Roget* (1966) and *Three Short Songs* (1971). Other crossover pieces include *Meeting Place* (1970) and *Nexus* (1971), for symphony orchestra and jazz quartet, along with *Take Eight* (1973), for combined string and jazz quartets. Another manifestation of this interest in combining different styles and mediums was the appropriately entitled *Intersections*, composed in 1969, which combined electronic sounds with a traditional orchestra. A piece called *Commentary*, from 1971, calls for tape and piano; while *Limbo*, from 1971, is scored for three singers, eight instruments and tape, setting words by the Australian poet Peter Porter.

After a period as director of Goldsmiths College in London in the late 1960s, Banks eventually returned to Australia in 1972, where he became even more committed to write specifically Australian music. Most characteristic of this quest is his piece for children's voices and orchestra called *Walkabout*, composed in 1972 (interestingly, it was composed only two years after Nicolas Roeg's Australian bush odyssey film of the same name, starring Jenny Agutter), and the orchestral *Prospects*, from 1973, which was commissioned to celebrate the opening of the Sydney Opera House.

Philip Martell hugely admired Don Banks and was of the firm opinion that he was one of the greatest composers he had ever worked with. (They worked together on seven Hammer films in all; *Nightmare* was supervised by John Hollingsworth), but there's very little in Banks' entire output for Hammer to suggest his relationship with the avant-garde. Following the example of Erich Wolfgang Korngold during the Golden Age of Hollywood, Banks began his career with Hammer with a swashbuckler, *Captain Clegg* (aka *Night Creatures*, dir. Peter Graham Scott, 1962). This is ideal Saturday matinée entertainment, in which

Peter Cushing gives a perfectly judged performance as Dr. Blyss—a smuggler-disguised-as-a-priest (who is actually the now reformed pirate Captain Clegg). Oliver Reed also appears in a supporting role, and ends up marrying Yvonne Romain, the actress who had played his unfortunate mother in *The Curse of the Werewolf*. In *Captain Clegg*, however, Romain plays Captain Clegg's daughter, Imogene.

This tale of smugglers outwitting Patrick Allen's band of sailors was beautifully filmed, and has its moments of horror—notably the opening scenes in which Milton Reid's mulatto is abandoned on a desert island, his tongue cut out as a punishment for seducing Clegg's wife. The marsh phantoms, who are really Blyss and his band of smugglers dressed in phosphorescent skeleton costumes, are also highly effective. Musically speaking, Banks sets up the style to which he will conform in nearly all his other films for Hammer: a swaggering main theme, with equally swaggering orchestrations, carefully observed responses to the editing of the film, and a sure grasp of what is needed from the music to aid, rather than merely accompany, the drama. But he avoids anything experimental, his poster-paint style here remaining strictly diatonic.

Don Banks during his Hammer period in the 1960s (photograph courtesy Phillipa Saraceno).

Gothic horror followed with *The Evil of Frankenstein*. In previous Frankenstein films, Hammer had always had to avoid any resemblance to the original Universal Studios makeup designed for Boris Karloff's monster, but, as this production was financed by Universal itself, Roy Ashton's makeup was permitted to nod in the direction of Jack P. Pierce's famous creation. Beneath Ashton's melange of paper, rags, old washers, empty bottles, boot lace, string and latex[11] was 238-pound wrestler Kiwi Kingston, who, like Don Banks, originated from Australasia (New Zealand, in Kingston's case). Not only did the Creature, as Hammer always preferred to call it, resemble the old Universal monster, but the sets were also similar to those of Universal's *The Bride of Frankenstein* (dir. James Whale, 1935). There was even a version of the apparatus that was known in *Bride of Frankenstein* as a "cosmic diffuser," as well as the lightning conductor from that film. However, unlike Franz Waxman, the composer of *The Bride of Frankenstein*, Don Banks refrained entirely from using music during the creation sequence, the film's most impressive scene. Waxman had been distraught when he discovered that his impressive music for this sequence had been virtually obliterated by the sound effects. Wisely, Banks leaves well enough alone for the creation scene of *The Evil of Frankenstein*, just as Malcolm Williamson would in *The Horror of Frankenstein* six years later; but such restraint isn't at all apparent during the main title music, during which Peter Cushing's Baron cuts out the heart of his latest piece of raw material. For this, Banks writes a swaggering, entirely tonal march, typical of the "uninhibited noisiness ... and plain, even naive lyricism" identified by William Mann as characteristic of his overall composition style. This theme recurs throughout the score, which, in contrast to Frankenstein himself, rarely ventures into anything remotely experimental.

On the run from the usual outraged villagers, the Baron returns to his old chateau in the hope of selling his possessions and buying new equipment with the proceeds. They pass through his hometown, Karlstadt, where the Feast of Carnival is in full swing. This is presumably in the vicinity of Chateau Ravna

Peter Cushing hard at work in ***The Evil of Frankenstein*** (dir. Freddie Francis, 1964).

(as visited in *The Kiss of the Vampire*), because several of the masks worn by the revelers in that film have been hung on the walls of the local inn! Perhaps Dr. Ravna had the same idea as Frankenstein and sold some of his assets to raise funds? During their escape from the police, who recognize their old enemy, Frankenstein and his assistant (played by Sandor Elès) come into contact with Peter Woodthorpe's stage hypnotist, Zoltan. After Frankenstein discovers the perfectly preserved body of his old Creature in a glacier, Zoltan's powers prove useful when the Baron needs to stimulate its brain. Inevitably, things begin to go wrong when Zoltan decides to use the Creature for his own ends, hypnotizing it to steal, from which crime it then graduates to murder.

As with the central creation scene, the other most effective moments of this film are actually those without any music at all. When, for example, the Baron enters his old home to find it ransacked and derelict, Banks puts away his march theme and allows the sound of footsteps and rustling leaves to complement the desolate atmosphere of the place. Similarly, as we follow Frankenstein down to his ransacked laboratory, a melancholy drip of water is all that accompanies this scene of devastation. Much of Banks' scoring is very simple, but also extremely effective. For example, he frequently employs harp *glissandi* and vibraphone *tremolos*, as in the introduction to the subsequent flashback, when the camera moves through the empty castle down to a now splendidly pristine laboratory set; and whenever Zoltan hypnotizes the Creature in subsequent scenes, Banks relies on a two-note oscillation accompanied with more harp *glissandi* and vibraphone trills. These techniques return to great effect in the hypnosis scenes of his sixth Hammer score, *Rasputin — The Mad Monk* (dir. Don Sharp, 1966).

Before that, however, Banks got down to work on *Nightmare*, a follow-up to the Hitchockian *Paranoiac* of the previous year. *Nightmare*, which first appeared as a support feature to *The Evil of Frankenstein*, even goes so far as to create an obvious homage to Hitchcock's *Psycho* in a scene later in the film that is shot from high above the set. To suggest its more modern credentials, *Nightmare* opens with no music at all. All we hear is a dog barking (anticipating, by three years, the opening of Joseph Losey's *Accident*). When the music does start with the main title card, the sequence is interrupted by dialogue, as Jenny Linden's character, Janet, wanders the corridors of an insane asylum in the nightmare that gives the film its name. "Janet, where are you?" calls the voice of her mother, who is incarcerated there. "Janet, I'm waiting"; and indeed the audience is kept waiting for a resolution to the film's cleverly constructed plot until the final moments.

Janet, who stands to inherit a fortune, is the victim of her unscrupulous ward, Henry Baxter (played by David Ward), and her "nurse," Grace Maddox (played by Moira Redmond). Having witnessed her father's murder at the hands of her own mother, Janet's nerves have become, understandably, overwrought. Henry and Grace plan to exploit this state of affairs to their own advantage. Grace not only pretends to be a nurse, but also imitates the wife of Janet's family doctor, a disguise that requires no little suspension of disbelief. (Can a latex face mask really be so convincing? In fact, we see Clytie Jessop, who had held the sheers of Fate in *Torture Garden*). Nonetheless, it certainly convinces Janet, who is so unnerved by this statuesque apparition that when Janet is introduced to the doctor's real wife (also played by Jessop) she drives the knife intended for her birthday cake into the unfortunate woman's stomach. When Janet is incarcerated in the same asylum as her mother, Henry and Grace think they've got away with it, but Janet's housekeeper, schoolteacher and chauffeur realize what has happened and plot revenge, sowing the seeds of marital jealously between Henry and Grace, a situation that ultimately leads to Grace killing her husband as well, bringing the film full circle.

One might have expected rather complex music for such a complex plot, but once again Banks remains securely tonal, restricting himself to mainly chamber orchestra textures in a score that's appropriately a lot less boisterous than his music for *The Evil of Frankenstein,* but no more experimental. Again, restraint pays off. For example, when Janet as a young girl runs in to see her mother laughing in front of the husband whom she has just murdered, there

Moira Redmond (left, as Grace Maddox), George A. Cooper (as John) and Jennie Linden (right as Janet) in *Nightmare* (dir. Freddie Francis, 1964).

is no music at all, and the dramatic effect is stunning. There is one moment of electronic music, heard as Janet is driven past her mother's asylum on her way back home from school; but modern though this timbre may be, it nonetheless plays the conventionally tonal main theme of the film. There is a good opportunity for Banks to enjoy some light jazz for the diegetic "radio music" in the scenes set in a hotel bar later in the film, but other than that there's little evidence of his other serial and experimental interests here.

Another thriller, *Hysteria*, and another swashbuckler, *The Brigand of Kandahar* (dir. John Gilling), kept Banks occupied during 1965, after which he and Hammer tried the hands at a different genre: the historical costume drama (though historical fact was hardly in the issue here). Loosely based on fact, *Rasputin — The Mad Monk* was originally released as part of a double-feature with the entirely fictional *The Reptile*, directed by John Gilling, and also scored by Banks.

Banks' highly proficient score for *Rasputin* again takes a conventional approach. Given the early twentieth-century Russian setting of this film about the faith-healing mystic, those equally mystic Scriabinesque constructs of fourths, to which this book has so often returned, would have been appropriate in more ways than one. Instead, Banks looked to Beethoven's Ninth Symphony for his main title sequence, which begins with a chromatic passage for lower tremolo strings that is very similar to this passage from the coda of the first movement of Beethoven's symphony:

Ludwig van Beethoven, *Ninth Symphony*—1st movement coda.

Needless to say, the rest of the score is highly proficient from a dramatic point of view, but steadfastly tonal from a musical one.

Nicholas and Alexandra, directed by Franklin Schaffner in 1971 took a much more historically accurate approach to the Rasputin story; but, of course, Hammer was making entertainment, and no one was much bothered about the facts, with the possible exception of Christopher Lee, who had been introduced to Rasputin's assassin, Prince Yusupof, when he was a boy, and who approached his role with his usual gravitas. (He presents Rasputin as a kind of mystical Stalin, which, in a way, he was.) The sets, redressed from *Dracula — Prince of Darkness*, and stock footage of an Imperial Ball weren't entirely convincing, however. Predictably, there is a great deal of diegetic balalaika music for the various café scenes, and, as mentioned above, the music Banks uses to cover Rasputin's several hypnosis scenes are in the manner of Zoltan's hypnosis cues in *The Evil of Frankenstein*.

The Reptile, one of Hammer's very low-budget masterpieces, introduced audiences to a new monster in the shape-shifting form of Jacqueline Pearce's Anna Franklyn, who turns into a snake woman at regular intervals. Her father, Dr. Franklyn (played with tremendously sinister dignity by Noel Willman), is a doctor of theology who has unfortunately discovered too much about the snake-people of Borneo while on his travels in the East. The shape-shifting natives promptly transformed his daughter into one of their own as a punishment, and Dr. Franklyn now keeps his reptilian offspring under his ever-watchful eye back in England in the overheated atmosphere of his opulent mansion, the exteriors of which were provided by Oakley Court, one of Hammer's favorite locations on the banks of the river Thames. The film opens with a typically strident fanfare from Banks to announce that this is a Hammer film, and we subsequently hear an oriental melody as we watch a man walking over heath land in the dark. The melody sounds oriental due to the scale from which it is derived: up a semitone, up a major third, and finally up a tone (i.e. C-sharp, D, F-sharp, G-sharp). We will hear this whenever any future victim of the Reptile wanders over lonely Clagmoor Heath. The first victim is one Charles Spalding (played by David Baron), the same man we have seen striding out over the moor at the beginning of the film. As Charles walks through Bernard Robinson's magnificent interior sets of Dr. Franklyn's mansion, Banks makes imaginative use of the celesta, an instrument that lends a suitably exotic timbre to the proceedings. After Charles' death at the fangs of the dreaded snake-woman, the main title music interestingly exploits a great deal of tuned percussion to suggest in a very general way the timbres of the entirely percussive Indonesian gamelan orchestra, which had also been imitated (rather more convincingly) by Benjamin Britten in his 1956 ballet *The Prince of the Pagodas*, and would feature in his last opera, *Death in Venice* (1971–3). Of course, Ravel and Debussy had also been inspired by the gamelan, but there are few examples of gamelan sounds in mainstream film music, even if only somewhat simplistic imitations, as is the case here. Banks' extravagant xylophone *glissandi* also combine with the thunder claps to create a stirring impression, and, as usual, Banks' score is very proficient but again resolutely tonal in harmonic idiom.

Charles Spalding's brother, Harry (played by another Australian, Ray Barrett), inherits Larkrise Cottage after Charles' death, and this is where Harry brings his wife, Valerie (played by Jennifer Daniel). Our first view of the cottage is accompanied by Romantic strings, with harp accompaniment, that could easily have been composed by Max Steiner; but things get a little more exotic in the middle of the film when we are presented with an oriental equivalent of the piano scene in *The Kiss of the Vampire*. Intriguingly, Noel Willman presides over both these unusual musical evenings, and also interrupts the music on each occasion. As Dr. Ravna in *The Kiss of the Vampire*, he politely requests his son Carl to stop playing James Bernard's "Vampire Rhapsody." In *The Reptile*, he rather more violently smashes the Sitar his daughter has been playing against one of the pillars of his living room when the music causes the reptilian side of his daughter's personality to come to the fore. Banks indicates this unfortunate development by weaving the Reptile theme into the sinister Sitar improvisation as Anna looks imperiously at her father, watched over by the sinister Malay servant (played with malevolent suavity by Marne Maitland, who was always useful in roles like these).

Philip Martell greatly admired Banks' last score for Hammer, *The Mummy's Shroud* (dir. John Gilling, 1967), and the music certainly has all the ingredients that Martell praised about Banks' work in general: elegance, style, strong melody and a sensitivity to the way in which the film has been edited. Imaginatively directed and skillfully photographed, *The Mummy's Shroud* creates an effectively claustrophobic impression of the back streets of Cairo; but basically the action revolves around a simple revenge plot, as is so often the case with Mummy movies. Banks creates a resonant texture for his main Egyptian theme with splashing cymbals, harp *glissandi* and another big tune, this time intoned by a choir alongside the orchestra in the manner of many an Egyptian epic before and after it (including Franz Reizenstein's impressive score for Hammer's first attempt at ancient Egyptian horror, *The Mummy*). Again there's nothing particularly novel about Banks' overall style here. He is, however, excellent at responding to details, such as the moment when the Mummy of Prem, the Pharaoh's devoted slave, first opens its eyes. After so many years asleep, these ancient eyelids take one or two attempts to open fully. The music responds to this accordingly, and also changes pace to match that of "the beat of the cloth-wrapped feet" (as the original publicity poster for this film put it). This Mummy (played by Eddie Powell) is genuinely rather sinister, due mainly to the way it is photographed, often from below, but also because of Powell's very restrained movements. No stomping around for Prem, just unstoppable persistence.

Another useful example of the excellent way in which Banks responds to the editing of the film occurs after the murder of the expedition photographer Harry Newton (played by Tim Barrett). As the flames rise up around his body after having been drenched with acid by the Mummy, high pitched strings frantically trill on a single note before we cut suddenly to a newspaper headline:

David Buck in *The Mummy's Shroud* (dir. John Gilling, 1967).

"Curse of Tomb Finds Second Victim." Instead of stopping the music dead there, Banks continues the trill into the new scene, raising the string trill by a tone at the moment of the cut. Only when we cut away from the newspaper does the music finally stop. By these simplest of means he expertly joins the two scenes together, and emphasizes the horror far more effectively than if the music had stopped with the cut. Banks' response to camera movements is also noteworthy. Towards the end of the film, the pompous expedition financier, Stanley Preston (played by John Phillips), has paid the Keeper of the Tomb, Hasmid (played with relish by *Dr. Who's* "the Master," Roger Delgado), to arrange transport to meet the ship, which he hopes will take him away from the danger posed by the Mummy. Preston doesn't realize who Hasmid is, and doesn't live long enough to find out, as Hasmid has sent the Mummy to murder him. After the murder, we see a hand pushing the bank note Preston had given Hasmid into the jacket of Preston's corpse. As the camera pans up to reveal the owner of the hand (Hasmid himself), Banks imitates this movement with a rising harp *glissando*, which makes the "reveal" so much more effective. Similarly, another harp *glissando* accompanies the camera's zoom as David Buck's Paul Preston touches the blood stains on the Mummy's hands. All these details demonstrate how Banks complements particular uses of the camera along with the film's overall editing style, and this is what makes him such an expert composer for film.

It is ironic, however, that both Banks and Williamson, for all their avant-garde credentials, were far more conventional in their harmonic approach to film music than James Bernard, who openly professed himself to be out of sympathy with atonality, serialism, and the avant-garde in general, yet nonetheless created far more extreme musical effects for horror films than either of them.

Notes

1. Malcolm Williamson, quoted on the entry about him on www.amcoz.com.au/composers.
2. Stanley Sadie (ed.), *The New Grove Dictionary of Music and Musicians* (London: Macmillan, 1980), vol. 2, p. 122.
3. James Bernard, in conversation with the author.
4. Randall Larson, "The Music of Hammer," in *Little Shoppe of Horrors* no. 10/11, p. 103 (ed. Richard Klemenson) (Des Moines, Iowa: Elmer Valo Appreciation Society).
5. Ibid.
6. Ibid., p. 102.
7. Ibid., p. 79.
8. Marcus Hearn and Alan Barnes, *The Hammer Story* (London: Titan Books, 1997), p. 138.
9. Randall Larson, "The Music of Hammer" (Note 4), p. 103.
10. Jimmy Sangster, *Inside Hammer* (Richmond: Reynolds & Hearn, 2001), p. 124.
11. Bruce Sachs and Russell Wall, *Greasepaint and Gore — The Hammer Monsters of Roy Ashton* (Sheffield: Tomahawk Press, 1991), p. 119.

NINE

Modern Gothic

Mike Vickers and John Cacavas

Scars of Dracula was Hammer's last attempt at a Dracula film set in the nineteenth century. (The later *The Legend of the Seven Golden Vampires* was actually set for the most part in 1904.) *Scars of Dracula*, however, was neither a commercial nor an artistic success, as David Pirie has explained:

> As must have been obvious to devotees, *The Scars of Dracula* was the product of a shift in Hammer's management and their production policy. The company was fast becoming rudderless and seemed intent on squandering its marketable assets as quickly as possible.[1]

In reconsidering its approach to the character who had given it so much success, Hammer was inspired by the example of the American International film starring Robert Quarry in the title role of *Count Yorga — Vampire* (dir. Bob Kelljan, 1970), which placed a vampire character in a contemporary Los Angeles setting. Hammer's corresponding attempt to pump fresh blood into their most famous franchise resulted in a film that was originally called *Dracula Today*. This was eventually released with the more imposing but inevitably soon-out-of-date title *Dracula A.D. 1972*. Some said at the time that the film was already dated, and since then it has often been criticized for its middle-aged approach to the youth culture, as though Inspector Murray's comment about "a bunch of spaced-out teenagers whose way of life is as foreign to me as..." ("As that of a vampire?" Van Helsing suggests) also applied to screenwriter Don Houghton. The police sergeant in the film who assists Murray even goes so far as to call the teenagers "fringe people"—as though hippies had never been a part of mainstream popular culture. However, put in the context of Hammer's overall conservative approach, this is hardly surprising. Middle-aged and middle-class values are actually held up as models to respect in all Hammer films. If the young people who are terrorized by the resurrected vampire Count in this film already seemed square on the film's release, this was perhaps appropriate, for the film's underlying message was to warn against the prevailing youth culture of the time. Fictional vampirism was firmly equated with the real "evils" of sex, drugs and all that was not professionally middle-class and traditionally Christian (the world, in fact, represented by Peter Cushing's authoritative Professor Lorrimer Van Helsing). Produced at the tail end of the swinging sixties, *Dracula A.D. 1972* merely confirmed what Hammer had been saying all along: that youth culture is generally a bad idea. Think of Professor Zimmer's anguish, in *The Kiss of the Vampire*, when he laments how a "smart set" corrupted his daughter, who returned home "riddled with disease"— a syphilitic metaphor if ever there was one. Indeed, the entire nineteenth-century decor of Hammer's Gothic horrors was a graphic rejection of modernity. As we have seen, these films were popular precisely because they offered a sense of stability and certainty in an increasingly unstable and uncertain world. For all the excitement of the swinging sixties, Rodgers and Hammerstein's *The Sound of Music* actually sold more records than anything by the Beatles. Most people wanted reassuring traditional values at this time of bewildering social change, and this explains the revival of interest in Victoriana that took place alongside the destruction of so much Victorian architecture (to say nothing of Victorian morality). While the young made fun of Victorian values, they also flirted with Victorian bric-a-brac. The Beatles themselves reflected the fashion trend for Victorian military uniforms on the cover of their *Sergeant Pepper* album. So did Michelangelo Antonioni, in the scene in *Blow Up* in which David Hemmings' photographer buys a propeller in an antique shop. Before Hemmings selects his eccentric purchase, Antonioni is keen to show us as much antique shop Victoriana as possible. Intriguingly, the shop is run by actress Susan Brodrick, who would later appear as in the role of prim and proper (and very Victorian) Susan Spencer in *Dr. Jekyll and Sister Hyde*.

In *Dracula A.D. 1972*, Van Helsing finds his granddaughter, Jessica (played by Stephanie Beacham), flipping through a *Treatise on the Black Mass* in his elegantly appointed study, and insists, "This is my place of work, not W.H. Smith and Son." When he adds, "It seems to me that you delight in deriding anything that is not on your particular wavelength," the implication, given what happens later in the film, is that such derision is foolish, immature and plainly wrong. Van Helsing, who, as Jessica puts it, "missed the big time as a comic" for suggesting her friends might like to come 'round to meet him in his "mausoleum" of a home, turns out to be the one who should have been taken seriously, for all his old-fashioned ways.[2] As I suggested above, the police are also out of their depth in this middle-class, academic world of "responsible" occult anthropology. Peter Hutchings has pointed out in his book *Hammer and Beyond* that the role of the middle-class professional is central to the overall ethos of Hammer's entire world-view:

> Authority in Hammer horror also has a clear class-dimension. Hammer's class structures are inflexible, with working, middle and upper classes

remaining totally separate social strata. Despite the plethora of aristocratic titles in these films (Count, Lord, Baron, etc.) the figures of valorised authority (that is Cushing and Lee) tend to be middle-class, if not in their actual social position then certainly in the values they espouse. The professionalism which, as we have seen, is an important aspect of their authority is dependent on their either having a profession in the conventional sense (the professor in *The Gorgon*, consulting detective in *The Hound of the Baskervilles*, archaeologist in *The Mummy*) or organising their obsessions in an ordered, methodical and altogether professional manner (Frankenstein and Van Helsing).[3]

Musically speaking, the style of Mike Vickers' score for *Dracula A.D. 1972* also conforms to this pattern. Hammer's tendency to use avant-garde techniques from a traditional perspective continued with this film, the avant-garde elements now blending with and sometimes being replaced by elements of pop and jazz. Vickers had originally worked with the pop group Manfred Mann before becoming a freelance arranger for the Beatles, the Scaffold, Tom Jones and Cilla Black. With the arrival of the Moog synthesizer (he was probably the first person in England to own one in 1968), he became something of a pioneer, and electronic music (though not, ironically, by Vickers himself) does indeed rub shoulders with the jazz, pop and more traditional idioms in the soundtrack of *Dracula A.D. 1972*.

Significantly, Vickers is not credited as "Mike" (how he's usually known), but the rather more formal "Michael Vickers," and the style of music he composed for *Dracula A.D. 1972* is a far cry from the kind of thing spaced-out teenagers were really listening to in the 1970s. The "rock" idiom here is really more indebted to the big band sound of Stan Kenton, with its punchy syncopated brass punctuating a quartet of saxophones that "swing" the main theme during the opening credits. It is presumably just the kind of thing that Christopher Neame's Johnny Alucard enjoyed with Gaynor (Marsha Hunt) at the "jazz spectacular at the Albert Hall," which he mentions half way through the film. Kenton, whose heyday as a progressive jazz arranger and pianist was in the 1940s and '50s, was also a huge influence on John Barry, who studied with one of Kenton's arrangers, Bill Russo, by means of a correspondence course while doing his national service. Intellectual and advanced, it's significant that Kenton's rather more esoteric approach to jazz eventually filtered into one of the most popular series of film scores ever composed for the James Bond films. By 1972, Barry's Bond music was far more well-known than Kenton's (Kenton died in 1979). However, by 1972, the Bond sound was no longer quite as novel as it had been in 1964 when *Goldfinger* appeared, and familiarity had perhaps weakened its impact, along with its once youthful, swinging significations; but Vickers was also influenced by Kenton's style in his Dracula score — not that he set out deliberately to pastiche it. He believed that a purely pop/rock score would not have been able to carry the narrative along, let alone successfully complement the integrity and weight brought to the proceedings by the presence of Lee and Cushing. So, a mixture of traditional elements in an overall jazz style seemed to him to be the best way to approach the music in general. (He was left largely to his own devices by Philip Martell and the film's producer, Josephine Douglas.)

Mike Vickers A.D. 2007. Mike Vickers in 2007 (photograph courtesy Mike Vickers).

The music was written in London at the end of December 1972, and Vickers recalls writing music for the Black Mass scene while carol singers were inappropriately serenading him in the street outside.[4] Contrary to subsequent rumor,[5] Martell laid the music into the film exactly as Vickers indicated in his orchestral score.

The prologue that precedes the main title sequence contains one of the most authoritative performances Cushing and Lee ever gave as Van Helsing and Dracula, and, as the scene is set in 1872, Vickers sensibly keeps modern musical elements to a minimum here. The main motif that recurs throughout the film is a triadic fanfare, scored for horns, which, apart from its closing interval of a fourth, is firmly in the heroic–Romantic tradition of which Siegfried's horn call from Wagner's *Ring* Cycle is a good example. Conventional instrumental forces are also spotlighted here (horns, snare drum, cellos, bases). However, the kind of percussion with which Vickers chooses to accompany this wild coach ride through Hyde Park hints at things to come later in the film. Tom-toms and conga drums subtly undercut the period texture of the score, preparing us for the eventual confirmation that this film will eventually have a contemporary setting. So, too, does the bass guitar that joins the lower strings a few bars into the scene; and when Dracula appears with the spoke of a carriage wheel in his chest, Vickers effectively accentuates the action with a very Kentonesque effect: muted horns and brass play a *fortissimo* chord, which then swoops down through a *glissando*. Kenton brings many of his arrangements to a close in much the same way, but its perhaps most famous manifestation occurs at the end of Henry Mancini's theme for Blake Edwards' numerous *Pink Panther* films.

An electric guitar then accompanies the moment when Alucard's ancestor collects Dracula's blood in a small glass vial. As he turns the vial, red flashes glint off its surface and the guitar slides down a tone. Vickers instructs the player to "USE FOOT VOLUME PEDAL, SILENT ATTACKS." As an ex–Manfred Mann guitarist, Vickers was certainly familiar with such effects from his career in pop music, and they provide an appropriately contemporary timbre while also operating harmonically in a very traditional way (for such semitones, which represent evil throughout the film, can be traced at least as far back as Wagner in the nineteenth century, or even Gluck in the eighteenth). Of course, Vickers is saving the full force of his more up-to-date idiom and instrumentation for the main title sequence.

The main title is actually one of Hammer's most interesting and imaginative opening sequences, with ironic references to crucifixes (the wings of an airplane, cranes and motorway overpasses), blood-red London buses and even a shot of a "London Steak House"; and the manner in which these images are introduced reworks the beginnings of several previous Hammer vampire films, several of which similarly begin with a funeral. *The Kiss of the Vampire* is one example. *Countess Dracula* is another. In *Countess Dracula*, like *Dracula A.D. 1972*, the tolling of a church bell leads into the main title music; but *Dracula A.D. 1972* is unique in the sudden change of style and period between prologue and main title. By the time the camera pans up from Van Helsing senior's grave into the sky, the credits in red Gothic script have already revealed the names of the two major stars. Now the word DRACULA appears. During the panning of the camera, timpani trills and celli play a dominant G-natural, accompanied by bongo drum rolls, all of which undergo a *crescendo* and resolve onto the tonic of C major as the crucifix form of a plane and the completion of the title — "A.D. 1972"—flash onto the screen. The big Kentonesque brass chords that introduce this are joined by, among other things, the electric guitar, marked "HARD SOUND SLIGHTLY DISTORTED." Drums with high-hat cymbal complete this musical leap through a century as we hurtle through a brutalist 1970s underpass somewhere in London and the saxophone quartet intones the main theme. The saxophones replace the traditional role of violins and violas, which, significantly, are rejected throughout the entire score, an absence that makes a major contribution to the contemporaneity of the sound. The syncopation used here is another way by which this modernity is indicated, breaking, as it does, with the regular rhythms of the prologue music. Vickers also asks for a much looser performance style than one would find in a James Bernard Dracula score, as he indicates that his players should improvise certain elements. For this, he was able to rely on the skills of the talented musicians who recorded the soundtrack, such as Steve Gray on organ, Alan Skidmore on tenor/soprano saxophones, and Stan Sulzman on tenor/soprano saxophones. Ronnie Verrell on drums was obviously left to his own devices within the general outline indicated, and the electric guitarist Alan Parker was also asked to fill out the harmony for himself.

The main theme, like that for Robinson's *Twins of Evil*, follows the typical pop-song structure of AABA. In the B section, horns intone a countermelody, investing the piece with a more symphonic, Romantic-heroic quality that is mixed with the sounds of 1970s city traffic; and this may serve to remind us of Van Helsing's heroic, and Dracula's antiheroic, nineteenth-century orientations, albeit that they now find themselves in a modern environment.

The party scenes that follow, featuring the rock group Stoneground, might have been more commercially successful if the original choice of Rod Stewart and the Faces had materialized, but Stoneground's two numbers here provide exactly what is needed from a dramatic point of view, i.e. a complete stylistic break from past Dracula films. These opening scenes also set out the underlying social message of the film: that youth culture is ultimately a dangerous and destructive phenomenon. On the surface, director Alan Gibson wants his presumably youthful target audience to identify with the teenagers, but on a deeper level, Don Houghton's script suggests we should actually feel more sympathy with the respectable inhabitants of the elegantly furnished drawing room in which the party takes place than the likes of Johnny Alucard, who deliberately smashes a valuable oriental figurine in front of chinless-wonder Charles' horrified mother. And, like Inspector Murray later (whose scenes bear a very watered-down resemblance to the British T.V. series *The Sweeney*), the police aren't particularly effective when they eventually arrive to sort things out. One

Alligator men. Stoneground in the recording studio for *Dracula A.D. 1972* (dir. Alan Gibson, 1972).

copper merely smiles at a canoodling couple under the table. A middle-class professional is obviously what's needed here to restore order and discipline.

The following morning, outside the Cavern coffee bar (the teenagers in this film rarely drink anything more intoxicating than Coca-Cola — until they start drinking blood, that is) we see a poster on the adjacent wall featuring two names, "Allery and Bernard," at which coincidence no keen-eyed devotee could help but think of James Bernard (whose famous Dracula theme accompanied [uncredited] this film's Warner Bros. logo). Meanwhile, Johnny returns to his satanically stylish flat (all blacks and reds), and Vickers brings the electric guitar back to accompany shots of Dracula's disciple holding up the vampire's ashes that are still safely secured in their glass vial.

So far, we've heard a good deal of diegetic music, such as Stoneground's two songs and the background music in the Cavern, neither of which Vickers was involved with. The next diegetic music wasn't scored by Vickers either. It occurs during the extended Black Mass scenes in St. Bartolph's Church, and the action suggests that the teenagers play it on the reel-to-reel tape recorder they've brought along to the church to liven things up a little. However, when the reel of tape runs out the music eerily continues, suggesting some other, supernatural origin of these disturbing sounds. The music was actually recorded by the cult electronic group the White Noise, brainchild of American musician David Vorhaus, who collaborated with the BBC Radiophonic Workshop's Delia Derbyshire (who had famously realized Ron Grainer's *Dr. Who* theme) on an album called *An Electric Storm*, which was released in 1968. The last of the seven tracks on *An Electric Storm*, called "The Black Mass—An Electric Storm in Hell," was apparently the product of a single day's jam session. The result is a truly unnerving track that is the perfect accompaniment to Johnny Alucard's distinctly over-the-top Black Mass (with its references to "the silken shrouds of death," etc.). In fact, this part of the soundtrack is the most contemporary musical element in the film, inspired, in part, by the example of the concept rock group Pink Floyd; but Vickers admirably segues out of this borrowing, bringing back his own music at the moment when Laura (played by Caroline Munro) volunteers for the sacrifice Johnny had originally planned for Jessica Van Helsing. Here Vickers' score starts to sound — and look — rather different, and, again, it emphasizes Hammer's conservative perspective on avant-garde techniques, for these experimental sounds are firmly equated with evil. This section of Vickers' score is really a blueprint for improvisation rather than an example of conventional notation. He writes: "ALL INSTRUMENTS — MAKE AN ATTACK AT EACH RED BAR LINE," which is about the only firm musical instruction here. The saxophone quartet are instructed to "stay in high register. Start fairly sparsely, gradually play more." The organ does have specific chords to play, but the Moog, vibraphone and percussion all perform "AD LIB RATTLES (HIGH SOUNDS)," which continue in their effectively trance-inducing way until the electric guitar returns with its falling "sighs" when the vial containing Dracula's ashes flashes red in Johnny's fingers. Johnny then produces a knife and slashes his wrist, filling a chalice with very glutinous Kensington Gore, which eventually spills over Laura's neck and breasts.

Vickers developed his interest in such musically generated sound effects in later films scores, such as that for the fantasy adventure film *Warlords of Atlantis* (dir. Kevin Connor, 1978). His brief for one scene in that film was to compose music evocative of a sub-aqueous domain:

> we put one musician in a water-tank [...] and got him to play instruments in the water. We recorded them from below; underwater. We tried everything—saxophone, violin, bassoon, post horn, French horn... The result is a series of strange whispering sounds—like echoes—blurred over so that you're never sure when one sound stops and another begins.[6]

He didn't resort to quite such extreme measures for *Dracula A.D. 1972*, but he did include a typically avant-garde effect for the long-awaited resurrection of Dracula after all the teenagers have run out in panic, leaving Laura screaming in the church and mystic smoke rising from Dracula's resting place outside. For this resurrection scene, Vickers employs an impressive tone cluster, in the manner of Penderecki. It's an extremely apt way to announce the Count's appearance in a twentieth-century graveyard. By 1972, Penderecki's apotheosis of the tone-cluster, *Threnody for the Victims of Hiroshima*, was twelve years old, and, as we have seen with regard to James Bernard's music for *The Quatermass Experiment*, the use of tone-clusters was nothing new to a Hammer film. However, that doesn't affect the considerable impact of this section of Vickers' score, providing, as it does, an eloquent example of how successfully avant-garde musical trends do indeed filter through to popular culture. Vickers concludes his tone-cluster with a triumphant C-minor chord as Dracula emerges fully reconstituted through the clearing mists of his resurrection, and, again, we can find a precedent for such a sudden contrast between atonal note cluster and a tonal chord in Penderecki's piece for orchestra and voices entitled *Kosmogonia*, which was premiered in New York only two years before *Dracula A.D. 1972* (on November 22, 1970, to be precise). *Kosmogonia* however, has nothing demonic about it, setting texts, as it does, by Copernicus, Leonardo da Vinci, Sophocles, Ovid and the astronaut Yuri Gagarin, among others, which compare the immensity of the universe with the genius of man. Having said that, the opening bars of John Williams' score for Steven Spielberg's science fiction epic about aliens and the mystery of the universe that is *Close Encounters of the Third Kind* similarly follows an extended note cluster with a tonal chord, perfectly in accord with Penderecki's cosmic intentions in *Kosmogonia*.

Back on the soundtrack of *Dracula A.D. 1972*, further diegetic music follows Dracula's resurrection, not only in the subsequent Cavern scenes, but also in Alucard's flat, to which Johnny and Gaynor return after their (off-screen) night out at the Albert Hall jazz spectacular. Gaynor said she was willing "to sell her soul" for that. "Come in for a bite," Johnny suggests, as he parks the car. The sax and piano improvisation he puts on the record player ("They were all zonked when they recorded this") is once more reminiscent of Pink Floyd, and again rather more like the kind of thing Johnny's genuine contemporaries might have been listening to at the time. (This library track, not composed by

The Prince of Darkness. Christopher Lee as Dracula *par excellence* in *Dracula A.D. 1972* (dir. Alan Gibson, 1972).

Vickers himself, actually resembles "The Great Gig in the Sky" from Pink Floyd's 1972 album *Dark Side of the Moon*. Pink Floyd's improvised rumination on death is, after all, an appropriate reference to make during a scene in which Johnny prepares Gloria for her encounter with the arch vampire himself.)

A final contemporary musical element remains to be pointed out, which occurs on several occasions: during Johnny's discussion with Dracula in which he pleads for immortality, during the athletic fight scene between Alucard and Van Helsing in Alucard's flat, and also when Jessica is attacked by Alucard and Bob in the deserted Cavern. The effect, created by guitar, is known as "wah-wah"— and it brings us to Hammer's next Dracula film, *The Satanic Rites of Dracula* (dir. Alan Gibson, 1973), as the composer for that film, John Cacavas, also made considerable use of it. The "wah-wah" sound is an important element in the soul classics of Barry White and others, and it had strong urban connotations of "hip" and "cool," as Philip Tagg has explained with regard to Isaac Hayes' use of the effect in *Shaft* (dir. Gordon Parks, 1971): "The title themes for both *Shaft* and *Baretta* are entirely in the soul/funk genre, and [...] both these heroes are portrayed as 'hip' [...] full of slang and 'street knowledge.'"[7]

The use of "wah-wah" in Cacavas' score for *The Satanic Rites of Dracula* is rather ironic because in this film teenage pop culture has completely vanished. Jessica Van Helsing, played this time by Joanna Lumley, is now a fully "reformed" young woman who wears respectable Laura Ashley dresses, dutifully makes coffee and has become her grandfather's "right hand." "I sometimes think she knows more about my work than I do myself," Van Helsing proudly explains. "She has an ingrained curiosity the hallmark of a true scientist." (It's important for screenwriter Don Houghton to point out her natural curiosity at this stage, because her curiosity is essential to the plot.) A further blow to teen culture is the fact that middle-aged police agents are now the only other male leads in the film, apart from Van Helsing himself. They are not "hip," sexually attractive policemen like Richard Roundtree's Shaft, but display the distinctly British, middle-aged establishment qualities of actors William Franklyn, Michael Coles and Richard Vernon, all of whom, at one stage, drink soup served in elegant china bowls from Van Helsing's antique silver tureen. Less trendy it would be hard to get. The only young male characters are the bike-riding Mod heavies who look after security at Pelham House, where Dracula's acolytes have been indulging in the satanic rites of the film's title. Originally, however, the film was to have been called *Dracula Is Dead... And Alive and Living in London*. "DRACULA IS DEAD..." is indeed rubber stamped in black ink all over Cacavas' score.[8] Christopher Lee disliked this title — and the film — so much that he vowed never to perform the role of Dracula again:

> I think it's fatuous. I can think of twenty adjectives ... fatuous, pointless, absurd. It's not a comedy ... [but] it's a comic title. I don't see the point. I don't see what they hope to achieve... I just hope they [the audience] realise

that I am struggling against insuperable odds on occasion to remain true to the author's original character.[9]

Lee's abandonment of Dracula is a pity, not only because of the authority he brought to the part but also because the film in which he performed his most celebrated role for the last time has many novel and ingenious ingredients: a group of middle-aged establishment figures, including an industrialist, a landowner, a high ranking army officer and a leading biochemist (the latter wonderfully performed by Freddie Jones), are all in thrall to the arch-vampire, who wishes to destroy the world in order to end his own suffering. His acolytes think that the plague bacillus Dracula has commissioned will only be used to hold governments to ransom, but they eventually find out that they have been duped. There is also a cellar full of female vampires, a female oriental High Priest of the coven, and, most intriguing of all, Dracula himself posing as a property developer by the name of D.D. Denham while residing amidst 1970s-style office furnishings at the top of a tower block, just like Howard Hughes. Lee even gives his Dracula a phony Russian accent before he is unmasked by Van Helsing by means of a crucifix and a silver bullet, the intended trajectory of which is sent off course by the timely intervention of two of Dracula's

Miss Stake. Joanna Lumley (at bottom) and Valerie van Ost in *The Satanic Rites of Dracula* (dir. Alan Gibson, 1973).

middle-aged acolytes. It's all a fantasy, of course, but, as Lord Byron was the first to say, truth is stranger than fiction. Today, in a world dominated by the fear of global assassins, such as Osama bin Laden, secret terrorist cells and suicide bombers, one could argue that *The Satanic Rites of Dracula*, for all its apparent absurdities, was actually rather prescient, and certainly no more absurd that the political realities of everyday life at the beginning of the twenty-first century. Dracula has indeed turned into a suicide bomber in this film (though his preferred method of dispatching humanity, and thus starving himself of blood, is germ warfare), and just like any fundamentalist, Dracula explains: "There is a group of us who are determined that the decadence of the present day can and will be halted. A new political regime is planned. To lend weight to one's arguments, amid the rush and whirl of humanity, it is sometimes necessary to be persuasive." (Lee was always very proud of his interpolations from Stoker's original novel.) The absence of hippies or anyone even remotely trendy in the film (unless motorcycle heavies in Afghan jackets can really make a claim in that direction) could be seen as a response to the death of sixties optimism. The Summer of Love in 1968 spawned the naive belief that teenagers, sex and positive thinking could save the world. Hammer seemed keen to point out in *Dracula A.D. 1972* that they very nearly destroyed it. Consequently, teenagers simply aren't allowed to interfere with or even appear in the even more serious business of *The Satanic Rites of Dracula*. This explains why there is no diegetic music drawn from hippie or pop culture on the soundtrack. John Cacavas' score is contemporary throughout, but in a much more mature way, the music once more rooted in the style of Stan Kenton, as Cacavas himself has explained:

> I started off as a band composer. I was an arranger in the Army Band in Washington D.C. That's when I started doing it and getting good recordings of my work and getting them published. I've probably got over two thousand published works for band, orchestra, choir. I still do four or five a year. One year my composition won the National Brass Band Contest. Everybody had to play it. It was called *Theme and Rock Out.*
> What happened was we were living in New York. From 1965 to 1970 I was General Manager of Chappell in New York, but I was also writing all the time, and I finally decided to go and move to London with the whole family. I had became very friendly with Telly Savalas. I'd made his record albums, and he got me into the movies as a film composer. He was doing something called *Pancho Villa* [dir. Eugenio Martin, 1972]. That was an Italian/Spanish co-production, and he tried to get me the job of writing the score, but it was one of those national pictures where the below-the-line people had to be the nationality of that country. But I could still write the title song, which I did, and the publishers really liked it and the orchestration, and it got me to Harold Shampan, who was running the music division of this film company. He recommended me for *Horror Express* [dir. Eugenio Martin, 1972]. It turned out very well, and then he engineered for

me to get *The Satanic Rites of Dracula*. Well, I was practically a novice then, and I knew the kind of scores Hammer had had before. I'm halfway through writing it under the guidance of Phil Martell, who was a wonderful musician. We had a big seventy-five piece orchestra. It was a Warner Brothers/Hammer co-production, and there was a guy named Robert Silver at Warner Brothers who decided that what this thing needed was a rock and roll score. Well, Phil Martell went through the roof. I figured, well, it could work but, you know, these Hammer films all have a certain style, and [James] Bernard did a great job with those scores. I personally think that mine was nowhere near as good as his. I had to go down the middle: half pop/rock and roll, half serious, and I don't think that Phil Martell liked it too much, but the studio did and we never heard any more about the rock and roll. It was a wonderful orchestra. I just sat in the booth. Because of a lot of the timings I used click tracks, and Phil wasn't really used to that. At that time a lot of British musicians didn't like them either, but if Phil was off a half-second he'd have had to do it again.

Then I got the chance to start doing movies in America. We moved to California — the whole family — in 1973. I've been there ever since. And then I did movies and television shows non-stop for about thirty-five years. I've done four hundred one-hour television shows, forty "Movies of the Week," fifteen features, eight mini-series, thirty specials. I'm getting tired! I was doing *Hawaii Five-0* and *Kojak* at the same time. I kept forgetting who was doing what. It didn't make any difference because they were always doing the same thing every week! On television you get three or four days to score an hour-long show. And that means laying it out, figuring out the timings, orchestrating it, conducting it.

I tried to make *Satanic Rites of Dracula* legit — the kind of style that they were used to. Dramatic, symphonic, which really works for stuff like that. Everybody was telling me what to do. That was the problem. I had Phil Martell, who I respected very much, and then you've got the editor, and then you've got the producer, and you have the director. I remember one time doing a picture in Hollywood and these people all had different ideas. I called my agent and he said, "Don't pay any attention to them. You just do what you think is right, because if you pay attention to them you'll get a mishmash and it will never work."

I might have met Alan Gibson, the director of *Satanic Rites*. I remember the producer, Roy Skeggs. Directors on television never turn up because they're working on another project unless it's a really high-profile thing; but episodic TV — they're off on the next project. I've found that directors are less music orientated than the producers. Producers see the whole picture. The director's only worried about preserving his dialogue.

Phil Martell was a perfectionist and a very good conductor. He knew his business backwards and forwards. A tough task master. Not really open to new ideas, I would think. He was steeped in the traditional British style of film scoring. American style has always been different from British style. British style was probably a little bit more legit, a little bit more symphonic. American composers tend to mix voicings and styles, depending

Nine: Modern Gothic (Vickers and Cacavas)

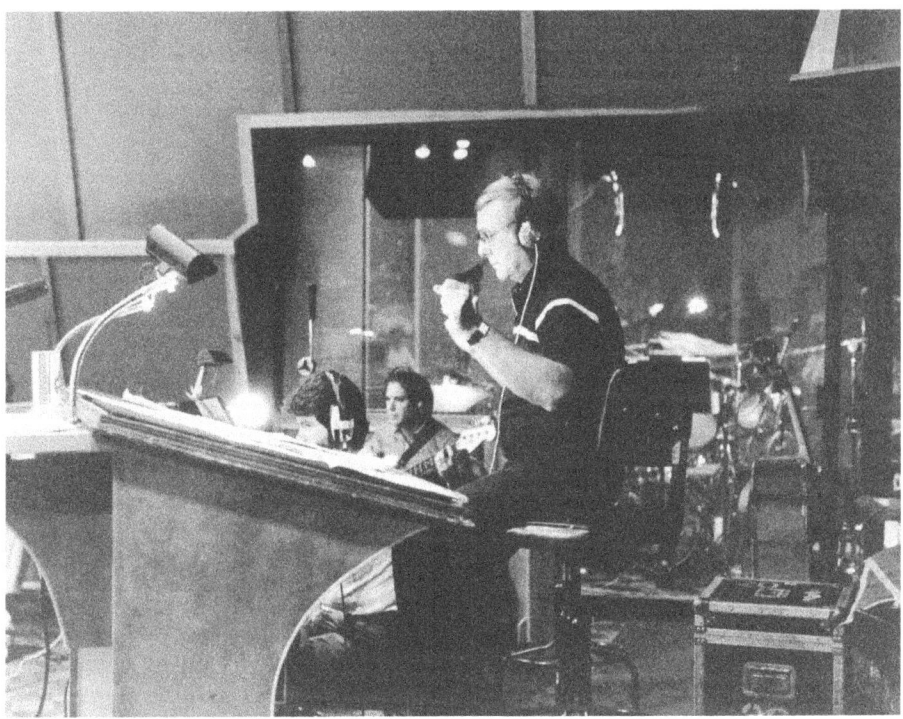

Beating time. John Cacavas conducting a recording session at MGM in the early 1980s for *Seven Brides for Seven Brothers*. The man playing guitar is Steve Carnelli, John's first-call guitarist (photograph courtesy John Cacavas).

on the scene. In my opinion, a lot of British composers overdid things all the time — had too much stuff going on. The Hollywood way was to make things more sparse and more transparent, because the moment you start putting in sound effects a lot of music is just lost. I remember one time I was doing a picture with a huge battle — machine guns and all that — and I thought nothing will come through. So what I did was I wrote a low C for two synthesizers, all the cellos, two basses and just held it for three minutes. It worked perfectly! You really have to be cognizant of what the sound effects are. I used to get so fed up at dubbing sessions. They would spend a half hour trying to get a door slam right on a car, and they would never take the time to run through the music by itself to sort out the various tracks. They didn't know and they didn't care. Henry Mancini once told me, "The last time you hear your music is when you record it." Music is like a piece of furniture to these people. They'll move it around.

The Hammer people allowed a lot of time for recording. In Hollywood, for an hour-long television show — an action show — you might end up having twenty-five minutes of music, and you're expected to do it in three hours. With *Kojak,* for example, I had the same orchestra, same engineer. Every episode had to have a fresh score.

Filming was all over by the time I got involved in *The Satanic Rites of Dracula.* A lot of times you'll see on the cue-sheets: "Scene missing," which means that they're re-shooting, something like that. I was doing something one time and the editor put in: "Plot missing"![10]

Cacavas' main title theme for *The Satanic Rites of Dracula* indeed brings a transatlantic quality to the proceedings that makes it rather different from what had gone before. During shots of London, a stylized shadow of Dracula gradually grows larger, suggesting, even at this early stage in the proceedings, his desire for world domination. Cacavas' main theme is introduced with the immediately contemporary significations of a riff on electric guitar and a rhythmic high-hat cymbal. Like Vickers' "Evil" theme, Cacavas' theme is simplicity itself: a dotted rhythm on a single note, followed by a falling semitone, which is played by the brass and supported by a swirl of harp *glissandi,* along with the important timbre of the electric harpsichord. Before the strings take over with a counter-melody, the electric bass guitar is exposed, further emphasizing the modernity of this particular Dracula story. The magical element provided by the harp *glissandi,* together with the "historical" element provided by the electric harpsichord, conversely suggest the traditional Gothic aspects of the film. (The harpsichord is actually associated with Dracula throughout, especially whenever there is a close-up of the woodcut portrait of him that hangs in Van Helsing's study. The fact that it is an *electric* harpsichord also suggests that this old-fashioned anti-hero has been brought up to date.) In order to create a magical quality, the harp is essential here, and Cacavas is careful to highlight its ethereal quality by removing the bass line during its opening flourish. A bass line gives music a sense of gravity, so to speak. Its absence suggests a more ethereal, even transcendental quality. When the harp *glissandi* stops, however, we are brought back to earth with an electric bass guitar line and a counter-melody on strings that is played in counterpoint with the electric harpsichord. Cacavas will make many such mythic/modern contrasts throughout the score in support of the film's similarly contrasting mythic/modern structure. The theme is then repeated two more times. On the second repeat, the strings take over the semitone theme (with timpani punctuating each phrase). The counter melody this time is played by horns, which are answered by violins in a very high register. The last repeat shares the semitone theme between the lower strings and violins, with low brass accompanying, before the upper strings take over the counter melody. This very straightforward structure is indeed made much more interesting through its orchestration, which is really a musical metaphor for the overall style of the film. Traditionally sinister brass, soaring strings, magical harps and a backward-looking (but simultaneously *electric*) harpsichord combine with jazzy high-hat cymbals and electric bass. In this way the significations of Cacavas' instrumentation perfectly complement this modernized Gothic narrative.

Nine: Modern Gothic (Vickers and Cacavas)

The contemporary aspects of Cacavas' approach include various other devices that recur throughout the score. As we have seen so often in the film scores explored in this book, fourths play an important role, and are also central to Cacavas' overall harmonic language. Chords built out of perfect and/or augmented fourths are what give it its particular quality. However, Cacavas' emphasis on brass and Kentonesque swing syncopations modernize these fourths still further. A useful demonstration of how he achieves this is to compare the music for the Black Mass scenes at Pelham House with the cue that covers the escape of police agent Hanson (played by Maurice O'Connell) from the upstairs room where he is being kept prisoner. These scenes are also usefully juxtaposed in the film itself.

The opening Black Mass scene, which is later broken up into eight flashbacks, features one of several *ostinati* in this score. The divided first violins play predominantly semitonal scalic passages of four notes in contrary motion, while the second violins oscillate between F-natural and G-flat in harmonics. Over this an organ intones the Black Mass theme, which is really a rumination on the interval of a fourth: B-natural, down to B-flat and F-natural, then up to A-natural (the fourth occurring between B-flat and F-natural). Cacavas harmonizes this organ theme with yet more fourths.

In the seventh flashback scene, in which the girl on the altar is sacrificed, we see the Chinese woman, Chin Yang (played by Barbara Yu Ling), raise the blade over the body of the girl, at which point Cacavas brings in trombones to punctuate the violence of the action. The punchy rhythm here is typical of how he will use the brass later, and again it derives from the swing style of Stan Kenton (and Cacavas' early days as a band composer). As the girl screams to the sound of thunder, Cacavas emphasizes the moment with high register violins in a figure again revolving around fourths, its initially wide leaps of pitch symbolizing the girl's extremis.

The occult significations of fourth-based harmonies can now be compared to the fourths used in the scene in which Hanson escapes from Pelham House. (This cue is later reprised when the other Mods kick-start their bikes to pursue Jane through the London streets.) An *ostinato*, based on fourths, is scored for wind, piano, marimba and a triangle (played with a metal whip snap), and the combined result is a glittering and highly distinctive sound, one made even more contemporary in effect when Cacavas brings in yet more fourths on horns and brass in his distinctive, syncopated style. Strings also appear in fourths, moving through a *glissando* from one chord to the next. The use of fourths here implies violence and brutality rather than anything occult, and they operate in much the same way as the fourths we frequently find in Stravinsky's *Rite of Spring*. Despite the antique pagan setting of that ballet, Stravinsky's music for it was self-consciously modern, and fourths provided just the angular, up-to-date harmony required. Cacavas' fourths similarly connote the modernity that Warner Brothers executives were so extremely concerned should feature throughout the score.

As we have seen, augmented fourths had formed the harmonic basis of James Bernard's celebrated Dracula theme, and Cacavas' use of them inevitably brings with them an echo of earlier, more traditional Dracula films. Indeed, at one point in 3M3X, the eighth flashback of the Black Mass, when the sacrificed girl's eyes open on coming back to life, Cacavas writes a chord for the organ that is identical to Bernard's Dracula chord: a tritone (spanning A and E-flat), with a D-flat squeezed in below the E-flat, creating a major second.

A very successful piece of atmospheric scoring occurs in 3M2 when Van Helsing walks down the steps in front of the Albert Hall on his way to visit his old college friend, Professor Julian Keeley (the biochemist played by Freddie Jones), whom he has been stunned to discover is involved in the black magic ceremonies at Pelham House. The scene takes full advantage of the chill November weather in which it was shot (the action is also set in November), and, together with Cacavas' score, an unnerving aura of anxiety is created, transforming what is an everyday environment into something much more troubling. Musically, this is achieved by unexpected and completely unrelated changes of tonality. A clarinet opens the scene, rising a semitone and then, perhaps predictably, up a tritone before falling back a semitone. The note the clarinet finally settles on is D-natural, which, together with the dominant A-natural above it, suggests a D major tonality. This is slightly blurred by horns, which punctuate

In step. The author follows Peter Cushing's path on the way to the "Keeley Foundation" in *The Satanic Rites of Dracula*— London's Albert Hall in the background (photograph by Markus Wallasvaara).

the next bar with major seconds (E-natural and F-sharp), but we're not at all prepared for the quietly intoned B-flat minor chord in the trombones when the camera cuts to a long shot of the Keeley Foundation building. The effect of this harmonic shift is very unsettling, all the more so due to its understated dynamic, and it suggests that all inside the Foundation building is not what is should be. After the trombone chord, Cacavas' *tremolo* strings wander around rather aimlessly; then a flute desolately rises through a tone, falls back to the original note, and tails off by falling a semitone, supported by fourths in the trombones and piano. The atonality and lack of motivic security here perfectly suggests the anxiety of Van Helsing at this point.

Van Helsing rings the doorbell of the Foundation building, but nobody seems to be at home. The flutes echo this apparent vacancy with another falling semitone, and this semitone quaver group is repeated before the final note literally disintegrates (Cacavas indicates this effect with a curving line on the last note to indicate a falling *glissando* that loses energy in its descent).

Unsurprisingly, tritones are all over this scene, and they recur in the strings while Van Helsing waits for an answer by the door. By instructing the strings to play *ponticello* (i.e. near the bridge of the violin) with no vibrato, Cacavas is able yet again to articulate such non-action by injecting a new sonority, thus providing the perfect musical counterpart to the tension of the moment. Van Helsing is about to give up hope of the door being answered, and the strings here vocalize his impatience by imitating a sigh, the first violins falling through a tone and their initial accent indicating Van Helsing's impatience. Cacavas is a master of such psychological detail, his approach to scoring being comparable to what Friedrich Nietzsche had to say about Wagner's *Parsifal*:

> Wagner is admirable and gracious only in the invention of what is smallest, in spinning out the details. Here one is entirely justified in proclaiming him a master of the first rank, as our greatest *miniaturist* in music who crowds into the smallest space an infinity of sense and sweetness. His wealth of colors, or half shadows, of the secrecies of dying light spoils one to such an extent that afterward almost all other musicians seem too robust.[11]

Cacavas' score is similarly constructed from small fragments which emphasize and articulate the on-screen action in much the same way that Wagner's music functions in his last music-drama. (*Parsifal* is dramatically very static for much of the time, too.) Indeed, Nietzsche's description of Wagner's music as being "not [...] music but language, instrument, *ancilla dramaturgica* [handmaiden of the drama]"[12] is also an apt definition of film music itself.

Van Helsing now gives up on the front door and tries around the back of the building. As he disappears through an open door, the camera pulls focus to reveal the reflection of a Mod in the wing mirror of his motorbike. Cacavas accompanies this with a chord constructed from three fourths, played on the suitably modern timbre of electric guitar. As was the case with Mike Vickers' score for *Dracula A.D. 1972*, modernity and aspects of popular culture are given a negative gloss throughout Cacavas' score, whereas the high point in the battle of good over evil in the music of *The Satanic Rites of Dracula* is manifested by a tonal chorale for strings in the manner of Bach, heard when Van Helsing forges a silver bullet from a crucifix. Despite the desire to capitalize on modernity in both these films, their overall implication is that modernity is not on the side of the angels.

3M2 now cuts to the interior of the Keeley Foundation, where the errant Professor is hard at work putting finishing touches to the plague bacillus on which Dracula has commissioned him to work. Here the analogy of evil with modernity is emphasized by Cacavas' ingenious use of quarter tones in the first violins as an acoustic correlate to the unspeakable ghastliness that lies within the innocuous Petrie dishes on Keeley's desk. As quarter tones unnervingly slide around in an uncertain pitch, *glissandi* in the cellos slide up and down through augmented fourths, while the trombones provide a syncopated punctuation of Cacavas' borrowing of Bernard's Dracula chord, mentioned above. However, the effect here is very different from Bernard's approach, due to the Kentonesque brass and the general sense of atonality.

Cacavas next indulges in a little thematic metamorphosis for the scene in which Dracula vampirizes Jane in one of the disused rooms in Pelham House.

The Keeley Foundation? Actually, Queen's Gate Lodge, 23A Elvaston Place, London, 1996, as filmed in *The Satanic Rites of Dracula* (photograph by the author).

According to the cue-sheets for 4M1, this scene was originally to have been preceded by an exterior shot of Professor Keeley silhouetted in the window of the Foundation building, with the camera then panning around the skyline of London before cutting to the exterior of Pelham House. Unfortunately this was cut from the final print, thus making the transition rather more abrupt. For the much more traditionally Gothic scene that follows, Cacavas' flutes quietly intone a transformed version of the main title theme over supporting string harmonics. Cacavas removes the initial dotted rhythm of the main theme, but its association with Dracula remains further to remind us of his presence. Cacavas also includes the electric harpsichord, which plays harmonically clashing decorations based, again, on fourths. A little later, when the door of the room starts to rattle, what Cacavas describes as "brassy" horns are introduced, which intone the falling semitone that opened the main title theme. Once more, this timbre adds a harder, Kentonesque edge to the more conventional Gothic style he has employed so far in this scene; and it returns, joined by equally brassy trumpets and trombones, when the main title theme, this time more like its old self, accompanies Dracula's appearance for the inevitable seduction that follows. Lee's misgivings about this film indeed have some justification, as we are already into the fourth reel of the film and this is his first appearance — though, to be fair, he has a lot more to say and do in the dénouement.[13]

For the seduction of Jane, Cacavas resorts to classically Bernardian effects: whole-tone harp *glissandi,* trills on the flutter-tongue flutes, and vibraphone ruminations on the same whole-tone scale as the harps; but we also hear the much more contemporary timbre of a "wha-wha" electric guitar, which falls through a semitone, again bringing this Gothic atmosphere suitably up to date. Later, as Dracula prepares to bite, Cacavas instructs the guitarist to "hit body [of the instrument] with palm [of player's hand]," creating further novelty of timbre, while everything else moves through the *crescendo* that is to be expected at moments like this. A nice touch is the musical equivalent of Jane's half horrified/half ecstatic scream when Dracula's fangs sink home. The violins leap from an F-natural at the top of the stave to a G-flat that's just above the upper octave F-natural in a manner that is worthy of Schoenberg himself. They then fall back to F-natural before passing through another tritone on their way back up to an E-flat, creating a graphic musical suggestion of vampiric coitus.

The main title theme will return when Dracula carries Jane's freshly vampirized body down one of Pelham House's corridors; but before that happens, back at the Keeley Foundation Van Helsing is beginning to find out what has been going on behind the closed doors of his old friend's research facility. During the climax of his confrontation with Keeley over the plague bacillus, the Mod who has been on surveillance outside enters the room and knocks Van Helsing unconscious with a bullet (evidence either of the Mod's embarrassing incompetence with firearms at this close range or his extremely accurate marksmanship; presumably Dracula wants Van Helsing alive to witness his final triumph). Anyway, when Van Helsing regains consciousness later that evening he discovers that Keeley has been hanged from the ceiling of his office, and Cacavas emphasizes the horror of the scene by superimposing different tritones in the brass, creating a far greater sense of discord—and contemporaneity—than if a single tritone had been played in unison. (The contemporaneity of the brass here is further emphasized by the electric guitar, which is instructed to "fuzz" its notes.)

Jessica Van Helsing's "ingrained curiosity," so much admired by her grandfather, is responsible for the next set-piece of the film. Accompanying Torrence and Inspector Morris to Pelham House at night, she wanders off to the cellar where she soon finds herself among a group of red-robed female vampires, hungry for blood. This cellar has an up-to-the-minute water sprinkler system in case of fire, which proves even more useful when the situation gets desperately out of hand a few minutes later—for, as Van Helsing had also reliably informed us in *Dracula A.D. 1972*, vampires cannot abide clear running water.

Musically, this section (5M2) is very atonal, and, at nearly four and half minutes, it contains some of Cacavas' most interesting and sustained writing:

> A lot of the classical writing I've done has been very modernistic. I don't think it's possible to have danger and terror with major chords, and jazz never works. Jazz is happy music, you know! Blues sometimes works, if it's like *film noir*. I did *The Return of Ironside* for Universal a couple of years ago, and the producer wanted me to keep using the theme; but I said, "Look, the theme is great at the beginning, great at the end, but when a guy's got a gun pointed at him you're not going to play that happy theme!" These guys don't seem to understand.[14]

The complexity of the writing here is handled with Cacavas' habitual care and professionalism:

> I'm an old-fashioned writer. I still write out full-scores. A lot the new directors don't really have much of a background in really good movie music. They like electronic music because it doesn't get in the way. It's impersonal.[15]

5M2 opens with a statement of the "vampire bride" theme that will eventually accompany the final scenes when Jessica lies on Dracula's sacrificial altar. Here the theme is associated with the female vampires in the cellar, and the principle part of its melodic line appropriately spans a tritone (F-sharp down through an E-natural to a C-natural). As Jessica wanders through the cellar, the electric bass guitar, double basses and piano alternate with a series of seemingly random pitches, but Cacavas is careful to include as many tritones as possible without forming a predictable pattern. This is a highly effective way of suggesting the apprehension experienced by Jessica (and presumably the audience as well). When Jessica lifts Jane's wrist, the seduction music returns, and as Jane turns to face Jessica, the electric guitar creates another very prominent "fuzz" effect. As Jane bares her fangs, Cacavas exploits the false relations of two chords built again out of fourths: the strings play F-natural, B-flat and D-natural (in fairly high register), while the piano plays F-natural, B-natural and D-natural.

The attack now begins. The tempo of the music changes to a lively *allegro* (crotchet=120), and the writing becomes very complex, consisting of syncopated fragments in Cacavas' most pointillistic compositional style. Over a "boogaloo" suspended cymbal, the horns intone syncopated statements of Bernard's Dracula chord, which broaden out into Scriabinesque chords built on augmented and perfect fourths. Beneath this, strings play oscillating semitone fragments, while, at the top of the score, wind sporadically decorate the whole with discordantly harmonized, rising semitone fragments. Fragmentation is indeed the operative word here, an apt musical signification for the chaos of the screen action, but there is nothing accidental about Cacavas' carefully contrived impression of chaos, all notated with his usual methodical care.

In the midst of the struggle, the "wah-wah" guitar returns, which Cacavas specifically marks "A LA SHAFT," and this leads into a contrapuntal section for strings. (The "wah-wah" on *The Satanic Rites of Dracula* was actually played by Vik Flick, who had played the original James Bond theme.[16]) Though not technically a fugue, this contrapuntal section suggests conflict in the same way that Wagner, for example, exploited a fugal style for the riot scene in his music-drama *Die Meistersinger von Nürnberg*. The term "fugue" derives from the Latin "*fuga*," meaning "fleeing" or "chasing," and fugues, or at least contrapuntalism of a less formal kind, are often used for scenes in which characters are similarly fleeing or chasing each other. Cacavas' contrapuntal section here is quite long (fifteen bars in all), and it is in marked contrast to the fragmented style of the preceding bars. It is extremely atonal in harmonic style, though the main theme on first violins has sufficient tonal shapes within it to make it stand out.

This contrapuntal passage leads up to oscillating tritones as Jessica's screams are heard by Torrence and Murray upstairs in the elegant hall of Pelham House. During the subsequent rescue of Jessica by these two men, Cacavas again punctuates the action with Kentonesque brass chords made up from fourths, and there is another excellent example of how Cacavas uses music to articulate the action when Jessica shouts, "She's a vampire!' to Torrence, who is in the process of trying to rescue Jane. A similar, though less extreme, musical articulation occurs in 7M1, when Torrence discovers the dead body of Colonel Matthews in the car during their surveillance of Pelham House.

As mentioned earlier, the central antidote to all this contemporaneous atonality and syncopation occurs in 7M2, when Van Helsing melts a crucifix in his study to forge the silver bullet with which he hopes to dispatch Dracula. However, instead of the music resolving into the perfect cadence we expect at the end of this chorale-like passage, we enter unexpected and unresolved harmonic territory when Van Helsing gazes at his woodcut of Dracula's portrait (again accompanied by the arch-vampire's obligatory harpsichord).

Cacavas' understated approach to the destruction of Dracula is quite unlike Bernard's. Quiet chromatic scales in the clarinets, accompanied by oscillating sextuplets in the flutes, are supported by equally hushed string harmonics. This is perhaps the weakest part of Cacavas' score, bringing Christopher Lee's last incarnation as Count Dracula to a rather depressing anticlimax. Van Helsing contemplates Dracula's silver ring (something Peter Cushing had been worried about, as his lines in the script specifically point out that Dracula lives "in mortal dread of silver"). He blows the dust off it, and the credits roll to a slightly modified version of the main title theme.

We will never know in what directions Hammer might have gone had Lee not been so reluctant to reprise the role of Dracula, and the British film industry hadn't collapsed a few years after the release of *The Satanic Rights of Dracula*. In 1979, however, a new American *Dracula* appeared, with Frank Langella in the title role. Directed by John Badham, Universal's remake of its own Bela Lugosi classic was accompanied by John Williams' score, which was for the most part in the Korngold/Steiner idiom that he had revived for *Star Wars* (dir. George Lucas, 1977), and which has had a major effect on film soundtracks ever since. But Hammer films had one more card to play—and it introduced the most extreme music that the company had ever commissioned.

Notes

1. David Pirie, *The Vampire Cinema* (Feltham: Galley Press, 1977), p. 93.
2. In a television interview about Dennis Wheatley (*Clive Barker's A-Z of Horror*), Christopher Lee significantly lamented "the complete [...] breakdown of discipline in this country."
3. Peter Hutchings, *Hammer and Beyond* (Manchester: Manchester University Press 1993), pp. 66–67.
4. Mike Vickers, in conversation with the author, January 31, 2007.
5. Marcus Hearn & Alan Barnes, *The Hammer Story* (London: Titan Books, 1997), p. 156. Hearn and Barnes repeat Philip Martell's own claim (in an interview in *Little Shoppe of Horrors*, No. 10/11, p. 97) that he brought in Don Banks to rewrite half of Vickers' score, but Martell's claim simply doesn't stand up to scrutiny of Vickers' original manuscript.
6. Mike Vickers quoted in Dez Skinn (ed.), *Hammer's Halls of Horror*, vol. 2, no. 10 (July 1978), p. 41.
7. Philip Tagg, *Kojak: 50 Seconds of Television Music* (Gothenburg: University of Gothenburg, 1979), p. 104.
8. The score itself is also written in black ink. In conversation with the author (November 8, 2006), Cacavas explained, "When I started working for Morton Gould, when I got out the army, he said, 'You use a pencil? Stop. Start writing in ink.' Because he always did. I said, 'Oh, Christ. I haven't got the confidence to do that!' He said, 'Paper is cheap. If you make a couple of mistakes, there's whiteout. Or just cross it out

and put it on another line.' He said the worst enemy of a composer or an arranger is the wrist. You can really hurt yourself over years on the wrist but if you use a pen there's hardly any pressure. With a pencil you have to apply pressure. And the object is not to have to apply pressure. And from that day on I started writing in ink. I never looked back. But you know, Beethoven wrote in ink. Stravinsky used a stubby pencil."

    9. Marcus Hearn and Alan Barnes, *The Hammer Story* (Note 4), p. 162.

    10. John Cacavas, in conversation with the author, November 8, 2006.

    11. Friedrich Nietzsche (trans. Walter Kaufmann), *The Birth of Tragedy, and the Case of Wagner* (New York: Vintage, 1967), p. 171.

    12. Ibid., p. 173.

    13. Christopher Lee, *Tall, Dark and Gruesome* (London: Victor Gollancz, 1997), p. 306. Lee described *The Satanic Rites of Dracula* as "a story with Dracula popped in almost as an afterthought."

    14. John Cacavas, in conversation with the author (Note 10).

    15. Ibid.

    16. Ibid.

TEN

Catching Up with the Future

Paul Glass

To the Devil a Daughter (dir. Peter Sykes, 1976) is a very different kind of film from Hammer's earlier Dennis Wheatley black magic tale, *The Devil Rides Out*. Director Peter Sykes was adamant that he didn't want to make a typical Hammer film. Indeed, the finished film also strayed considerably from Wheatley's original novel, whereas Terence Fisher's 1968 adaptation of *The Devil Rides Out* had been remarkably faithful to its source. Consequently, Wheatley was not happy with Sykes' film,[1] and critics at first were somewhat dismissive of this last, late bloom from the blood red rose garden of Hammer Films, complaining (unjustly) of an anticlimax in the final scenes. But as Jonathan Rigby points out, "the film's atmosphere is so disquieting and its tone so oddly cerebral that a more slam-bang climax would seem out of place. Cerebral disquiet, however, was hardly the recipe for Hammer's commercial salvation."[2] This cerebral approach also required very different music from what had gone before, and Paul Glass' astonishingly contemporary score indeed proved to be unlike any previous Hammer film soundtracks.

Born in 1934 in Los Angeles, Glass studied with Ingolf Dahl and then with Boris Blacher at Tanglewood before graduating from the University of Southern California in 1956. He later went on to study with, among others, the celebrated film composer and orchestrator Hugo Friedhofer, Goffredo Peprassi in Rome, Roger Sessions at Princeton, and Witold Lutosławski in Warsaw. He returned to America in 1962, writing film and concert music (he scored Otto Preminger's *Bunny Lake Is Missing* in 1965), and settled in Switzerland in 1973 after spending four years in France studying the work of Anton Webern. Today he teaches music composition and music history, and continues to compose. His considerable output of concert music includes chamber music for various instrumental combinations, pieces for piano (including a piano concerto for

Ten: Catching Up with the Future (Glass)

Paul Glass, 2007 (photograph courtesy Paul Glass and Müller und Schade).

improvised piano composed in 1982), a cello concerto, a short ballet (*Eschatos*, composed in 1957) and six symphonies. Glass' setting for baritone of his own text (*5 chansons pour une princesse errante*) dates from 1968, and his vocal work includes several choral works, such as his setting for *Psalm LXXXIII* (1957), along with *Sahassavagga* for children's choir (1976). A choir also makes a significant contribution to the overall effect of his score for *To the Devil a Daughter*.

His own opinion of this film has changed with the years:

> I never saw *To the Devil a Daughter* when it was finished. I trusted Philip Martell to dub it in the way I had planned. Only a few years ago I saw the DVD. I looked at the film, and lo and behold Philip had done it to the mark exactly. It was perfect. I looked at the picture. It's beautifully made. I'd remembered it being very ordinary stuff at the time.[3]

Peter Sykes didn't have any influence over the style of the music. He described Glass as "one of the most highly qualified musicians I've ever met,"[4] and left the music entirely to musical supervisor Philip Martell and Glass himself. In fact, as Glass makes clear below, Martell left the job almost entirely to the composer:

> I did meet Peter Sykes. A lovely guy. I've lost contact with him. I did not discuss the music with him. I was trying to push what I was experimenting

with in those days, more than what someone would ask me to do, and Philip gave absolutely complete stylistic freedom, which is not the case too often. Harry Martell, Philip's brother, was the greatest orchestral "fixer" of them all. My first encounter with him was on a film called *The Test of Violence* [dir. Stuart Cooper, 1970], and there Harry brought me an orchestra with the superstars of all time. Incredible sight-readers. People like clarinetist Jack Brymer, Philip Jones the trumpeter, and others. He was a lovely man, Harry; and working with Philip meant working with someone who did not bar anything. He did not tell you, "I think you better go here or there."

Harry had also fixed a fantastic orchestra for one of the best films I was ever involved with, called *Overlord* [dir. Stuart Cooper, 1975]. It was probably because of that, or *A Test of Violence*, that Philip liked what I was doing. He knew that I was a fervent admirer of his brother Harry. Harry was one of the most incredibly calm, tranquil people. Philip was not. Philip got very upset and excited. Philip was very very uptight about how late I was. I only finished the score at 6:28 A.M. on the day of the recording. Philip called Paul Patterson to help me one night on *To the Devil a Daughter*. I actually conducted the score at the recording session.

Philip Martell had extraordinary musical tastes to have chosen such extraordinary musicians. I sometimes teach a course on film music at the university where I live, and also on contemporary music, and in my teaching I've found that students—nineteen, twenty years old—seem to relate any kind of contemporary music (you play them Luciano Berio, György Ligeti) to horror film music. It's back to front. It's so unfortunate. Though I have to say that I, myself, tried out the experimental things first in film music. The first time I used quarter tones was in a film called *Catch My Soul* [dir. Patrick McGoohan, 1974], and I most definitely used quarter tones in *To the Devil a Daughter*—they're quite up front. In *To the Devil a Daughter* I do use what we call those little *ritornelli*, those repetition signs that you put in to create a kind of aleatoric feeling. My teacher Lutosławski used them too. I used those in the score, but I did not use spacial notation. I actually conducted *To the Devil a Daughter* because Philip wanted me to do it.

I found that the use of triads would be banal. I tried to go out into some really way-out place with this film score. The main thing in the music for *To the Devil a Daughter* is that I needed a sound structure. I simply took four semitones arranged with only the intervals of a major second or a semitone, but never making a chromatic scale. The simple one would be C, D, C-sharp, B and all of its possible inversions and so on, and that transposed three times will give you twelve pitches. And that, of course, is what happens in the B.A.C.H. motif of the Webern String Quartet. Those are B-flat, A, C, B-natural.[5] That does have the minor third in it—it has to, to make the B.A.C.H.—but I did it just making it the smallest intervals. This is the best way to avoid consonance. So the idea was to avoid consonance at all costs. It takes time to control, but there is not a vertical sound in there that is going to be consonant. All of a sudden, by controlling it that way, you come up with a sound that Hammer didn't have. You've got a completely controlled musical continuity, and any kind of linear things that happen are, instead of the Schoenberg concept of as many skips as possible, hardly any! Almost what we call conjunct motion.

Obviously we're talking about clusters. There are not many times when one hears any single instruments, so it's a very thick, fat texture. The idea of the choir was always there. We recorded it overdubbed. The people we had were amazing. They could come in on a quarter-tone cluster *in tune*! This is only possible with absolutely the super-best musicians. Not as in rock and roll, when for the first time in history dilettantes often run the show. We're talking about super-pros! In order to have the full symphonic sound which the number of men given would never have permitted, I used two different groups on two different sessions, one which used four horns, four trumpets, three trombones and a tuba, percussion, and strings; and the second group basically a Mozart orchestra, consisting of two flutes, two oboes, two clarinets, alto sax, and two bassoons, with the normal doublings, percussion and strings. So that was the idea.

We used these repetitions, they have little phrases and come in at different times in different lengths. It didn't bother anybody. I don't think we even had to rehearse it. We just asked, "Can you do it? Do you guys understand it?" And they said, "Oh yes, no problem." I also used those other signs for the world's highest notes, incessant *glissandi*, and the harmonic language hardly ever uses widespread harmonies. The harmonies are very thick. I also used the technique of writing a lot of notes in a line, and they keep getting closer and closer together. It means that the players should, at will, constantly get faster or slower. That's used a lot. If there are any sonorities, there are almost always twelve notes. So it was thick. I did go from time to time into lighter textures: the old rule of contrasts.

But the scoring was so clear that we were able to record it without any mistakes in record time.[6]

Christopher Wicking's radical reworking of Wheatley's *To the Devil a Daughter* concerns the attempts of Father Michael Raynor (played by Christopher Lee) to create an avatar of the demon Astaroth. He baptizes a baby girl, called Catherine (played by Nastassja Kinski) in the blood of her dead mother. Afterwards, he impregnates another woman while possessed by the spirit of Astaroth. The avatar of Astaroth is then born by ripping its way out of the woman's womb. The demon creature is subsequently killed and its blood used to re-baptize Catherine, who will become Astaroth in human form.

At first uncertain as to whether he should accept the job of composing music for such a disturbing film, Glass finally overcame his doubts by interpreting the film's conclusion as a representation of the triumph of good over evil. (Richard Widmark, who plays the hero, John Verney, was famous for playing "bad guys" in many of his previous films, but in this story he's very much on the side of the angels.)

Like other Hammer films that wished to differentiate themselves from the

Gothic horror tradition for which the company had been so well known, *To the Devil a Daughter* begins with no music. Instead, a bell tolls in time with each main title card (two bells for the actual main title, and two bells for longer cast listings that are grouped together on a single card). This not only establishes the ecclesiastical atmosphere of the first scene but also creates the same ambivalent mood that we witnessed in the opening of *The Nanny*. The audience is

Would this go with Wellingtons? Nastassja Kinski in *To the Devil a Daughter* (dir. Peter Sykes, 1976).

therefore not quite sure what to expect. Things become clearer when Derek Francis' Bishop pronounces the word *"excommunicatus,"* for this is exactly what is happening: the excommunication of Christopher Lee's Father Michael Raynor for a crime we can only guess at this stage. Glass' first music cue doesn't start until the Bishop closes the book from which he has been reading the excommunication ritual and the camera rises up over the figure of Christ behind the altar of the church. Here, Glass demonstrates a technique he uses throughout the film, for the purposes of unity and organization, which reacts to cuts and changing camera angles with contrasts of textures. One could argue that such a technique is related to Schoenberg's idea of *Klangfarbenmelodie*, wherein the function of traditional melody is replaced by the effect of filtering the pitches of a single chord through contrasting orchestral timbres. (One of Schoenberg's most notable examples of the technique is the appropriately named "*Farben*" ["Colors"] in his *Five Pieces for Orchestra*, Op. 16. [1909, revised 1949].) Though not limiting himself to the notes of a single chord, as Schoenberg suggested, Glass nonetheless relies on tone color (and contrasting rates of pitch agitation), rather than traditional melody, to articulate the structure of the film. The score is far from an arbitrary overlay of broad "moods," but is actually related very specifically to the structure of the editing. So, as the book from which the Bishop has been reading the excommunication ritual is closed, we hear rumblings in the lower strings; as the camera starts to rise up over the crucifix the choir is introduced, along with a highly symbolic tubular bell, and the choir grows louder as the camera rises up to Christ's head. The choir is then removed for the subsequent shot of Christopher Lee sitting beneath the left arm of the crucifix, and another change of texture follows with the wide angle shot of the priests leaving Lee alone at the altar. For the close-up of Christ's head, the bell returns, and the scene's final close-up of Lee is accompanied by much higher string activity, which grows quieter as we fade out to the boat crossing the lake in the next scene, set in Germany.

By emphasizing the editing in this way, Glass' score might be said to go against one of the cardinal rules of classic Hollywood tradition that required film music to create what Claudia Gorbman has called "formal and rhythmic continuity" by means of what she terms music's "spatiotemporal connective tissue." In this traditional aesthetic, "Music," Gorbman explains, "smooths discontinuities of editing within scenes and sequences. The discontinuity of a cheat cut or a temporal ellipse will be slightly less jarring or noticeable because of music, this flexible and pleasurable auditory substance (this 'cohesive') in the background. As an auditory continuity it seems to mitigate visual, spatial, or temporal discontinuity."[7] The master of the classical approach identified by Gorbman here was Max Steiner, the composer who has been dubbed "the father of film music" during the Golden Age of Hollywood, and whom, incidentally, Glass had met during the recording of his first score for a film in Hollywood.

In one way, Steiner's approach wasn't so different from Glass.' As Gorbman puts it, Steiner's music for a transition between scenes in *The Big Sleep* (dir. Howard Hawks, 1946) "has no particularly musical form of its own, since it must obey the rhythm of the editing and the rapid change of locations it is illustrating and connoting [...] but it is still one uncut piece of music, a continuous substance that compensates for the spatiotemporal discontinuities—necessary for narrative coherence, efficiently getting Marlowe from one place to another."[8] In general terms, this could well be a description of Glass' approach, but Steiner's ultimate aim was to use music to disguise the editing process. Glass, however, uses music to emphasize it. More significantly, as Gorbman also points out, in *King Kong* Steiner breaks up continuity in the scene in which Ann (Fay Wray) and Jack (Bruce Cabot) embrace on the deck of the ship that has taken them to Skull Island in search of the giant gorilla. Because, for Steiner, strings signified the presence of women, and therefore "romance," he felt it inappropriate to continue to use them in prosaic "male" environments. The love scene is interrupted by several cuts to the captain on the bridge of the ship, and Steiner consequently breaks up the distinctly Viennese waltz he uses to accompany the love scene so that the "male" dialogue on the bridge isn't contaminated, so to speak, by romantic strings.[9] This, however, is very much an exception that proves Steiner's general rule. By contrast to that general rule, it is not only Glass' use of a consistently atonal language, but also his continual emphasis of the "jarring" effect of the editing that makes a significant contribution to what Jonathan Rigby describes as the film's overall "cerebral disquiet." This approach is initiated right at the start of the film with the tolling bell during the main titles. While the music itself may seem to lack definite rhythmic patterns, we soon realize, if only instinctively at first, that the music's most significant rhythms are those that are created by contrasts of timbre, which respond to the narrative structure of the film.

There are also more straightforward responses to the action. When, for example, Nastassja Kinski's Catherine prepares to go to bed in John Verney's flat towards the middle of the film (just before her nightmare), she rests her head in her hands. Glass reflects this action with a descending string *glissando*. Though the musical style is modern, this is, in effect, an example of old-fashioned, Steineresque "mickey-mousing." Glass has a rather low opinion of mickey-mousing, but nonetheless believes that it can be redeemed if the style of music used is atonal. There are several other examples of such atonal mickey-mousing. During the juxtaposition of two different locations (one concerning Margaret, played by Isabella Telezynska, who is the woman who is to give birth to the avatar of Astaroth; and the other concerning Catherine, who is having her nightmare back in John Verney's flat), Glass not only emphasizes the cutting with subtle changes of timbre, but also mickey-mouses a camera zoom into Margaret's swelling belly with a *sforzando* cluster chord for strings. When Lee's Father Michael ignites a small pile of herbs on a plate decorated with an image of the Goat of Mendes, Glass emphasizes the flames with agitated string patterns. Similarly, when Margaret dies, Glass provides quiet, rhythmically unpredictable string chords to imitate her exhausted final breaths. Such a device could be traced back to the opening bars of Richard Strauss' tone poem *Tod und Verklärung* (1889), which represent the dying breaths of the Artist who is the subject of that programmatic work. Though the harmonic language used by Glass is far more advanced than Strauss', the musico-dramatic allusion is indeed the same.

There now follows the scene in which Father Michael launches a psychic attack on Catherine's father, Henry Beddows (played by Denholm Elliot). Father Michael wraps a rope around the telephone receiver, and Beddows is persuaded to believe that a snake is writhing around his own handset. For this, Glass provides a sustained atonal cluster that seems to be, but is not, electronically generated.

"I was terribly worried about electronics coming in and taking our orchestras away," said Glass, "and so my idea was to have fun and write a score with absolutely no electronics."[10]

Just as Glass creates an overall rhythm by means of contrasting timbres, he also replaces the Wagnerian practice of creating *leitmotifs* out of melodic ideas with *leitmotifs* of timbre. For example, a percussion effect is associated with Henry Beddows. We hear it first while Father Michael baptizes the infant Catherine in the blood of her dead mother, Isabella. Beddows interrupts this ceremony, but before he is discovered, we observe him watching the proceedings from behind a curtain. Glass's percussion effect accompanies the close-ups of Beddows' face, and it returns later in the film when Anthony Valentine's David is possessed by Beddows personality just before he takes hold of the pact that will cause him to burst into flames. David repeats the words that Beddows first spoke to him in the art gallery right at the beginning of the film ("Do you have any other pictures?"), and the percussion effect here helps us understand what has happened: that David has indeed "become" Beddows. Glass's use of *leitmotif* is nothing novel in itself, but the use of a *leitmotif* of timbre rather than one of melody is certainly evidence of a less orthodox approach.

The scene in which Catherine is baptized in her mother's own blood takes place in one of the film's several flashback sequences. When this flashback ends, naturalistic sound effects are treated in a musical fashion to help us return to "present" time. "Live in dread, Henry Beddows," Father Michael threatens. "Mend your ways." We then hear a police siren, but one that has been subjected to a great deal of reverberation, which consequently confuses our perception of what it is. As the scene dissolves back to 1970s London, in which the main action of the film is set, the reverberation is gradually removed and we recognize the true identity of the sound. Normality is restored to us, so to speak. This was the work of sound mixer Dennis Whitlock, but the effect has a musical as well as purely naturalistic function, and is, of course, an example of what we would now call "sound design."

When Father Michael later attempts to summon Catherine back to his temple, Glass again contrasts different timbres to emphasize cutting between different locations. A flurry of string *glissandi* accompanies the shots of Catherine pulling at her fingers, to suggest that Father Michael's invocation is taking effect. Glass initially restricts the scenes with Catherine to strings, but when we cut back to Father Michael at work on his telepathic summons, wind and percussion join in to add resonance and reflect the acoustic space of the hall in which the invocation is being worked. When Catherine leaves Verney's flat, the choir returns, and the eventual climax is abruptly interrupted as Verney, having caught up with Catherine, snatches the amulet of Astaroth that hangs around her neck.

Another flashback occurs a little later, in which the avatar of Astaroth is conceived, and this is where Tristan Fry was asked to create another percussion effect:

> It was nearly Christmas, and before we started recording, the percussionists were playing carols on slide-whistles. There was an orgy scene, which was pretty disgusting; so at the appropriate moment I signalled Tristan Fry to play a *glissando* on the slide-whistle, along with the strings. Again, this was mickey-mousing, but you can do that when the textures are so complex. I put loads of footnotes in the score, which reading after years I found ridiculous. There's one which says, "Old Franz Liszt used this harmonic device before Schoenberg was born!" I realize that there is a kind of tongue-in-cheek element in the score, sending up contemporary music. I was having fun with these avant-garde guys, because here they were doing this sort of stuff so seriously for small audiences, and this music would be heard 'round the world. Those things were happening at the time. I was living there right in the middle of all that. I was at the first performance of Penderecki's *Threni* in Poland, where half the audience was not in agreement. Those things were happening.[11]

For Catherine's murder of Anna Fountain (played by Honor Blackman), high-pitched string sounds accompany Catherine opening her eyes, and Glass articulates the action by altering their pitch. As Catherine sits up, the pitch rises. For the actual stabbing of Anna in the neck with the pointed end of a metal comb, the choir returns. Contrasting string pitches continue to articulate the shots of Catherine running away, each cut emphasized by different pitch groups.

The solo voice that is introduced at the end of the film is reminiscent (though not in melodic style) of James Bernard's use of a solo voice in *The Gorgon* (dir. Terence Fisher, 1964). Coincidentally, *To the Devil a Daughter* features the actor Michael Goodcliffe, who also appeared in *The Gorgon*, alongside Christopher Lee.

There was only one place where Philip suggested something. This was for a disgusting scene with Nastassja Kinski and a small reddish creature [the avatar of Astaroth]. Philip said, "I think we should have a voice." That was a good idea! So we called in a star singer whom we overdubbed later.[12]

The final example of Glass's use of timbre and pitch to suggest contrasting spaces and locations occurs at the end of the film when Father Michael confronts Verney from inside a circle of blood in the devil worshippers' temple (actually the Dashwood Memorial near High Wycombe in Buckinghamshire). After a highly cacophonous music cue, during which Verney kills Father Michael and rescues Catherine, the end titles roll, and the score ends on a unison note in the choir and orchestra, which brings with it an appropriate sense of finality and resolution. The finality of the drama itself is ambivalent, however, as it is implied that Catherine has already "become" Astaroth when two drops of the demon's blood dripped onto her forehead before Verney interrupted the ceremony. She now wipes these away and smiles, equally ambivalently, up at Verney as he carries her away.

Hammer's final horror film and most experimental film score thus comes to an end. It seems fitting that the company's last feature film in a genre that had brought so many audiences into contact with so many avant-garde techniques should have a score that was so very modern in its sound and overall approach. Though Glass himself complained, with good reason, that the popular equation of avant-garde techniques with "horror" films was "back to front," his score for *To the Devil a Daughter* certainly nurtured that connection in the minds of popular audiences. While adventurously encouraging his composer to write in such an advanced style, Philip Martell could once more be said to have simultaneously (though unintentionally) undermined the aspirations of avant-garde composers who had hoped to liberate contemporary musical style from traditional significations. Whereas Penderecki was equally happy to use his cluster style for a piece about Hiroshima and for a setting of the St. Luke Passion, in the minds of cinema audiences such a style was more suitable for horror and science fiction. Indeed, Penderecki's music has featured in two very high-profile horror films: William Friedkin's *The Exorcist*, released in 1973, and Stanley Kubrick's *The Shining* in 1980.

"Roy Skeggs wanted the manuscript of *To the Devil a Daughter*," Glass explained. "So Penelope Margaret, who became my wife, tied it up with a beautiful pink ribbon!"[13] And with that, Hammer films also wrapped up its thirty-year history of horror films; but its adventurous patronage of contemporary music wasn't over yet. A few years later, Hammer would reemerge as a television production company, for which other contemporary composers would be equally in demand.

Notes

1. Richard Klemensen (ed.), *Little Shoppe of Horrors*, vol. 12, 1994, p. 69. Christopher Lee is quoted as saying that Wheatley was "very unhappy with it ... because he felt the sexual perverseness of it was gratuitous. He wasn't angry with me, but he was very disappointed in the movie."
2. Jonathan Rigby, *Christopher Lee — The Authorised Screen History* (Richmond: Reynolds and Hearn, 2001), p. 168.
3. Paul Glass, in conversation with the author, November 20, 2006.
4. Marjorie Bilbow, *The Facts About a Feature Film* (London: André Deutsch, 1978), p. 43.
5. In German, B-natural is referred to as "H."
6. Paul Glass (Note 2).
7. Claudia Gorbman, *Unheard Melodies* (London: British Film Institute, 1987), p. 89.
8. Claudia Gorbman, *Unheard Melodies* (Note 7), p. 90.
9. Ibid., p. 80.
10. Paul Glass (Note 2).
11. Ibid., Glass here refers to Penderecki's *Threnody to the Victims of Hiroshima* (1960).
12. Ibid.
13. Ibid.

Eleven

Television Terror

John McCabe, Paul Patterson and David Bedford

When Hammer rose from the grave as a television concern in the 1980s, a group of contemporary composers lent their support to the company's two TV series, *Hammer House of Horror* and *Hammer House of Mystery and Suspense*. Hammer's house style is pervasive throughout these episodes in their very English locations and the many familiar British actors who feature in them, although the second series required American stars to meet the demands of the American backer, Twentieth Century–Fox. Many of the British actors had been involved in the heyday of Hammer, and they were joined by old crew members, as well as established Hammer composers such as James Bernard and Leonard Salzedo. The latter had taken over from Bernard for the music of *The Revenge of Frankenstein* (dir. Terence Fisher, 1958), and his score for "The Silent Scream," an episode from the first television series, follows the same dramatically effective but musically fairly conventional approach of his Frankenstein score. Bernard's score for "The House That Bled to Death" is also instantly recognizable. In one way, this was appropriate, for despite their then-contemporary settings, many of the episodes from these series operated within a traditionally Gothic framework. "The Silent Scream," for example, is a typically Gothic plot of entrapment. (An ex-concentration camp officer [played by Peter Cushing] traps an ex-convict [Brian Cox] as part of an experiment to use fear of electrocution as a way of making conventional prisons obsolete.) The main title sequence that introduces all the episodes of the first series features shots of mist-shrouded battlements and a mysterious, shadowy figure at a candlelit castle window, and is designed to remind the audience of Hammer's past reputation and achievements, though none of the stories had period settings. To reflect this duality of past achievements and contemporaneity, the popular music idiom of the title music, composed by Roger Webb (drums, electric guitar, etc.), is combined with traditional symphonic elements. The melody, however, avoids obvious tritones and overt discords, and is based on scales and perfect fifths. The result is atmospheric but rather blander than the more full-blooded musical style of Hammer's earlier films. As a piece of Gothic pop it made sense to release the theme as a seven-inch single at the time of the series' original broadcast.

Salzedo and Bernard were only two of several Hammer composers who were brought back to the fold for these T.V. episodes. Paul Glass also contributed a score, for one of the episodes of the second series called "The Late Nancy Irving." In this, a golf star with a rare blood type (played by Christina Raines) is kidnapped by Marius Goring's wealthy businessman who shares her blood group but also suffers from an equally rare form of anaemia. In a novel variation on a vampire story, the businessman has her blood transfused into him to keep his degenerative disease under control. Glass' score for this episode was modestly scored for one flute (doubling with alto flute), one clarinet (doubling with bass clarinet), one trumpet, two horns, percussion, seven violins, seven violas, three cellos and two basses. At certain points, however, it manages to sound as though scored for larger forces, and it often sounds rather more conventional than the consistently contemporary *To the Devil a Daughter*, including traditional Romantic elements for the scenes featuring the golfer and her boyfriend (played by Simon Williams). Also, Marius Goring's businessman has sent one of his employees to stalk Nancy Irving, and whenever we see the stalker in his car, Glass provides conventionally "sinister" music on the bass clarinet (played by Jack Brymer), sometimes accompanied with *col legno* string effects. For the various hallucination and dream sequences, however, Glass returns to the more atonal string writing of *To the Devil a Daughter*. He also makes a point of highlighting solo wind timbres (clarinet and flute in particular), which help create the atmosphere of desolation and abandonment experienced by Nancy Irving. Certain cues (and they are mostly all very short) even echo the styles of Berg and Shostakovitch. The use of a solo violin when Nancy Irving wakes up in the clinic after her abduction and looks at the view through her bedroom window is briefly reminiscent of passages in Berg's Violin Concerto (Glass had been experimenting with diatonic elements in tone rows in his concert music around this time); while the slow and rather lonely solo trumpet that we hear when the businessman's car draws up outside his mansion one night has something of the trumpet writing in Shostakovitch's first Piano Concerto about it. When Nancy Irving eventually escapes her hospital bedroom, she discovers that she has not been in a hospital at all. The room has been made to look as though it is part of a hospital but is, in fact, part of the businessman's luxurious mansion. As she makes her way into his study, Glass nicely treats the various bleeps and whirrings from a computer system as part of his writing for xylophone.

Philip Martell was well aware that, despite their basic Gothic structure, these contemporary horror films also needed fresh ideas from the musical department:

I've brought a lot of new people into the film business. I brought in John McCabe — gave him his first picture. He wrote a brilliant piano concerto — fantastic — and he gave me a ticket to go and hear it. Roy Skeggs, the producer, heard this conversation, and later on some time said to me, "You know, I'd like to go and hear that piano concerto." He didn't know what a concerto is, but that doesn't matter. So I phoned up John and asked for another ticket and he gave it to me, and I said to Roy, "I've got you a ticket. I'll go on my own and I'll meet you in the foyer of the Festival Hall." He never turned up. This has happened before.

When we came to do that last two TV series, I decided that the films were so way-out that they needed avant-garde composers, with their weird, strange harmonic non-structures. I thought Hammer will go mad; but I think that if I'd said, "That was written by Beethoven," they would have believed me.

Hammer films have changed. They're still horror films, but they've changed. They have a different feeling. They're much more contemporary in feeling, so you've got to go along with the period. It wasn't until I saw the sort of treatment that the horrors were getting that I realized that we've got to come into atonal music; and it's absolutely crucial unless you want to color the pictures with the nineteenth century. The only reason we don't use that kind of music for a love scene is because we're not prepared to accept it yet, that's all. I can't imagine putting a theme like [James Bernard's] *She* into a contemporary Hammer film. It's the wrong harmonic construction. It's the wrong emotional interpretation. For what it is it was exceedingly brilliant, but even I, who belong to the past generation, want to hear new music, new approaches, new sounds. I want mental stimulation to give me a direction. Jimmy [Bernard] had a pattern that he would never deviate from. I'm very fond of Jimmy, but he couldn't possibly have done an avant-garde score. It's not his world. Now, I don't think it's very good for him *not* to try, but he doesn't try. I think he should! I'm older than Jimmy, and yet I realize I've got to find out what's going on. The first time I heard Messiaen, I went out and bought some records of his and listened to them and finally got myself into a mood when I could accept them, because prior to that I would have said, "Oh no, that's not film music," but it is film music. Anything is film music if it lives with the picture, if it helps the picture.[1]

John McCabe was born in 1939 and had written thirteen juvenile symphonies by the time he was eleven years old. His approach to composition is generally an eclectic one, largely independent of British and Continental trends. His interest in film prefigured his actual experience of film composition, as he demonstrated in 1971 with his Second Symphony, which was in part inspired by Sam Peckinpah's film *The Wild Bunch* (1969). McCabe's association with Hammer began with his score for the psychological shocker *Fear in the Night* (dir. Jimmy Sangster, 1972). Richard Rodney Bennett had originally been asked to score this film but wasn't available at the time, and so recommended McCabe.

McCabe worked closely with Philip Martell, who would regularly come to his house to hear McCabe play through what he'd written and discuss details of orchestration. McCabe fondly recalls the stimulating discussions about music in general that they enjoyed, and he was delighted to have the opportunity to invite Martell to be his guest at the London Philharmonic Orchestra's premiere of his Concerto for Orchestra, and introduce him to the conductor Sir Georg Solti, whom Martell revered.

For *Fear in the Night*, McCabe composed a hauntingly lyrical melody that perfectly complemented the sense of lonely melancholy experienced by the heroine (played by Judy Geeson) as she wanders through the deserted school in which she finds herself half way through the film. The more acerbic music for the pursuit scenes is highly effective but not particularly different from the approach of Bernard and Robinson, and it certainly never ventures into more extreme harmonic territory. McCabe recalled how the director, Jimmy Sangster, thought this was the most Romantic music to have graced the soundtrack of any Hammer film. Said McCabe:

> For *Fear*, we had I think a 28-piece band. The larger ensemble didn't affect the way we worked, though, except that at a few moments it enabled one to create more elaborate textures. I enjoyed the whole process very much — the discipline of working to such a tight time-frame is a valuable one for honing one's technique. I didn't find I was trying out things for use in concert music later on, which I know some composers have done — I just wrote what seemed to me appropriate for the scenes concerned. It is possible that the disciplines, and the stylistic range, I sometimes needed to use helped me when I came to write full-length ballets later on, and gave me a technical edge I mightn't have had (in terms of being aware of time and durations, for instance).[2]

John McCabe, 2006 (photograph by Peter Thompson, courtesy Novello & Co. Ltd.).

In *Fear in the Night*, Geeson's character is terrorized into killing Peter Cushing's apparently sinister Headmaster (he is actually a red herring), so that Ralph Bates (playing Geeson's husband)

Ralph Bates double-crossing Judy Geeson in *Fear in the Night* (dir. Jimmy Sangster, 1972).

and Joan Collins (playing Cushing's wife) can get their hands on the Headmaster's money. In many ways, the film was the same kind of modern-dress suspense story that Hammer would develop in its television productions. It's appropriate, therefore, that McCabe should have been asked to score episodes for both *The Hammer House of Horror* and *Hammer House of Mystery and Suspense*. Two episodes from the first series, "The Thirteenth Reunion" and "Guardian of the Abyss," are particularly interesting. The latter story was really a reworking of Hammer's two Dennis Wheatley black magic adaptations, in which an occult organization attempts to incarnate the demon Choronzon (a demon that real-life occultist Aleister Crowley claimed to have actually conjured up himself).[3] Not only does "Guardian of the Abyss" feature Rosalyn Landor, who had played the little girl Peggy in *The Devil Rides Out*, but also John Carson as Randolph, who plays a modern day version of Charles Gray's black magician, Mocata. At one stage in "Guardian of the Abyss" a situation from *The Devil Rides Out* (in which Mocata uses hypnosis to bring back the girl Tanith) is reprised. Similarly, Rosalyn Landor's character in "Guardian of the Abyss" also attacks an antique dealer, played by Barbara Ewing, just as

Nastassja Kinski's Catherine had attacked (and actually murdered) Honor Blackman's character, Anna Fountain, in *To the Devil a Daughter*.

McCabe's score for "Guardian of the Abyss" is also somewhere in between James Bernard's for *The Devil Rides Out* and Paul Glass' for *To the Devil a Daughter*. It is structured around six "wildtracks" (cues that are recorded separately and can be used on their own or superimposed over the orchestral score):

> The use of wildtracks in *Guardian* was Phil's idea. Mostly he would suggest one or two instruments (always the same ones: bass clarinet or bass flute for menace, e.g.) and leave me to my own devices once we'd decided what to do; though, as I say, he did come and hear the music through at home. He didn't make many alterations, though. He was quite reluctant to have a harpsichord in one score (*13th Reunion*, if I recall), and I had to work hard to persuade him (I wasn't going to give way, though).
>
> I find the level of invention in film and TV music very poor at the moment. The major composers derive their ideas by imitating much better composers, and not doing it so well, while the producers and directors very often seem to have no idea of the aptness of a particular style for the film. A rock score is not always an ironic post-modern joke — it's very often just cultural laziness, it seems to me.
>
> I do remember Phil saying to me, "Remember, everybody in the film business knows about their own job plus music," and I did get some woeful advice from one or two people about what to write (film editors, for instance) — which I ignored. My disenchantment with Hammer came from the fact that though the TV series' shooting schedule got later and later in each series, the music recording dates could never be postponed, so on two (maybe three) occasions I ended up writing 20 minutes of music in two days. You can't do good work in those circumstances, and I simply said, "No more." But it was a good time, nonetheless.[4]

Wildtrack one, for synthesizer, is based on superimposed consecutive fifths and tritones. Wildtrack two combines the synthesizer and a vocal chant based on similar material for choir. Wildtrack three presents the chant for choir alone. Wildtrack four is a chord for the organ. Wildtrack five is for alto flute, vibraphone, marimba and divided strings, representing the swirling mist we see in the scrying glass that is central to the story; and wildtrack six is a small, high pitched-note cluster of D-sharp, E-natural and F-natural, which represents the scrying glass itself.

McCabe also uses a variety of other techniques. For example, in 4M1, when Randolph first looks into the scrying glass, McCabe asks for a low-pitched *glissandi* on piano, which come with the explanatory footnote, "Quick glissandi (both hands) with fingers on strings bottom 2 octaves; no rhythm, continuous sound, brush strings with fingers always upwards, overlapping." In 3M1, during the scene in which Michael (played by Ray Lonnen) reads about the Choronzon ritual, McCabe is also able to make strings resemble electronically generated sound, with note clusters played by divided muted strings, *sul ponticello*. In

Eleven: Television (McCabe, Patterson and Bedford) 195

3M2, when Alison tries to throw the scrying glass away, McCabe also calls for cluster chords in the piano ("Cluster over bottom 2 octaves played with flat of hand on strings [i.e. inside piano]").

McCabe also uses more traditional material. For example, in 2M1, when Alison runs away from the Choronzon Society, McCabe, a pianist himself, places the piano center-stage in a cue that would not be out of place in the Piano

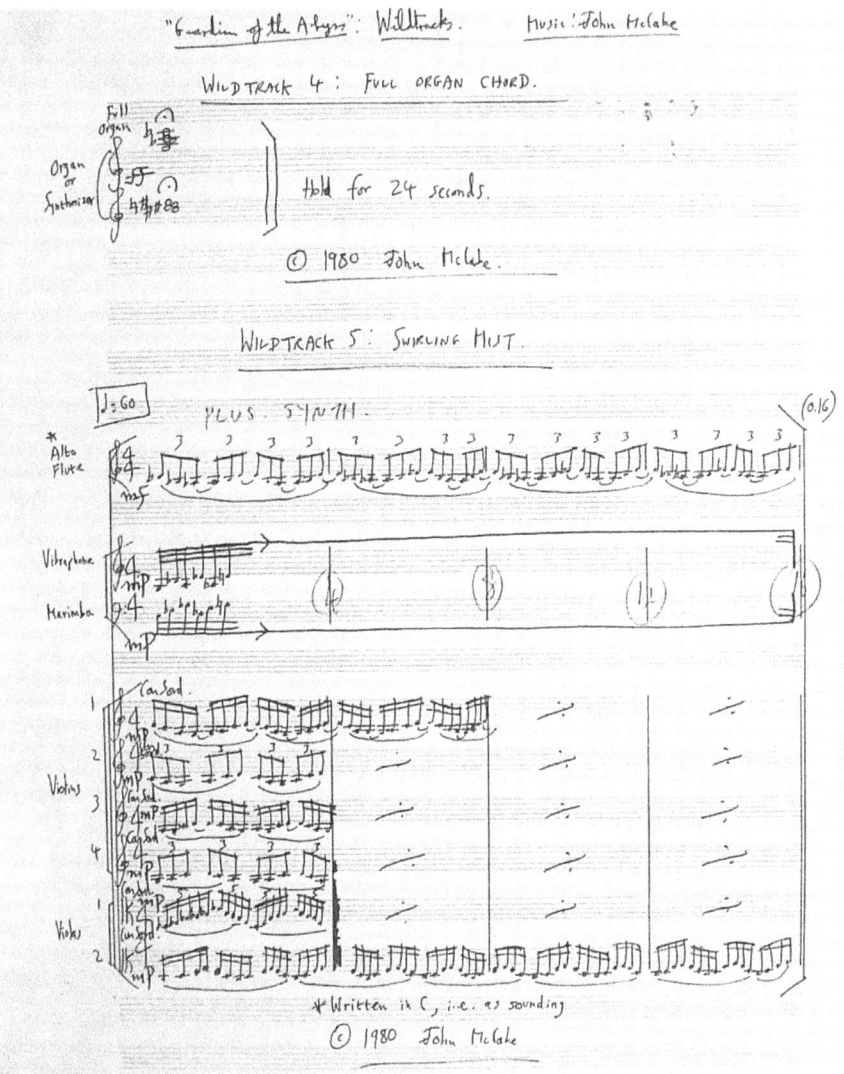

John McCabe's original manuscript for two of the wildtracks in his score for "Guardian of the Abyss" (1980) (photograph by author, courtesy John McCabe).

Concerto Martell so much admired. It features a brisk *ostinato* in the instrument's low register, which is punctuated with timpani and tam-tams. At other times, McCabe combines wildtracks with orchestral sections. In 2M2, for example, when Michael is driving his car and comes under the influence of the scrying glass beside him, wildtrack six is combined with fragments for alto flute (featuring another "modern" and unnerving fourth).

The centerpiece of the score is 4M3, for the ritual initiated by Randolph, during which Michael and Alison are brought together by means of psychic suggestion and the symbolic voodoo effigies Randolph has made of them. (This is something with which actor John Carson would have been familiar from his role as voodoo-master Squire Hamilton in Hammer's *Plague of the Zombies*.) 4M3 begins with low-pitched, dissonant strings playing harmonics beneath wildtracks one and six. The wildtracks continue throughout the cue, but as the love scene between Alison and Michael gets under way, McCabe's style becomes rather more traditional, and is reminiscent of the early twentieth-century composer John Ireland. The harmonies here (consecutive seventh chords and chords emphasizing major seconds) indeed resemble Ireland's "The Palm and the May" from his piano collection *Green Ways* (1938).

When Alison, under Randolph's malign influence, stabs Michael (or thinks she is stabbing him: Michael actually escapes), McCabe resorts to more "modern" consecutive fourths for the attack.

Seventh chords return during the scene in which Randolph hypnotizes Michael in an attempt to make him release Alison. He asks for water, bread and salt (an established occult means of gaining influence over others), and when Randolph tilts his head in close-up, McCabe instructs these seventh chords to move down a tone through a *glissando*, to highly disorienting effect.

Note clusters also move through *glissandi* in 6M1, the section that accompanies the final ritual to raise Choronzon, and here the textures and sonorities resemble a Pendereckian model, with the added element of McCabe's wildtracks.

McCabe's score for "The Thirteenth Reunion" is less adventurous than "Guardian of the Abyss." The story, horrific but not supernatural, concerns the survivors of a plane crash who celebrate their deliverance with regular reunions. A dinner party is arranged at which they consume a meal of human flesh, having acquired a taste for it after the crash. Journalist Ruth (played by Julia Foster) accompanies Gerrard Kelly's Andrew into a vault to find out what has happened to the body of the man she met and fell in love with at a rather sinister clinic that plays host to an organization devoted to weight-loss. The most interesting modernistic element in McCabe's score for this story is his use of extended *ostinati*, which are somewhat minimalist in style. In 1984, four years after the first transmission of *The Hammer House of Horror*, Philip Glass' popular minimalist opera *Akhnaten* received its world premiere; and while McCabe's music here is not formally minimalistic, it is interesting to place his *ostinati* patterns in the context of the time in which they were written.

McCabe also makes effective use of cluster chords, particularly when Ruth later observes the surgeon Jack Rothwell (played by Kevin Stoney) removing a corpse from a hook (the corpse is to be the main course of that night's reunion dinner); and a minimalist *ostinato* pattern on the violins returns under a motif consisting of E-flat, D-natural, and C-natural, which resembles the opening notes of the ever-useful *Dies Irae* chant. The *ostinato* consists of a rising quaver pattern of F-sharp, A-natural, B-natural, C-natural and then down to G-natural, accompanied by a descending quaver pattern of F-natural, D-natural, C-sharp, B-flat, and A-natural.

Ruth follows Rothwell to the mansion at which the reunion is to take place and enters an elaborate dining room, set for a banquet. As she steps inside, McCabe insistently repeats a single chord (built on C-natural, with, over it, E-flat, G-flat, B-natural and F-natural) in which the tritone between C-natural and G-flat clashes with the tritone between B-natural and F-natural, to particularly disturbing effect.

Philip Martell also brought in David Bedford for three of the episodes of *Hammer House of Mystery and Suspense.* Bedford was born in 1937 and came from a musical family (his grandmother was Victorian composer Liza Lehmann, famous for her various song cycles, such as her setting of verses by Omar Khayyam, called *In a Persian Garden*). A student of Lennox Berkeley at the Royal Academy of Music, and of Luigi Nono in Venice, he also spent a year at RAI Electronic Music Studio in Milan in 1962. Bedford has always taken a diverse approach to composition, having worked with and been commissioned by such diverse musicians and organizations as Elvis Costello, Mike Oldfield, the Royal Philharmonic Orchestra, Sir Peter Pears, the Aldeburgh Festival, the Cheltenham Festival and the BBC. His scores for Hammer's T.V. series include the episodes

David Bedford in 2007 (courtesy David Bedford).

"Child's Play," "Mark of the Devil" (both directed by Val Guest) and "The Corvini Inheritance" (dir. Gabrielle Beaumont).

"Child's Play" is set in the future, in an extremely advanced, very realistic doll house, though we don't know this until the dénouement in which the characters are revealed to be diminutive automatons rather than human beings. We also learn that the house has been inappropriately stored in the heating shaft of a real, full-sized house in the future, hence trapping its inhabitants behind what to them seems a mysterious and impenetrable grey shield. Unable to escape the increasing heat, as the doors and windows are all blocked by the walls of the heating shaft, the story concerns the plight and growing desperation of the automatons. The most novel aspects of Bedford's score here are those sections that rely solely on percussion effects: timpani *glissandi*, cymbals and tam-tams; but Bedford alternates these sections with more conventional, rather Romantic string writing. The string writing does become more unusual from time to time, with string *glissandi* during the scene in which the automaton Michael (played by Nicholas Clay) tries to break out of the house by causing an explosion. But much more musically interesting is Bedford's score for "The Mark of the Devil," in which Dirk Benedict plays a man who murders an oriental tattooist for his money, only to find that a hideous tattoo subsequently begins to cover his entire body, ruining his marriage and eventually leading him to his death. Again, the score begins with percussion, but this is actually drawn from an unused track from James Bernard's score for *She*, featuring native drumming and a vocal chant. It is appropriately used to cover the opening shots of an African black magic ritual, presided over by the oriental tattooist (played by Burt Kwouk). Bedford provides fairly standard suspense music for the scene in which Benedict steals the money, but during the subsequent fight scene Bedford indulges in more string *glissandi*, along with an odd effect to complement an African fetish that swings in sinister fashion as Benedict brushes past it. (String *glissandi* prove to be the characteristic timbre of this episode, just as a harpsichord and synthesized *ostinato* characterize much of his less interesting music for "The Corvini Inheritance.") Bedford later mixes his string *glissandi* with Bernard's *She* chant during Benedict's flashback of the murder, and later distorts them electronically for the final scene in which Benedict is killed by Burt Kwouk's vengeful ghost. Another interesting timbre here is the cimbalom, used once more for its troubling, alien quality, and therefore most appropriate for the scenes in which we learn that the tattoo is growing ever larger.

Perhaps the most interesting music in Hammer's two T.V. series was composed by Paul Patterson, who was born in 1947 and later became a student at the Royal Academy of Music in 1964, and later a pupil of both Elisabeth Lutyens and Richard Rodney Bennett. He was introduced to Bennett when Bennett was one of the judges of the South West Arts Competition at which Patterson's Wind Quintet, Op. 2 won first prize. A Trumpet Concerto and Horn Concerto followed, along with an organ piece, *Visions*, Op. 9, written especially for Malcolm Williamson. Patterson returned to wind instruments for his *Comedy*, Op. 14, which employed jazz idioms; while his *Kyrie*, Op. 13, went on to explore aleatoric devices. Penderecki and Lutosławski also exerted an important influence on his style, which is made particularly manifest in the Op. 34 Clarinet Concerto; *Timepiece*, Op. 16; and *Cracowian Counterpoint*, Op. 38.

Patterson's *Requiem*, Op. 19, was composed to commemorate the assassination of John F. Kennedy, and includes the novel effects of simulated rifle shots and a screaming chorus. Electronic music is also central to Patterson's interests. In the 1970s he was head of electronics with the London Sinfonietta, working with Boulez, Hans Werner Henze, Berio and Stockhausen. The result of this was a series of works that incorporated electronic elements, such as *Fusions*, Op. 23; *Shadows*, Op. 27; *Wildfire*, Op. 33; and the appropriately entitled *Brain Storm*, Op. 39.

While only partly representative of his music as a whole, Patterson's music for Hammer nonetheless brought his work to a very different, and much larger, audience than his concert pieces have ever attracted. His score for what was originally called "Doppelgänger," but which was later changed to "The Two Faces of Evil" (presumably in case anyone wasn't entirely sure what "Doppelgänger" meant), employs a variety of avant-garde techniques. There are two main themes, which both share a similar pitch contour. The first consists of the rising semiquaver group of C-natural, F-natural, C-natural, and a falling B-natural, followed by a minim B-flat. The second is a triplet grouping (the first group consisting of a rest, a C-sharp and E-natural, the second group moving down from B-natural through a B-flat, and F-sharp, ending on an F-natural crotchet).

Patterson transforms this material into many permutations throughout the score. The drifting string writing of 3M1, for example, is derived from the pitch contours of both themes, and it accompanies Anna Calder-Marshall's Janet as she prepares

Paul Patterson, circa 2007 (photograph by Alistair Patterson, used by permission of Josef Weinberger, Limited).

to burn the clothes she has collected from the hospital where she, her husband and her son have been treated after a car accident caused by a hitchhiker in a yellow oilskin coat, who turns out to be the husband's sinister double.

It is salutary to realize how detailed and elaborate the orchestration of Patterson's scores for television episodes are. Unfortunately, sound effects and dialogue often obliterate some of his detailed cues, but even when the music is given opportunities to shine through, few people would have had any idea of the amount of work involved to create a mere thirty seconds of sound. Scored for a flute, clarinet, brass and horns, string orchestra, percussion and two synthesizers, Patterson's interesting orchestral effects here include string harmonics and *sul ponticelli* writing for strings, timpani *glissandi,* bowed vibraphones, note clusters, and improvisatory sections in which, for example, the vibraphone player is given several notes enclosed by a square and instructed to improvise with them, to a very slow, irregular rhythm. This occurs in the middle of the scene in which Janet distractedly grabs the belongings that have been piled in a room in the hospital where her husband is being treated after the accident.

These elements of improvisation, which Paul Glass also exploited in his score for *To the Devil a Daughter,* are indebted to techniques pioneered by John Cage in America, and Lutosławsky in Poland, during the middle years of the twentieth century. As Michael Hall has pointed out, Lutosławsky "never wanted to forfeit control over pitch. All he wanted was a way of loosening his control over rhythm. He realized that in passages which did not need to be rhythmically tight, the texture would be richer and less predictable if the players had the freedom to play the notes in their own time and independently of one another."[5]

Of course, improvisation in a film score is a technically problematic thing to achieve because film music is constrained by timing that must be accurate to a fraction of a second. Jazz soundtracks, for example, cannot be true jazz, as Elmer Bernstein readily confessed with regard to his jazz-inspired music for *The Man with the Golden Arm* (dir. Otto Preminger, 1956), which was the first of its kind. Improvisation is central to the aesthetic of jazz, but Bernstein had to compose an impression of jazz for this film. Similarly, aleatoric elements in film music can never be allowed too much room to maneuver, but, within certain confines, can be highly effective.

Patterson's percussion for "The Two Faces of Evil" is very varied. As well as the instruments mentioned so far, he includes a glockenspiel, marimba, bass drum, suspended cymbal, xylophone, tubular bells, bell tree, Bali gong and tam-tam. Harmonically, things are rather more dense (and cacophonous when the clusters take over) than McCabe's more restrained musical language. Fourths and tritones are still important, but rarely in the more obviously exposed manner of James Bernard. For example, at one point during the final chase sequence of 6M1, Patterson writes fourths in the right hand of the synthesizer line and fifths in the left. A vibraphone also brings the score to an end with a series of layered fourths (E-flat, A-flat, D-flat). The atonal approach to harmony is therefore somewhat compromised by Patterson's use of traditional intervals, and even more by his reliance on certain traditional methods of developing his main theme (as, for example, when he subjects it to chromatic sequencing during the scene in which Janet grabs a knife to protect herself after seeing her husband's sharpened fingernail; the fingernail is the same as that of the double, suggesting that the double has taken over her husband's body.) Patterson's music therefore differs considerably from Glass' score for *To the Devil a Daughter* (which avoids entirely any sense of consonance or traditional structural patterns), while being simultaneously far more extreme in its harmonic language than McCabe.

In "The Mark of Satan," Patterson also resorts to fairly traditional sequencing devices that are based on the three basic themes in the score. These are, in fact, all related to one another. The first theme rises a tone from A-flat to B-flat, then falls a semitone to A-natural, and this relationship of a tone and semitone informs the other themes. Such thematic unity is an important part of the overall concision of Patterson's approach. The brevity and thematic unity of many of his cues for this episode do indeed relate them to the style of Anton Webern, a composer whose main aim was to achieve the greatest unity by means of the minimum of material, frequently limiting himself to semitones and thirds. Despite the distinctly anti–Webern elements of traditional sequencing, and the use of far more theatrical orchestral effects than Webern would ever have countenanced, one can nonetheless regard Patterson's short, thematically condensed and highly fragmented cues for "The Mark of Satan" (particularly if they are taken out of the context of the film) as evocative of Webern's aesthetic. Particularly Webernesque cues include 1M3, when we first see Edwin (played by Peter McEnery) reacting to the "demonic" number nine as he stores a cadaver in the mortuary where he works. Also, in 3M3, when Edwin finds that the numerical value of the letters of his own name also add up to nine, Patterson achieves another distinctly Webernesque texture.

Webern is still regarded as a challenge for concert promoters and audiences alike, the extreme brevity of his pieces suggesting to many that there isn't much going on; but the point of Webern's music is the quality of its nuances of timbre, as well as its thematic compression. Rather than bringing to it traditional expectations of thematic development *through* time, Webern intended his audiences to experience a single musical moment *in* time. If the present moment is all that matters to a composer, the length of duration is hardly the point. Of course, no music can exist outside time, but Webern's aim was to condense time to *approximate* a moment outside time. Via Patterson's score for "The Mark of Satan," a television audience was able to experience, as part of a tale of demonic possession, a musical style that may well have baffled many of its members in a concert hall environment.

Having said that, the dramatic function of the music is never overlooked. A particularly effective synchronization occurs in 2M3, when Edwin reacts to the sight of six people wearing sunglasses. (He interprets this as a sign that they are all in league with the Devil.) As the camera cuts from one person to another, Patterson effectively adds another higher pitch. A-sharp in the cellos is joined by F-natural in the violas to create a fifth (if we interpret A-sharp enharmonically as B-flat). The second violins then join in with a C-sharp, interrupting the pure cycle of fifths Patterson leads us to expect. (C-natural would have made another perfect fifth, but Patterson avoids this.) This C-sharp is then joined by a G-sharp in the first violins to form another fifth. The strings then move up to higher pitches, the first and second violins in fifths, the violas and cellos in tritones.

The unfortunate consequences of what Paul Glass referred to as the "back-to-front" reception of contemporary music is also in evidence in Patterson's scores for Hammer. By actually writing the words "painful chord," "distorted mental thinking," and "strange" over certain bars (admittedly highly appropriate markings for a story such as "The Mark of Satan"), he, too, undermines the attempt of the avant-garde to liberate atonality from such conventional significations.

Of all the music in Hammer's T.V. output, the most astonishing example occurs in the episode from the second series, called "In Possession." For this, Patterson created one of the longest and most extreme sections of music in all of Hammer's T.V. output, if not of T.V. drama in general. "In Possession" was directed by Val Guest, and stars Carol Lynley and Christopher Casenove as a couple who are haunted by ghosts from the past, which materialize on the eve of their departure from their London flat to start a new life abroad. Towards the end of the episode, Lynley and Casenove are filmed in slow-motion as they flee from the ghost of a murderous former inhabitant, whom they have seen attempting to drown an old woman in the bath. They rush out through the front door and run upstairs, only to find the ghost lugging a trunk, in which they suspect the corpse of his victim lies. These shots are accompanied by ponderously grinding cello *ostinati*, which form just one of the myriad of avant-garde effects that Patterson piles up on the soundtrack of this astonishing four-and-a-half-minute nightmare sequence. He makes no concessions to traditional styles here, combining electronically generated sounds with violent orchestral material that includes furious, widely-spaced *glissandi* and heavily reverberated *pizzicati* on strings (reminiscent of, but much more anarchic than, the *pizzicato* passages in the *Adagio* section of Schoenberg's *Verklärte Nacht*). There are also advanced atonal harmonies and a great many percussion effects. No other television score had ever been quite like it in its sustained, uninterrupted flow. No sound effects or dialogue get in the way of the music, which is a testament not only to Patterson's inventiveness but also to Philip Martell's (and Hammer's) progressive policy of commissioning extremely adventurous music for these popular entertainments.

This musical vision was one of the things that singled out Hammer from the rest of the British film industry at the time, and from the majority of those who followed. Hammer's musical legacy is unique, not only in individual scores that were the result of its musical policy, but also in the fact that it maintained its patronage of contemporary music right from the start of its success with *The Quatermass Experiment* up through *The Hammer House of Mystery and Suspense*, after which Hammer ceased production altogether. Around the time of Hammer's collapse, however, popular culture itself began to turn its back on musical modernism, looking instead either to popular music or the Golden Age of Hollywood for its inspiration. As we have seen, Hammer was one of the most significant patrons of contemporary music in England, and, thanks to the company's immense success, its musical policy still has a world-wide influence. When discussing the history of twentieth-century music, the contribution of Hammer Films to its dissemination and development should never be underestimated.

Notes

1. Philip Martell, in conversation with the author, August 24, 1988.
2. John McCabe, in email correspondence with the author.
3. Aleister Crowley (ed. John Symonds & Kenneth Grant), *The Confessions of Aleister Crowley* (Harmondsworth: Arkana (Penguin), 1979), p. 23: "Choronzon, the demon of all disharmony and confusion, whom Crowley had conjured up in the form of a naked savage." Like Wheatley's novels, the occult aspects of this story were carefully researched and largely based on information derived from Crowley.
4. John McCabe, in email correspondence with the author.
5. Michael Hall, *Leaving Home — A Conducted Tour of Twentieth-Century Music with Simon Rattle* (London: Faber and Faber, 1996), p. 154.

Conclusion

It is ironic that the exclusive ideals of composers who followed the example of Arnold Schoenberg (who himself referred dismissively to the tastes of "ordinary people" with regard to the cinema) have ultimately found the greatest audience for their musical ideas in film. Joan Peyser, in her study of Pierre Boulez, defined the quest of much of the avant-garde in the 1950s as a desire to create a "refined, inaccessible language" in order "to resist the increasing popularization and vulgarization of art which had flourished under neo-classicism and socialist realism and had been encouraged by radio and films, perhaps to restore a more intellectually aristocratic elite."[1] Yet, as I have attempted to demonstrate, such refined and inaccessible musical grammars have indeed filtered down into mainstream popular culture, where they coexist quite happily with tonality and popular Romanticism. Far more than in the world of popular music, which remains impregnably tonal, film music was the twentieth-century's most eclectic arena.

Twentieth-century avant-garde composers undeniably extended the language and expressive potential of music; but far from *replacing* traditional styles and approaches, as Schoenberg and Schoenberg's avant-garde "opponent," Pierre Boulez, hoped, such music has been absorbed into the commercial mainstream. Tonality is not dead, but neither has it overwhelmed and destroyed its opposite. The combative and even vandalistic vocabulary employed by Boulez and Stockhausen in their expressions of a desire to liquidate the music of the past has been made to look rather ridiculous in the face of late-twentieth and early twenty-first century commercial culture. Boulez, with his desire to "strip music of its accumulated dirt," "to construct a musical language from scratch,"[2] and his arrogant statement that "Anyone who has not felt — I do not say understand — but felt the necessity of the dodecaphonic language is *useless*; For everything he writes will fall short of the imperatives of his time"[3] has been proved hopelessly wrong-headed in a post-modern, commercially-orientated culture. The twentieth-century film soundtrack has proved to be the greatest concert platform there has ever been. It was the most significant arena of twentieth-century musical life, with no aesthetic limitations, no manifestos, no excommunications of style and musical language; and it remained free from the cults of musical dictatorship. Though Boulez once said, "I am not a fascist. I hate Tchaikovsky and I will not conduct him. But if the audience wants him, it can have him,"[4] his desire was nonetheless to dictate the tastes of others. "We have to fight the music of the past," he insisted, believing that tonality was utterly exhausted and irrelevant to modern life; but as Boulez himself now admits, the history of twentieth-century music has proved—in both popular and art traditions—that this has patently not been the case. As the twentieth century drew to a close, Boulez set his own personal record straight:

> If you had asked me fifty years ago where music would be in 1998 I would have told you maybe a nonsense: "Everything will be organized, serialised and so on"—and it wasn't the case. At least experience makes you modest.[5]

Tonality, which, like Dracula, was once thought to be dead, simply won't lie down. No amount of serial staking has been able to destroy it. Democratic and eclectic, film music, which so fascinatingly has one foot in art music and one in popular music, has proved to be the great musical Colossus of the twentieth century, happily striding tonality, serialism, atonality, the popular and the esoteric, electronic and acoustic music. Consequently, it has brought the astonishing adventures of avant-garde twentieth-century music to a wider public than any amount of *recherché* concerts and academic treatises. In so doing, it has nonetheless redefined (some might also say constricted) the aesthetic ambitions of the avant-garde. While exposing popular audiences to modern ideas, forward-looking film scores simultaneously consolidated a specific response to such music, which, in the case of Ligeti's *Requiem* in *2001— A Space Odyssey*, for example, gave the music of Ligeti connotations the composer never intended. However, it is self-evident that all languages (musical and otherwise) change and adapt through usage, and it is frequently the case that while the original intention behind a new technique is lost, the technique itself nonetheless enters the mainstream and fertilizes new developments. Film music in general, and the music composed for that once most critically dishonored genre of the Hammer horror film in particular, is where Schoenberg and the composers who followed in his wake have found their greatest vindication.

Notes

1. Joan Peyser, *Boulez— Composer, Conductor, Enigma* (London: Cassell, 1976), p. 80.
2. Ibid., p. 63.
3. Ibid., p. 70.
4. Ibid., p. 11.
5. Michael Oliver (ed.), *Settling the Score— A Journey Through the Music of the 20th Century* (London: Faber and Faber, 1999), p. 148.

Glossary of Musical Terms

Allegro "fast."

Appoggiatura a melodic note alien to the underlying harmony, usually a semitone or a tone away from the "correct" note onto which it eventually resolves. The appoggiatura therefore creates a dissonance with powerful emotional effect.

Arpeggio the notes of a chord played one after the other instead of together.

Atonality music that is in no specific key.

Bossa-nova Brazilian dance dating from the late 1950s, based on the Samba.

Broken chord the notes of a chord played consecutively rather than together (see **arpeggio**).

Cadence two chords that bring a phrase or piece to a close.

Chorale typically a Lutheran hymn, as harmonized by Bach, or in this style.

Chord a group of notes played together, not necessarily concordant.

Chord of the added sixth i.e. C, E, G and A. The first three notes form a major chord, the A is the added sixth (being six tones from the fundamental).

Chromatic scale a scale which moves consecutively through twelve semitones.

Chromaticism music which introduces notes alien to the key in which the piece is based, and which often moves through different keys.

Col legno the use of the back of the violin bow on the strings.

Con intensita "with intensity."

Conjunct motion notes that are successive degrees of the scale, as opposed to "disjunct" when the pitches form intervals larger than a second.

Consecutive triads i.e. a C-major chord, followed by a D-major chord, followed by an E-major chord.

Contrapuntal in the style of counterpoint.

Crescendo increase in loudness.

Crotchet a quarter note.

Diatonic/diatonicism another name for tonality.

Diegetic music that is heard by the characters on-screen, as opposed to **non-diegetic** music, of which only the audience is aware.

Dies Irae a rhymed sequence sung in the Requiem Mass concerning the Last Judgement.

Diminished seventh chord a chord created from four minor thirds. (Another way of looking at it is that it consists of two interlocking tritones.)

Diminuendo growing quieter.

Dissonance harmonic elements that are contrary to the tonality of a chord.

Divided strings groups of string players who are subdivided into smaller groups.

Dolce cantabile "softly singing."

Dotted rhythm placing a dot after a note extends its value by half.

Dynamics loudness or softness.

11/8 11 quavers to the bar.

False relations the juxtaposition of a natural tone with either its sharpened or flattened form.

Fandango Spanish dance in three beats in the bar.

Flattened a note lowered by a semitone.

Flutter-tongue the effect of rolling the tongue when playing the flute.

Fortissimo very loud.

4/4 four crotchets to the bar.

fp< an indication to begin loudly, immediately become quiet and then increase in loudness.

Fugue a most elaborate form of counterpoint usually blending four separate "voices."

Glissando/glissandi the execution of rapid scales, literally "sliding."

Grottesco "grotesque."

Intervals intervals are relationships between the pitches of scale. There are different kinds of interval: major, minor, perfect, diminished and augmented, all of which refer to whether the pitch is sharpened or flattened. Intervals are defined by their relationship with the first (or fundamental) note of the scale. In C major, a third would be E (i.e. three tones from the fundamental). A fifth would be G. A fourth would be A. A minor third would imply that the E-natural has been flattened. A perfect fifth (or an open fifth, as it is also known) remains in its natural form (i.e. not sharpened or flattened). An augmented fourth would imply that the A has been sharpened. The augmented fourth is also known as a tritone (as it spans three superimposed tones), and over the centuries it has acquired the connotation of diabolism, evil and ambivalence, hence its other name of "*diabolus in musica*"— or "the devil in music." A diminished fifth is the equivalent of the augmented fourth (i.e. the fifth has been flattened).

Key the scale in which a piece is written.

Klangfarbenmelodie "Sound-color-melody"— Schoenberg's term for the coloration of a chord by means of passing the notes of that chord through different timbres.

Ländler a German folk-dance in three beats in the bar that was the precursor to the waltz.

Leitmotif literally "leading-motif," derived from the practice of Richard Wagner. A leitmotif is a short melodic or rhythmical idea that signifies a dramatic character, an idea or a phenomenon.

Maestoso "majestically."

Martellato literally, "hammered."

Mickey-mousing in film music, the literal imitation of movements and actions.

Mistico "mystically."

Musique concrète music created from recorded sounds of all kinds.

Nocturne usually a quiet, often slow piece, nocturnal in mood, typified by the Nocturnes of Chopin.

Ostinato an insistently repeated phrase.

Overtone series naturally occurring frequencies that resonate sympathetically above the fundamental tone.

Passacaglia 17th-century Spanish dance characterized by a repeated four-bar phrase in the the bass.

Pianissimo "very softly."

Piano "soft."

Pizzicato plucked, as opposed to bowed.

Quarter tones pitches between semitones.

Quaver an eighth note.

Rests silences.

Ritardando slowing down.

Ritornelli literally "a little return"—a repeat.

Scherzo literally "joke"—a fast, often humorous movement (usually the third) in sonatas and symphonies, but can also refer to a lively self-standing piece or musical section.

Semiquaver a sixteenth note.

Semitone half a tone.

Serialism compositional principle based on a note-row derived from the twelve notes of a chromatic scale.

Sextuplet a group of six notes which have the value of one beat.

Sforzando "forcing," with a sudden, strong accent.

Sharpened a note raised by a semitone.

Sul ponticello an instruction for a string player to draw the bow "near the bridge" of the instrument.

Tempo the speed of a piece.

Tenuto "held," sustained to its full value.

3/4 three crotchets to the bar.

Tonality music written in major and minor keys.

Tone (or note) cluster a (usually dense) grouping of tones creating a dissonant effect.

Transposing the transposition of a piece or phrase into a different key.

Tremolo the rapid repetition of a single tone (usually applied to string instruments).

Trill the rapid oscillation of a note with one either immediately above or below it.

Triplet a group of three notes that has the value of a single beat.

Twelve-tone (or note) row the basis of serial composition.

Unison playing the same notes together.

Vibrato a slight, rapid fluctuation of pitch on sustained string notes.

Wrong side of the bridge in string and viola playing, the bow is drawn over the side of the bridge closest to the player's chin.

Select Discography

Blood from the Mummy's Tomb — Original Motion Picture Soundtrack (music by Tristram Cary), GDI Records, GDICD019, 2002.
Curse of the Werewolf and Other Film Music by Benjamin Frankel, Naxos, 8.557850, 2006.
The Devil Rides Out — Horror, Adventure and Romance (music by James Bernard), Silva Screen, FILMCD174, 1996.
The Devil Rides Out — Original Motion Picture Soundtrack (music by James Bernard), GDI Records, GDICD013, 2000.
Hammer Film Music Collection, Vol. 1 (contains music by James Bernard, Harry Robinson, Mario Nascimbene, Tristram Cary, Malcolm Williamson), GDI Records, GDICD002, 1998.
Hammer Film Music Collection, Vol. 2 (contains music by Don Banks, Richard Rodney Bennett, James Bernard, Mario Nascimbene, John McCabe, Paul Glass, Humphrey Searle, Michael Vickers, Malcolm Williamson, John Cacavas, Harry Robinson), GDI Records, GDICD005, 1999.
The Hammer Frankenstein Film Music Collection (contains music by Don Banks, James Bernard, Malcolm Williamson), GDI Records, GDICD011, 2000.
Hammer — The Studio That Dripped Blood! (contains music by James Bernard, Mario Nascimbene, Humphrey Searle), Silva Screen, FILMXCD357, 2002.
The Hammer Vampire Film Music Collection (contains music by James Bernard, Harry Robinson), GDI Records, GDICD017, 2001.
Horror! (contains music by James Bernard, Humphrey Searle, Gerard Schurmann, Benjamin Frankel, Buxton Orr), Silva Screen, FILMCD 175, 1996.
The Lost Continent — Original Motion Picture Soundtrack (music by Gerard Schurmann), GDI Records, GDICD015, 2000.
Love from a Stranger — Four British Film Scores (contains Elisabeth Lutyens music for *The Skull*), NCM, NMC D073, 2004.
Quatermass and the Pit (music by Tristram Cary), Cloud Nine Records, CNS5009, 1996.
She and The Vengeance of She — Original Motion Picture Soundtracks (music by James Bernard and Mario Nascimbene), GDI Records, GDICD018, 2001.
Twins of Evil — Original Motion Picture Soundtrack (music by Harry Robinson), GDI Records, GDICD012.

Select Bibliography

Ayles, Allen, Robert Adkinson, and Nicholas Fry. *The House of Horror*. London: Lorrimer, 1984.
Bilbow, Marjorie. *The Facts About a Feature Film*. London: André Deutsch, 1978.
Boulez, Pierre. *Orientations* (trans. Martin Cooper). London: Faber and Faber, 1986.
Bronson, John. *The Horror People*. London: Macdonald and Jane's, 1976.
Burke, Edmund. *A Philosophical Enquiry into the Origin of Our Ideas of the Sublime and the Beautiful*. Oxford: Oxford University Press, 1990.
Buscombe, Edward. *Making "Legend of the Werewolf."* London: British Film Institute, 1976.
Caute, David. *Joseph Losey — A Revenge on Life*. London: Faber and Faber, 1994.
Crowley, Aleister (ed. John Symonds & Kenneth Grant). *The Confessions of Aleister Crowley*. Harmondsworth: Arkana (Penguin), 1979.
Dahlhaus, Carl. *Schoenberg and the New Music*. Cambridge: Cambridge University Press, 1987.
Eisler, Hanns. *Composing for Films*. Oxford: Oxford University Press, 1948.
Fiegel, Eddi. *John Barry — A Sixties Theme*. London: Boxtree/Pan-Macmillan, 2001.
Freud, Sigmund. *Art and Literature*. Harmondsworth: Penguin, 1985.
Gorbman, Claudia. *Unheard Melodies*. London: British Film Institute, 1987.
Griffiths, Paul. *György Ligeti*. London: Robson Books, 1983.
Haining, Peter (ed.). *The Frankenstein Omnibus*. London: Orion, 1994.
Hall, Michael (ed.). *Leaving Home — A Conducted Tour of Twentieth-Century Music with Simon Rattle*. London: Faber and Faber, 1996.
Harries, Meirion, and Susan Harries. *Elisabeth Lutyens, a Pilgrim Soul*. London: Michael Joseph, 1989.
Hearn, Marcus, and Alan Barnes. *The Hammer Story*. London: Titan Books, 1997.
Huckvale, David. *James Bernard, Composer to Count Dracula: A Critical Biography*. Jefferson: McFarland, 2006.
Hutchings, Peter. *Hammer and Beyond: the British Horror Film*. Manchester: Manchester University Press, 1993.
Kennedy, Michael. *The Works of Ralph Vaughan Williams*. Oxford: Oxford University Press, 1992.
Krzywinska, Tanya. *A Skin for Dancing In*. Trowbridge: Flicks Books, 2000.
Lee, Christopher. *Tall, Dark and Gruesome*. London: Victor Gollancz, 1997.
Levant, Oscar. *A Smattering of Ignorance*. New York: Doubleday, 1940.
Lutyens, Elisabeth. *A Goldfish Bowl*. London: Cassell, 1972.
Mann, Thomas (trans. H.T. Lowe-Porter). *Dr Faustus*. London: Secker and Warburg, 1976.
Mann, Thomas (trans. Allan Blunden). *Pro and Contra Wagner*. London: Faber and Faber, 1985.

Manvell, Roger, and John Huntley. *The Technique of Film Music*. London: Focal Press, 1975.
Nietzsche, Friedrich (trans. Walter Kaufmann). *The Birth of Tragedy, and the Case of Wagner*. New York: Vintage, 1967.
Oliver, Michael (ed.). *Settling the Score—a Journey Through the Music of the 20th Century*. London: Faber and Faber, 1999.
Peyser, Joan. *Boulez, Composer, Conductor, Enigma*. London: Cassell, 1976.
Pirie, David. *The Vampire Cinema*. Feltham: Galley Press, 1977.
Prawer, S.S. *Caligari's Children*. Oxford: Oxford University Press, 1980.
Prendergast, Roy M. *Film Music, A Neglected Art*. New York: Norton, 1977.
Rigby, Jonathan. *Christopher Lee—the Authorised Screen History*. Reynolds and Hearn, Richmond, 2001.
Rigby, Jonathan. *English Gothic*. Richmond: Reynolds & Hearn, 2000.
Sachs, Bruce, and Russell Wall. *Greasepaint and Gore—The Hammer Monster of Roy Ashton*. Sheffield: Tomahawk Press, 1991.
Sadie, Stanley (ed.). *The New Grove Dictionary of Music and Musicians*. London: MacMillan, 1980.
Sangster, Jimmy. *Inside Hammer*. Richmond: Reynolds & Hearn, 2001.
Schoenberg, Arnold. *Style and Idea* (ed. L. Black). London: Faber and Faber, 1975.
Schoenberg, Arnold. *Theory of Harmony* (trans. Roy E. Carter). London: Faber and Faber, 1975.
Smith-Brindle, Reginald. *The New Music*. Oxford: Oxford University Press, 1982.
Tagg, Philip. *Kojak—50 Minutes of Television Music*. Gothenburg: Gothenburg University Press, 1979.
Viertel, Salka. *The Kindness of Strangers*. New York: Holt, 1940.
Villiers de l'Isle Adam, Count Philippe Auguste. *Cruel Tales* (trans. Robert Baldick). Oxford: Oxford University Press, 1985.
Wagner, Cosima. *Diaries*, Vol. 2 (trans. Geoffrey Skelton). London: Collins, 1978.
Wagner, Richard. *My Life* (trans. Andrew Gray). Cambridge: Cambridge University Press, 1983.
Wagner, Richard. *Selected Letters of Richard Wagner* (ed. Barry Millington, trans. Stewart Spencer). London: Dent, 1987.
Watkin, David. *English Architecture*. London: Thames and Hudson, 1992.

Journals and E-Publications

Cary, Tristram. "Electronic Music," in *Audio Annual '71*, London, 1971.
Huckvale, David. "Wagner and Vampires," in *Wagner—Journal of the Wagner Society* (ed. Stewart Spencer), Vol. 18, No. 3, September 1997.
Larson, Randall. "The Music of Hammer," in *Little Shoppe of Horrors* (ed. Richard Klemenson), nos. 10/11 & 12 (Des Moines, Iowa: Elmer Valo Appreciation Society).
Searle, Humphrey. *Quadrille with a Raven—Memoirs by Humphrey Searle*, www.musicweb-international.com/searle.

Index

Numbers in **_bold italics_** indicate pages with photographs.

The Abominable Snowman 55, 69
Accident 66, 67, 77, 147
Ackland, Joss 139
Addinsell, Richard: "Warsaw Concerto" 138, 139, 140, 141
Adkinson, Robert 53
Adrian, Max 63
Agutter, Jenny 144
Akhnaten 196
Alexander the Great 119
Alfvén, Hugo 8
Allen, Maud 125
Allen, Patrick 145
Also Sprach Zarathustra 131
Alwyn, William 40
Anderson, Gail-Nina vii
Anderson, Judith 83
Anderson, Lindsay 67
Andress, Ursula 115, 122
Andrews, Dana 123
Animal Farm 143
Antonioni, Michelangelo 67, 155
Arliss, Leslie 140
Arnold, Sir Malcolm 55, 134; *Tam O'Shanter Overture* 8
Arrigi, Niké 102
Asher, Jack 135
Ashton, Roy 60, 145
Asquith, Anthony 38
Asther, Nils 72
Astley, Edwin: "High Wire" 80
Atilla 8
Auric, Georges 58, 78, 79
The Avengers 80
Avery, Tex 31
The Awakening 24, 124
Ayles, Allen 53

Babbitt, Milton 143
Bach, Johann Sebastian 80, 172; *Toccata and Fugue in D Minor* 143

Bacon, Francis 49
Badham, John 36, 37, 176
Baker, Roy Ward 41, 89, 118, 128, 138
Banks, Don ix, 2, 14, 59, 133, 142, 143, 144–153, 176; *Commentary* 144; *Duo* 144; *Equations* 144; *Four Pieces for Orchestra* 143, Horn Concerto 144; Horn Trio 144; *Intersections* 144; *Limbo* 144; *Meeting Place* 144; *Nexus* 144; *Pezzo dramatico* 144; *Prospects* 144; *Settings from Roget* 144; *Sonata da Camera* 144; *Take Eight* 144; *Three Short Songs* 144; *Walkabout* 144
Barabbas 119
Baretta 163
Barnes, Alan 87, 153, 176, 177
Baron, David 150
Barrett, Ray 151
Barrett, Tim 152
Barron, Bebe 122, 123, 132
Barron, Louis 122, 123, 132
Barry, John 64, 68, 70, 80, 99, 156
Bart, Lionel 88
Barth, Herbert 51
Bartók, Bela 32, 72, 97, 100
Batchelor, Joy 143
Bates, Ralph 137, 138, 192, **_193_**
Bath, Hubert: "Cornish Rhapsody" 140
Bathory, Countess Elizabeth 97
Battleship Potemkin 49
Baudelaire, Charles 36
BBC Radiophonic Workshop 123, 160
Beacham, Stephanie 155
The Beast with Five Fingers 142
"The Beast with Five Fingers" 62
The Beatles 88, 155, 156; *Sergeant Pepper's Lonely Hearts Club Band* 155
Beaumont, Gabrielle 198
Bedford, David vii, ix, 197, **_197_**, 198
Beethoven, Ludwig van 177, 191; *Für Elise* 143; "Moonlight" Sonata 141; Ninth Symphony 131, 149

Index

Begleitungsmusik zu einer Lichtspielszene 26, 27
"The Bells" 36
Benedict, Dirk 198
Bennett, Compton 38
Bennett, Jill 84
Bennett, Richard Rodney ix, 2, 15, 70–87, **73**, 107, 120, 134, 191, 198
Berg, Alban 33, 71, 72; Violin Concerto 4, 5, 43, 44, 47, 190
Berio, Luciano 34, 118, 180, 199
Berkeley, Sir Lennox 197
Berlioz, Hector 36
Bernard, James vii, ix, 1, 3, 4, 5, 7, **11**, 16, 24, 56, 58, 65, 70, 71, 74, 78, 82, 83, 87, **105**, 105–113, **113**, 136, 138, 142,153, 158, 160, 161, 166, 170, 172, 175, 176, 186, 189, 194, 198, 200; *Passacaglia* 4, 109, 110; *Spur of the Moment* 106; "Vampire Rhapsody" 141, 151
Bernard, Katherine 106
Bernard, Col. Ronald Playfair St. Vincent 106
Bernstein, Elmer 200
Bernstein, Leonard 72
Berova, Olinka 122
Beswick, Martine 132
The Big Sleep 184
Bilbow, Marjorie 188
Billion Dollar Brain 72
The Birds 58, 122
Blacher, Boris 178
Black, Cilla 156
Black, Isobel 124
Blackman, Honor 129, 186, 194
Bliss, Sir Arthur 55, 56, 134
Blom, Eric 57
The Blood Countess 98
Blood from the Mummy's Tomb 16, 24, 124, 125
Blow Up 67, 155
"Blue Danube" Waltz 120
Böcklin, Arnold: *The Isle of the Dead* 36
Bogarde, Sir Dirk 66, 67, 77
Bolling, Claude 24
Boulez, Pierre 2, 3, 4, 32, 33, 34, 37, 51, 53, 71, 87, 108, 111, 113, 118, 126, 132, 134, 135, 199, 204, 205; *Le Marteau sans Maître* 2, 71, 108
Boult, Sir Adrian 143
Boulting, John 113
Bradley, Scott 31
Bradshaw, Susan 71
Brahm, John 141
Brainstorm 199
Bram Stoker's Legend of the Mummy 124
Brandy, Howard 125
The Bride of Frankenstein 145, 146
The Brides of Dracula 41, 135–137
The Brigand of Kandahar 149
Britten, (Edward) Benjamin 34, 36, 56, 84, 106, 134, 136, 150; *Death in Venice* 150; *Owen Wingrave* 36, 37; *Peter Grimes* 84, 106; *The Prince of the Pagodas* 150
Broderick, Susan 155
Bronson, John 53
Browning, Robert: "Summum Bonum" 17, 18
Browning, Tod 52, 65
Brusse, Liliane 58
Buck, David 152, 153
Buck, Pearl S. 29
Bulwer, Edward (Lord Lytton): *The Last Days of Pompeii* 17
Bunny Lake Is Missing 178
Bürger, Gottfried: "Lenore" 36
Burgess, Anthony: *A Clockwork Orange* 131
Les Burgraves 17
Burke, Edmund 102–4
Byron, George Gordon, 6th Lord 165

The Cabinet of Dr. Caligari 25, 26
Cabot, Bruce 184
Cacavas, John vii, ix, 75, 163, 165–177, **167**; *Theme and Rock Out* 165
Caesar 17
Cage, John 34; *4'33"* 34, 200
Caine, Michael 64
Calder-Marshall, Anna 199
The Camp on Blood Island 49
Caplet, André: *Conte fantastique* 36, 125
Captain Clegg 144, 145
Carlos, Walter: *Switched-on Bach* 131
"Carmilla" 90
Carnelli, Steven 167
Carradine, John 141, 142
Carreras, Sir James 2
Carreras, Michael **11**, 49, 51, 116, 117
Carry On films 122
Carson, John 193, 196
Cary, Joyce 125
Cary, Tristram vii, ix, 115, 118, **123**, 124–129, 132
Casenove, Christopher 202
Cass, Henry 140
Castle, Roy 62
The Cat Who Hated People 31
Catch My Soul 180
Caute, David 67, 70
Cello Concerto (Glass) 179
Chaffey, Don 115, 116, 129
Chaplin, Charles **30**
Char, René 2
Children of the Damned 134
"Child's Play" 198
Chopin, Fryderyk (Franciszek) 58; "Marche funèbre" 142, 143
Churchill, Sir Winston 7
Ciment, Michel 67
5 chansons pour une princesse errante 179
Clarinet Concerto (Patterson) 199
Clark, Edward 54

Index

Clay, Nicholas 198
Clayton, Jack 58
A Clockwork Orange 131
Close Encounters of the Third Kind 119–21, 161
The Cobweb 31
Coles, Michael 163
Collins, Joan 193
Comedy 199
Commentary 144
Concerto for improvised piano (Glass) 179
Concerto for Orchestra (McCabe) 192
"Concerto Macabre" (Herrmann) 140, 141
Connor, Kevin 161
Conte fantastique 36, 125
Continuum 108
Cooper, George C. **148**
Cooper, Merian C. 27
Cooper, Stuart 180
Copernicus 161
Copland, Aaron: *Grogh* 36
"Cornish Rhapsody" 140
Corridors of Blood 53
"The Corvini Inheritance" 198
Costello, Elvis 197
Count Yorga — Vampire 154
Countess Dracula 65, 89, 90, 96–104, **101**, 158
Court, Hazel 73
Cowell, Henry 123, 139; Piano Concerto 139
Cox, Brian 189
Crabtree, Arthur 49
Cracowian Counterpoint 199
Craig, Wendy 82
Cregar, Laird 141
Crescendo 15, 16, 62, 138–140
Crossland, Alan 27
Crowley, Aleister 193, 203
Cruel Tales 34, 37
Csók, István: *The Blood Countess* 98
Cummings, Lionel vii, 105
The Curse of Frankenstein 73, 88, 108, 111
Curse of the Mummy 124
The Curse of the Werewolf 1, 2, 4, 5, 23, 38, 40–52, **41**, **50**, 54, 56, 57, 69, 145
Cushing, Helen 125
Cushing, Peter 52, 60, 61, 63, 64, 93, 95, 96, 112, 119, 125, 135, 143, 145, 146, **146**, 155, 157, 170, 176, 189, 192, 193

Dahl, Ingolf 178
Dahlhaus, Carl 37
Dalí, Salvador 31
Dangerman 80
Dangerous Moonlight 139, 140
Daniel, Jennifer 59, **141**, 151
Dankworth, John 66, 77, 83, 144
Danot, Serge 53
Danse macabre 36
Danse sacré et danse profane 137
Dapnis et Chloë 139

Dark Side of the Moon 118, 163
Daves, Delmer 122
Davis, Bette 76, 78, 80–82, **81**
Dawson, Anthony 43
Day, Doris 140
Day, Robert 53, 115
The Day the Earth Stood Still 128
"Death and the Maiden," String Quartet No. 14, in D Minor 143
Death in Venice 150
Debussy, Claude Achille 36, 72, 137, 141, 150; *Danse sacré et danse profane* 137; *Khamma* 125; *Six épigraphs antiques* 125
Dehn, Paul 7, 8, 23, 74, 113
Delgado, Roger 153
Demons of the Mind 89
Denberg, Susan 112
Denham, Maurice **59**
Department S 80
Derbyshire, Delia 124, 160
Déserts 128
The Devil Rides Out 87, 108, 178, 193, 194
Dickens, Charles 79
Dido and Aeneas 35
Diffring, Anton 72, 73, 75, **76**
"Dir töne Lob" 99
Dix, William 76
Dr. Blood's Coffin 53
Dr. Faustus 42, 53
Dr. Jekyll and Sister Hyde 41, 58, 89, 155
Dr. Terror's House of Horrors 4, 60–69, 143
Dr. Who 123, 124, 129, 153, 160
Dodds, Marcus ix, 7, 8, 23, 24
Don Giovanni 35
"Don't You Rock Me, Daddio" 88
Döppler, Franz 64, 100
Dostoyevsky, Fyodor M. 79
Dotrice, Michelle 85
Dougal and the Blue Cat 53
Douglas, Josephine 10, 157
Dracula (John Badham, 1979) 36, 176
Dracula (Terence Fisher, 1958) 62, 73, 88, 106, 135
Dracula (Tod Browning, 1931) 52, 65, 78
Dracula A.D. 1972 10, 52, 154–162, **162**, 165, 172, 174
Dracula Is Dead ... and Alive and Living in London see *The Satanic Rites of Dracula*
Dracula Prince of Darkness 82, 150
"The Dream of Olwen" 140
Duchamp, Marcel 3
The Duchess of Malfi 106
Duffell, Peter 143
Duo 144
Dyke, Katie van vii, 73

Earle, Terry 8
East of Eden 72
Eddington, Paul 110
Edison, Thomas Alva 112

Edwards, Blake 157
Eisenstein, Sergei 49
An Electric Storm 160
Elegiac Melodies 8
Elès, Sandor **101**, 102, 147
Elgar, Sir Edward 14
Elliot, Denholm 185
The Empire of Lights 77
Endore, Guy: *The Werewolf of Paris* 42
Die Entführung aus dem Serail 51
Equations 144
Erwartung 25, 27
Eschatos 179
Etude 128, 129
Evans, Clifford 43
Everett, Kenny 143
The Evil of Frankenstein 62, 145–148, **146**, 150
Ewing, Barbara 142, 193
The Exorcist 187
Eye of the Devil 77
Eyerly, Scott 37

Fairchild, Edgar 141
Fear in the Night 191–193, **193**
Feller, Catherine 45
Fennell, Albert 89
Fess, Eike vii
Fiegel, Eddi 64, 70
First Piano Concerto (Shostakovitch) 190
First Piano Sonata (Williamson) 135
Fisher, Terence 1, 38, 40–42, 48, 71, 73–76, 82, 87, 106, 108, 112, 136, 178, 186, 189
Five Pieces for Orchestra 183
Fleischer, Richard 119
Flick, Vic 175
Florey, Robert 142
Fontaine, Joan 83, 84, **85**
Forbes, Bryan 64
Forbidden Planet 122, 123, 132
Foster, Julia 196
Four Pieces for Orchestra 143
4'33" 34, 200
Fourth Symphony (Searle) 64
Francen, Victor 142
Francis, Derek 183
Francis, Freddie 2, 9, 25, 58–60, 63, 67, 77, 142, 146, 148
Frankel, Benjamin ix, 1–5, 23, 38–54, **39**, 57, 58, 69, 71, 74, 135
Frankel, Cyril 60, 79, 85, 87
Frankel, Xenia vii, 39, 50
Frankenstein 2, 3
Frankenstein Created Woman 74, 112
Franklyn, William 163
Freeman, Alan 62, 143
Der Freischütz 35
Frend, Charles 55
Freud, Sigmund 78, 79, 87
Friedhofer, Hugo 178
Friedkin, William 131, 187

Fry, Nicholas 53
Fry, Tristan 100, 186
Für Elise 143
Fury, Sidney J. 53, 64
Fusions 199
The Future Eve 112, 114

Gagarin, Yuri 161
Gallu, Sam 67
Gamley, Douglas 14, 130, 131
Garland, Judy 88
Gasken, John: *Golem* 36
Geeson, Judy 192, **193**
Gerhard, Roberto 67
Gershwin, George 139
Gesang der Jünglinge 118
Gibson, Alan 10, 15, 16, 62, 75, 159, 162–164, 166
Gilling, John 108, 149, 151, 152
Glass, Paul vii, ix, 178–190 **179**, 194, 200–202; Cello Concerto 179; *5 chansons pour une princesse errante* 179; Concerto for improvised piano 179; *Eschatos* 179; *Psalm LXXXIII* 179; *Sahassavagga* 179
Glass, Penelope Margaret 187
Glass, Philip 65, 78; *Akhnaten* 196
The Glass Mountain 140
Glennie, Ian 54
Glenville, Peter 38
Glover, Julian **128**, 129
Gluck, Christoph Willibald von 158
Die glückliche Hand 26–28
Gogol, Nicolai 79
Goldfinger 23, 68, 156
Goldoni, Lelia 69
Golem 36
Good, Maurice 64
The Good Earth 29
The Good, the Bad and the Ugly 96, 121
Goodcliffe, Michael 186
Goode, Frederic 92
Gorbman, Claudia 183, 184, 188
The Gorgon 186
Gossett, Louis, Jr. 124
Gough, Michael 49, 62, 65
Gould, Morton 176
Grainer, Ron 124, 160
Gray, Charles 110, 193
Green, Kenneth 106
Green Ways 196
Grey, Steve 158
Grieg, Edvard: *Elegiac Melodies* 8
Griffiths, Paul 120, 121, 132
Gringoire 17
Grogh 36
Groupe de Recherches Musicales 117–119
"Guardian of the Abyss" 193, 194, **195**
Guest, Val 2, 9, 49, 55, 69, 115, 116, 122, 198, 202
Gurrelieder 31

Hadfield, Hurd 72
Haese, Geraldine vii
Halas, John 143
Hall, Michael 37, 200, 203
Hamburger Hill 65
Hamilton, Guy 23
Hammer House of Horror 189, 193, 196, 203
Hammer House of Mystery and Suspense 189, 193, 197, 203
Hammerstein, Oscar 155
Hand, Slim 54
Hangover Square 141
The Happy Prince 9
Hardy, Robin 84
Harlequin 133
Harlow, John 140
Harries, Meirion 4, 70
Harries, Susan 4, 70
Harryhausen, Ray 155
Harvey, W(illiam) F(ryer): "The Beast with Five Fingers" 62
"The Haunted Palace" 36
The Haunting 56, 69
Hawaii Five-O 166
Hawks, Howard 184
Hawthorne, Nathaniel: *The House of Seven Gables* 37
Hayes, Isaac 163
Hayes, Tubby 62, 139, 140
"Hear My Prayer" 58
Hearn, Marcus vii, 87, 115, 131, 153, 176, 177
Hemmings, David 67, 155
Henderson, Russ 62
Henze, Hans Werner 199
Herrmann, Bernard 3, 4, 47, 58, 68, 76, 83, 84, 106, 108, 122, 128; "Concerto Macabre" 140, 141
Hessler, Gordon 90
Heston, Charlton 124
"High Wire" 80
Hilton, Ronnie 88
Hinds, Anthony 3, 106
Hitchcock, Alfred 3, 31, 47, 58, 76, 83, 122, 140, 147
Hitler, Adolf 32
Holbrooke, Joseph 36
Hollander, Benoit 9, 16–21; *Les Burgraves* 17; *Caesar* 17; *Gringoire* 17; *Pompeii* 19; *Roland* 17; *Sappho* 17; *Sardanapalus* 17; "Summum Bonum" 17, **18**
Hollingsworth, John ix, 7, 8, 23, 55, 59, 74, 136, 144
Holt, Seth 2, 16, 76, 77, 81, 125
"Hoots Mon" 88
Horn Concerto (Banks) 144, 198
Horn Concerto: Banks 144; Patterson 198
Horror Express 165
The Horror of Frankenstein 137, 146
Horrors of the Black Museum 49
Hot Butter 131

Hough, John 89
Houghton, Don 154, 159, 163
The Hound of the Baskervilles (Terence Fisher, 1959) 106, 136
House of Dracula 141
The House of Seven Gables 37
"The House That Bled to Death" 189
The House That Dripped Blood 143
Howe, Hubert S., Jr. 124
Huckvale, David 37, 70, 87, 114, **170**
Huckvale, Iris vii
Huckvale, John vii
Hughes, Christopher vii
Hughes, Howard 164
Hugo, Victor 40
Hungarian Rhapsody No. 2 100
Hungarian Rhapsody No. 6 64, 100
Hunt, Marsha 156
Hunt, Martitia 135
Huntley, John 40, 49, 53, 70, 132
Hurst, Brian Desmond 38, 139
Huston, John 38
Hutchings, Peter 52, 53, 155, 176
Hysteria 142, 149

The Importance of Being Earnest 38
In a Persian Garden 197
"In Possession" 202
The In Sound from Way Out 130
The Innocents 58, 78, 79
Institut de Recherche et de Coordination Acoustique/Musique (IRCAM) 124
International Society for Contemporary Music (ISCM) 51, 54, 55, 144
Intersections 144
Introduction and Allegro 125
The Ipcress File 64, 99
Ireland, John: *Green Ways* 196
Irvin, John 65
Isis and Osiris 4
The Isle of the Dead 36
It's Trad, Dad! 60

James, Henry: "The Turn of the Screw" 36, 58
The Japanese Fishermen 129
The Jazz Singer 27, 119
Jessop, Clytie 142, 148
The Jewel of Seven Stars 124, 132
Johnson, Laurie 80, 89, 90
Jolson, Al 25, 27, 119
Jones, Freddie 164, 170
Jones, Philip 180
Jones, Tom 156
Jordan, Louis 140
Joseph II, Emperor 51
Julie 140
Jungle Marriners 59

Karloff, Boris 36, 145
Keats, John 41

Keir, Andrew 125
Kelljan, Bob 154
Kelly, Gerrard 196
Kemp, Jeremy 62
Kennaway, Dimitri vii, 49, 53
Kennedy, John F. 199
Kennedy, Michael 70
Kenton, Erle C. 141
Kenton, Stan 156, 165, 169
Kerr, Deborah 78, 79
Khamma 125
King Kong 27, 184
King Rat 64
Kingsley, Gershon 130; *The In Sound from Way Out* 130; *Music to Moog By* 130; "Popcorn" 130
Kingston, Kiwi 145
Kinski, Nastassja 181, **182**, 184, 187, 194
The Kiss of the Vampire 59, 62, 73, 124, 141, **141**, 142, 147, 151, 155, 158
Kitchin, Margaret 144
Kneale, Nigel 2, 87, 125, 129
Kodály, Zoltán 97, 100, 143
Kojak 98, 99, 166, 168
Korda, Sir Alexander 55
Korngold, Erich Wolfgang 144, 176
Kosmogonia 161
Koyaanisqatsi 65
Kraftwerk 131
Krishnamurti 61
Krzywinska, Tanya 77, 87
Kubrick, Stanley 120, 121, 131, 187
Kwouk, Burt 198
Kyrie (Patterson) 199

Landor, Rosalyn 110, 193
Lang, Fritz 25, 78
Langbein, Brenton 144
Langella, Frank 176
Lapotaire, Janes 140
Larson, Randall 137, 153
The Last Days of Pompeii 17
"The Late Nancy Irving" 190
Laura 123
Law, Phyllida 53
Lawrence, Andrea 102
Lawrence, Delphi 75
Lawson, Sarah 110
Leader, Anton M. 134
Lee, Christopher 52, 54, 60, 62–64, 67, 68, 70, 72, 73, 86, 90, 110, 132, 135, 136, 150, 157, **162**, 163–165, 176, 177, 181, 183, 184, 186
Lee-Thompson, J. 77
Lees, Jeremy vii
Lees, Lady Mary vii
Le Fanu, J. Sheridan: "Carmilla" 90
"The Legend of the Glass Mountain" 140
The Legend of the Seven Golden Vampires 113, 154

Lehár, Franz 13
Lehmann, Liza 197; *In a Persian Garden* 197
Leigh, Janet 108
"Lenore" 36
Leo, Serafina di 46
Leonard, Harry 123
Leone, Sergio 96
Lester, Richard 60
Levant, Oscar 37
Lewin, Albert 72
Lewton, Val 36
Ligeti, György 35, 112, 113, 120, 121, 180, 205; *Continuum* 108; *Lontano* 112, 113; *Requiem* 120, 205
Limbo 144
Linden, Jennie 147, **148**
Ling, Barbara Yu 169
Liszt, Franz 35–36, 55, 64, 86, 97, 99, 126, 141, 186; *Hungarian Rhapsody No. 2* 100; *Hungarian Rhapsody No. 6* 64, 100; *Missa Choralis* 86
Lithgoe, Clive 139
London Philharmonic Orchestra 192
London Sinfonietta 199
London Symphony Orchestra 130, 131, 139, 143
Lonnen, Ray 194
Lontano 112, 113
Lorre, Peter 142
Losey, Joseph 66, 67, 70, 77, 147
Loss, Joe 15
The Lost Continent 49
Love Story 140
Lubin, Arthur 140
Lucas, George 176
Lugosi, Bela 176
"Lullaby of the Bells Piano Concerto" 140
Lumet, Sidney 23
Lumley, Joanna 75, 163, **164**
Lust for a Vampire 89, 95
Lustigman, Anthony vii
Lutosławski, Witold 90, 112, 113, 178, 180, 199, 200
Lutyens, Sir Edwin 57
Lutyens, Elisabeth ix, 2, 4, 5, 16, 54, 56–71, 57, 80, 83, 92, 99, 134, 198; *Isis and Osiris* 4
Lyndon, Barré 72
Lynley, Carol 202
Lytton, Lord *see* Bulwer, Edward

Macbeth 129
MacGregor, Scott 15
MacMillan, Kenneth 55
Madden, Peter 62
The Magic Roundabout Story 53
Magritte, René: *The Empire of Lights* 77
Maitland, Marne 151
Malcolm, George 80
The Man in Half Moon Street 72

The Man Who Could Cheat Death 71–76, **76**, 80, 84
The Man with the Golden Arm 200
Mancini, Henry 157, 167
Manfred Mann 156, 158
Mann, Thomas 113; *Dr. Faustus* 42, 53
Mann, William S. 133, 146
Mantovani 140
Manvell, Roger 49, 70, 113
"Marche funèbre" (Chopin) 142, 143
Margo, Sid 64
"The Mark of Satan" 201, 202
"Mark of the Devil" 198
Marle, Arnold 75, **76**
Marschner, Heinrich: *Der Vampyr* 35
Le Marteau sans Maître 2, 71, 108
Martell, Harry 180
Martell, Philip vii, ix, 5, 7, 9–17, **11**, 21–24, 115, 116, 119, 120, 125, 129, 132, 138, 144, 151, 157, 166, 176, 179, 180, 187, 190, 192, 194, 197, 202, 203
Martin, Eugenio 165
"The Masque of the Red Death" 36, 125
Mathieson, Muir 7, 55, 92
Mathieu, André: "Quebec Concerto" 140
Mazzarini, Gianni 119
McCabe, John vii, ix, 191–197, **192**, 200, 201, 203; Concerto for Orchestra 192; Second Symphony 191
McCallum, Neil 62
McCowan, Alec 85
McEnery, Peter 201
McGoohan, Patrick 180
McNally, Raymond T. 97
Meeting Place 144
Meisel, Edmund 49
Die Meistersinger von Nürnberg 175
Mendelssohn, Felix: "Hear My Prayer" 58
Meredith, Burgess 142
Messiaen, Olivier 111, 112, 118, 134, 135, 191; *Poèmes pour Mi* 134
Meyerbeer, Giacomo: *Robert le diable* 36
Meyrinck, Gustav: *The Golem* 36
"Midnight on the Cliffs" 140
Miller, Glenn 15
Millington, Barry 37
Minelli, Liza 88
Minelli, Vincente 31
Mirbeau, Octave: *The Torture Garden* 142
Miss Julie 52
Missa Choralis (Liszt) 86
Mitchell, Lewis vii
Moog, Robert 131
Moog Indigo 130
"Moonlight" Sonata 141
Morricone, Ennio 90, 96, 121
Morris, Aubrey 124
Morris, Robert 112
Morrison, Van: "Don't You Rock Me, Daddio" 88

Morross, Jerome 90
Mozart, Wolfgang Amadeus 181; *Die Entführung aus dem Serail* 51; *Don Giovanni* 35
The Mummy 73, 151
The Mummy's Shroud 151, **152**
Munroe, Caroline 160
Murder on the Orient Express 23, 74
Murnau, F(riedrich) W. 36, 60
Music to Moog By 130
Mussorgsky, Modest: *Pictures at an Exhibition* 131
My Nights with Susan, Sandra, Olga and Julie 60

Nana 52
The Nanny 2, 74, 76, 77, 79–84, **80**, 86, 182
Nascimbene, Mario ix, 62, 115–117, 119–122, 131
Neame, Christopher 156
The Net 38
Never Take Sweets from a Stranger 60
Newell, Mike 24, 124
Nexus 144
Die Nibelungenlied 25
Nicholas and Alexandra 150
Nielsen, Carl 8
Nietzsche, Friedrich 171, 177
Night Creatures see *Captain Clegg*
The Night of the Iguana 38
Nightmare 25, 77, 144, 147, **148**
Ninth Symphony (Beethoven) 131, 149
Niven, David 77
Noctambules 55
Nono, Luigi 197
Norman, Leslie 58
North, Alex 72, 120, 121
North by Northwest 47
Nosferatu 36, 60
Nothing but the Night 86
The Nutcracker 8, 72, 99, 205
Nyby, Christian 123

The Oblong Box 90
O'Connell, Maurice 169
Ogilvie, Gertrude 125
Oldfield, Mike 197
Oliver, Michael 37, 53, 87
Olivier, Sir Laurence (Lord Olivier) 83, 205
Olsen, James **16**, 138
On the Waterfront 72
One Million Years B.C. (Don Chaffey, 1966) 115–117, **115**, 119–122, 126, 132
One Million Years B.C. (Hal Roach, 1940) 115
Organ Concerto (Williamson) 135, 137
Orr, Buxton vii, 38, 53
Orwell, George: *Animal Farm* 143
Ost, Valerie van 164
Overlord 180

Ovid 161
Owen, Cliff 62, 122
Owen Wingrave 36, 37
Ozep, Fedor 140

Paal, Alexander 97, 99, 103
Paganini, Niccolo 126
Palestrina, Giovanni Pierluigi da 86
Pancho Villa 165
Pappenheim, Marie 25
Parker, Alan 158
Parks, Gordon 163
Parra, Pim de la 60
Parry, Sir Hubert 14
Parsifal 26 27, 35, 36, 41, 171
Passacaglia 4, 109, 110
Patterson, Paul ix, 2, 16, 180, 198–202, **199**; Brainstorm 199; Clarinet Concerto 199; *Comedy* 199; *Cracowian Counterpoint* 199; *Fusions* 199; Horn Concerto 198; *Kyrie* 199; *Requiem* 199; *Shadows* 199; *Timepiece* 199; Trumpet Concerto 198; *Visions* 199; *Wildfire* 199; Wind Quintet 198
Paul, Jeremy 97
Payne, Anthony 56, 57, 70
Pearce, Jacqueline 108, 150
Pears, Sir Peter 197
Peckinpah, Sam 191
The Peddlers 51
Peel, David 135
Penderecki, Krzystof 3, 5, 35, 106, 112, 113, 161, 187, 199; *Kosmogonia* 161; *St. Luke Passion* 199; *Threnody for the Victims of Hiroshima* 5, 161, 186, 188
Pennario, Leonard: "Midnight on the Cliffs" 140
Penny and the Pownall Case 54
Perrey, Jean-Jacques 130; *The In Sound from Way Out* 130; *Moog Indigo* 130
Peter Grimes 84, 106
Peyser, Joan 37, 87, 204, 205
Pezzo dramatico 144
The Phantom of the Opera 140
Phillips, John 153
Phillips, Roy 51
Piano Concerto (Cowell) 139
Picnic at Hanging Rock 133
The Picture of Dorian Gray 72
Pictures at an Exhibition 131
Pierce, Jack P. 145
Pierrot Lunnaire 230
Pink Floyd 118, 160, 162; *Dark Side of the Moon* 118, 163
Pink Panther films 157
Pinter, Harold 77
Pirie, David 154, 176
"The Pit and the Pendulum" 66
Pitt, Ingrid 90, **101**, 102
The Plague of the Zombies 108, 196
Poe, Edgar Allan 143; "The Bells" 36; "The Haunted Palace" 36; "The Masque of the Red Death" 36, 125; "The Pit and the Pendulum" 66; "The Raven" 36; "Ulalume" 36
Poèmes pour Mi 134
Pompeii 19
"Popcorn" 130
Porter, Peter 144
Powell, Eddie 151
Powell, Robert 133
Powers, Stephanie **16**, 138, 139
Preminger, Otto 11–15, 123, 178, 200
Prendergast, Roy M. 37, 53
Price, Dennis 137
The Prince of the Pagodas 150
The Prisoner 38
Prospects 144
Prowse, Dave 137
Psalm LXXXIII 179
Psycho 3, 83, 86, 106, 108, 147
Puccini, Giacomo 36, 90
Purcell, Henry: *Dido and Aeneas* 35

Quarry, Robert 154
Quatermass and the Pit 118, 125, 126, 128, 129
The Quatermass Experiment 2–5, 74, 83, 106, 161, 203
Quatermass II 108
"Quebec Concerto" 140

Rachmaninoff, Sergei 13, 36, 72; Second Piano Concerto 125
Radio Parade of 1935 38
RAI Electronic Music Studios 197
Raines, Christina 190
Raksin, David **30**, 123
Rascher, Sigurd 4, 109, 110
Rasputin, Grigory Efimovich 133
Rasputin — The Mad Monk 147, 149
Ravel, Maurice 150; *Dapnis et Chloë* 139; *Introduction and Allegro* 125
"The Raven" 36
Rebecca 83, 84
The Red House 122
Redgrave, Vanessa 14, 67
Redmond, Moira 147, **148**
Reed, Oliver 4, **41**, 43, 48, 58, **59**, 145
Reggio, Geoffrey 65
Reich, Steve 33, 34
Reid, Lesley vii, 89, 90, 97
Reid, Milton 145
Reizenstein, Franz 151
The Reptile 149–151
Requiem: Ligeti 120, 205; Patterson 199
The Return of Ironside 174
The Revenge of Frankenstein 189
Das Rheingold 113
Richardson, John 122
Rigby, Jonathan 63, 70, 178, 184, 188
Der Ring des Nibelungen 96, 157

The Rite of Spring 108, 169
Ritt, Martin 23
Roach, Hal 115
Robert le diable 36
Robinson, Bernard 73, 135, 150
Robinson, Harry vii, ix, 16, 56, 64, 88, **89**, 89–104, **91**, **97**, 113, 159, 192; "Hoots Mon" 88
Rockingham, Lord *see* Robinson, Harry
Rod Stewart and the Faces 159
Roeg, Nicolas 144
Rogers, Richard 155
Rohe, Mies van der 51
Roland 17
Romain, Yvonne 43, 145
Roosevelt, Theodore, Jr. 7
Rosenberg, Max 60
Rosenman, Leonard 33, 34, 37, 72
Rossen, Robert 119
Rósza, Miklós 122; "Spellbound Concerto" 140
Rota, Nino: "The Legend of the Glass Mountain" 140
Roundtree, Richard 163
Royal Philharmonic Orchestra 197
Rufer, Josef 53
Russell, Ken 72
Russo, Bill 156

Sachs, Bruce 153
Sadie, Stanley 53, 70, 132, 153
Sahassavagga 179
St. Joan 11
St. Luke Passion 199
Saint-Saëns, Camille 16, 17; *Danse macabre* 36
Sala, Oskar 58, 122
Salzedo, Leonard 189, 190
Sangster, Jimmy 73, 77, 87, 89, 137, 138, 153, 191–193
Sappho 17
Saraceno, Phillipa vii, 145
Sardanapalus 17
Sargent, Sir Malcolm 7
Sasdy, Peter 9, 65, 86, 97, 101
Sassard, Jacqueline 67
The Satanic Rites of Dracula 52, 75, 163, 164–166, **164** 168–177
Savalas, Telly 165
Scaffold 156
Scars of Dracula 138, 154
Schaeffer, Pierre 117–119; *Symphonie pour un homme seil* 118
Schaffner, Franklin 150
Schelling, Friedrich Wilhelm Joseph von 79, 80
Schlesinger, John 14, 15
Schmitt, Florent 36
Schoenberg, Arnold ix, 4, 25–34, **30**, 37, 38, 42, 44, 53, 56, 57, 71, 134, 140, 173, 181, 183, 186, 204, 205; *Begleitungsmusik zu einer Lichtspielszene* 26, 27; *Erwartung* 25, 27; *Five Pieces for Orchestra* 183; *Die glückliche Hand* 26–28; *Gurrelieder* 31; *Pierrot Lunaire* 230; *Verklärte Nacht* 29, 202; *Von Heute auf Morgen* 27, 28
Schoenberg, Gertrude **30**
Schreck, Max 60
Schubert, Franz: String Quartet No. 14, in D Minor, "Death and the Maiden" 143
Schuller, Gunther 2
Schumann, Robert (Alexander): "Träumerei" 143
Schurmann, Gerard vii, 49, 51, 53; *Six Studies of Francis Bacon* 49
Scott, Janette 58
Scott, Margaretta 138
Scott, Peter Graham 144
Scott of the Antarctic 55
Scriabin, Alexander 75, 106, 136, 142
Searle, Humphrey ix, 54–58, **55**, 69, 70; Fourth Symphony 64; *Noctambules* 55
Second Piano Concerto: Rachmaninoff 125; Williamson 137
Second Piano Sonata (Williamson) 135
Second Symphony: McCabe 191; Williamson 140
Secrets of Naughty Susan see My Nights with Susan, Sandra, Olga and Julie
Seiber, Mátyás 143
Sellors, Anthony vii
Sergeant Pepper's Lonely Hearts Club Band 155
Sessions, Roger 178
Settings from Roget 144
Seven Brides for Seven Brothers 167
Seven Days to Noon 113
The Seventh Veil 38
Seyrig, Delphine 77
Shadows 199
Shaft 163, 175
Shakespeare, William: *Macbeth* 129
Shampan, Harold 165
Sharp, Don 59, 141, 147
Shaw, George Bernard: *St. Joan* 11
She 115, 122, 191, 198
Shelley, Mary: *Frankenstein* 2, 3
The Shining 187
Shostakovitch, Dmitri 34; First Piano Concerto 190; Tenth Symphony 48
Sibelius, Jean 8
"The Silent Scream" 189
Silver, Robert 166
Six épigraphs antiques 125
Six-Five Special 88
Six Studies of Francis Bacon 49
Skeggs, Roy 116, 125, 166, 187, 191
Skidmore, Alan 158
Skinn, Dez 176
The Skull 5, 63–68, 99

The Sleeping Beauty 8
Sloane, Edward van 52
Small, Victoria vii
Smith-Brindle, Reginald 2, 5, 118, 119, 131, 132
Smithson, Peter and Alison 51
So Long at the Fair 38
The Society for the Promotion of New Music 55
Solomon and Sheba 119, 122
Solti, Sir Georg 192
Sonata da Camera (Banks) 144
Sophocles 161
Sorcerer 131
The Sound of Music 56, 155
Sounds Astounding LP **130**, 131
Souza, Edward, de 59, **141**
Spellbound 31, 122, 140
"Spellbound Concerto" 140
Spence, Sir Basil 51
Spiby, Ian vii
Spielberg, Steven 120
Spoliansky, Mischa 11, 13
Spur of the Moment 106
The Spy Who Came In from the Cold 23
Stalin, Joseph 7, 48, 150
Standing, John 142
Stanford, Sir Charles Villiers 14
Stapleton, Cyril 80
Star Wars 176
Steele, Tommy 88
Steiner, Max 92, 137, 151, 176, 183, 184
Steurmann, Eduard 29
Stockhausen, Karlheinz 113, 118, 119, 128, 204; *Etude* 128, 129; *Gesang der Jünglinge* 118
Stoker, Bram 125, 132, 165; *The Jewel of Seven Stars* 124, 132
Stone, Andrew 140
Stoneground 159, **159**, 160
Stoney, Kevin 197
Strauss, Johann, Jr.: "Blue Danube" Waltz 120
Strauss, Richard 120; *Also Sprach Zarathustra* 131; *Tod und Verklärung* 185
Stravinsky, Igor 4, 32, 72, 134, 139, 177; *The Rite of Spring* 108, 169; *Threni* 4
A Streetcar Named Desire 72
Strindberg, August: *Miss Julie* 52; *To Damascus* 26
Subotsky, Milton 60
Sulzman, Stan 158
"Summum Bonum" 17, **18**
Sutherland, Donald 63
Svendsen, Johan 8
Swan Lake 8, 78
The Sweeney 159
Switched-on Bach 131
Sykes, Peter 89, 178, 179, 182
Symphonie pour un homme seil 118

Tagg, Philip 93, 98, 99, 163, 176
Take Eight 144
Tales from the Crypt 9
Tam O'Shanter Overture 8
Tangerine Dream 131
Tannhäuser 99
Taste the Blood of Dracula 9, 135
Tchaikovsky, Pyotr Il'ytch: *The Nutcracker* 8, 72, 99, 205; *The Sleeping Beauty* 8; *Swan Lake* 8, 78; "The Waltz of the Flowers" 99
Telezynska, Isabella 184
Tenth Symphony (Shostakovich) 48
The Test of Violence 180
The Testament of Dr. Mabuse 78
Thalberg, Irving 29, 30
Theatre of Death 67, 68
Theme and Rock Out 165
Thérémin, Léon 122
The Thing from Another World 123
"The Thirteenth Reunion" 193, 194, 196
This Sporting Life 67
Thompson, Eric 53
Thompson, Peter 192
Threadgould, Merryn 53
Three Short Songs 144
Threni 4
Threnody for the Victims of Hiroshima 5, 161, 186, 188
Till, Jenny 69
Tiomkin, Dimitri 122
Timepiece 199
To Damascus 26
To the Devil a Daughter 178–187, **182**, 190, 194, 200, 201
Toccata and Fugue in D Minor 143
Tod und Verklärung 185
Torture Garden 142, 143, 148
Toscanini, Arturo 67
"Träumerei" 143
Trevor-Roper, Hugh 55
Trottie True 38
Trumpet Concerto (Patterson) 198
Tuckwell, Barry 144
"The Turn of the Screw" 36, 58
Twins of Evil 89, 90, 93, 98, 102, 159
A Twist of Sand 129
"The Two Faces of Evil" 199, 200
2001: A Space Odyssey 120, 121, 205

"The Ugly Bug Ball" 89
"Ulalume" 36
Uncharted Seas 89

Valentine, Anthony 185
The Valley of the Kings 92
Vampire Circus 58
The Vampire Lovers 89
"Vampire Rhapsody" 141, 151
Der Vampyr 35
Varèse, Edgar 118, 126; *Déserts* 128
Vaughan Williams, Ralph 14, 55, 56, 70
Veidt, Conrad 25

Venables, Philip vii
The Vengeance of She 62, 122
Verdi, Guiseppe 36, 119; *Atilla* 8
Verklärte Nacht 29, 202
Vernon, Richard 163
Verrell, Ronnie 158
Vetri, Victoria 122
Vickers, Mike vii, ix, 156–163, *157*, 172, 176
Vidor, King 119
Viertel, Salka 29, 37
The Vikings 119
Villiers, James 82, 124
Villiers de l'Isle Adam, Phillippe Auguste: *Cruel Tales* 34, 37; *The Future Eve* 112, 114
Vinci, Leonardo da 3, 161
Violin Concerto (Berg) 4, 5, 43, 44, 47, 190
The Violins of Saint Jacques 140
Visions 199
Von Heute auf Morgen 27, 28
Vorhaus, David 160

Wagner, Cosima 53
Wagner, (Wilhelm) Richard 17, 25, 27, 28, 32, 35, 37, 41, 42, 54, 158, 171; "Dir töne Lob" 99; *Die Meistersinger von Nürnberg* 175; *Parsifal* 26 27, 35, 36, 41, 171; *Das Rheingold* 113; *Der Ring des Nibelungen* 96, 157; *Tannhäuser* 99; *Die Walküre* 94
Walbrook, Anton 139
Walkabout 144
Die Walküre 94
Wall, Russell 153
Wallis, Jacquie *141*
Walton, Sir William 55, 56, 134
"The Waltz of the Flowers" 99
Ward, David 147
Ward, Edward: "Lullaby of the Bells Piano Concerto" 140
Warlords of Atlantis 161
Warren, Barry 58, *141*
"Warsaw Concerto" 138, 139, 140, 141
Watkin, David 51, 53
Waxman, Franz 83, 84, 146
Webb, Roger 189
Weber, Carl Maria von: *Der Freischütz* 35
Webern, Anton (Friedrich Wilhelm von) 33, 54, 140, 178, 201; String Quartet 180
Webster, John: *The Duchess of Malfi* 106
Wegener, Paul 36
Weir, Peter 133
Welch, Rachel 115, *116*
The Werewolf of Paris 42
Wesendonck, Mathilde 37
West Side Story 56
Whale, James 145

Wheatley, Dennis 49, 176, 178, 181, 188, 193, 203; *Uncharted Seas* 89
When Dinosaurs Ruled the Earth 121, 122, 131
Where the Spies Are 115
While I Live 140
Whispering City 140
Whitaker, David 58
White, Barry 163
White Noise: An Electric Storm 160
Whitlock, Dennis 185
The Wicker Man 84
Wicking, Christopher 125, 132, 181
Widmark, Richard 181
Wiene, Robert 25, 26
Wilcock, Samuel vii
Wilcox, Fred M. 122
Wild, Katy 62
The Wild Bunch 191
Wilde, Oscar 72
Wilder, Billy 122
Wildfire 199
Williams, Charles: "The Dream of Olwen" 140
Williams, John 36, 37, 119–121, 161, 176
Williams, Simon 190
Williamson, Malcolm ix, 9, 21, 62, 107, 133–140, 142, 146, 153, 199; First Piano Sonata 135; *The Happy Prince* 9; Organ Concerto 135, 137; Second Piano Concerto 137; Second Piano Sonata 135; Second Symphony 140; *The Violins of Saint Jacques* 140
Willman, Noel 141, *141*, 150, 151
Wincer, Simon 133
Wind Quintet (Patterson) 198
"A Windmill in Old Amsterdam" 89
Wise, Robert 56, 128
The Witches 79, 80, 83–87, **85**
Woodbridge, George 46
Woods, Arthur B. 38
Woodthorpe, Peter 147
Wordsworth, Richard 4, 42, 46
Wray, Fay 184
Wright, Basil 59
Wymark, Patrick 65

X— The Unknown 58, 74, 106
Xenakis, Yannis 118

Yanks 14
Young, Robert 58
Ysaÿe, Eugène 21
Yusupov, Prince Felix 150

Zamphir, George 97
Zimbalist, Stephanie 124
Zola, Émile 52; *Nana* 52

www.ingramcontent.com/pod-product-compliance
Ingram Content Group UK Ltd.
Pitfield, Milton Keynes, MK11 3LW, UK
UKHW041948140426
5217IPUK00014B/702